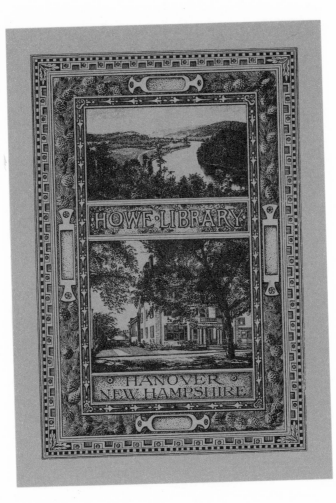

SWIMMING
TO
ANTARCTICA

This Large Print Book carries the
Seal of Approval of N.A.V.H.

SWIMMING TO ANTARCTICA

Tales of a Long-Distance Swimmer

LYNNE COX

Thorndike Press • Waterville, Maine

Published in 2004 by arrangement with Alfred A. Knopf, Inc.

Thorndike Press® Large Print Biography.

The tree indicium is a trademark of Thorndike Press.

The text of this Large Print edition is unabridged.
Other aspects of the book may vary from the original edition.

Set in 16 pt. Plantin by Liana M. Walker.

Printed in the United States on permanent paper.

Library of Congress Cataloging-in-Publication Data

Cox, Lynne, 1957–
    Swimming to Antarctica : tales of a long-distance
swimmer / Lynne Cox.
      p. cm.
    Originally published: New York : Knopf, 2004.
    ISBN 0-7862-6421-7 (lg. print : hc : alk. paper)
    1. Cox, Lynne, 1957– 2. Swimmers — United States —
Biography. 3. Long distance swimming. I. Title.
GV838.C69A3 2004b
797.2′1′092—dc22
  [B]   2004043980

To Mom and Dad

As the Founder/CEO of NAVH, the only national health agency solely devoted to those who, although not totally blind, have an eye disease which could lead to serious visual impairment, I am pleased to recognize Thorndike Press* as one of the leading publishers in the large print field.

Founded in 1954 in San Francisco to prepare large print textbooks for partially seeing children, NAVH became the pioneer and standard setting agency in the preparation of large type.

Today, those publishers who meet our standards carry the prestigious "Seal of Approval" indicating high quality large print. We are delighted that Thorndike Press is one of the publishers whose titles meet these standards. We are also pleased to recognize the significant contribution Thorndike Press is making in this important and growing field.

Lorraine H. Marchi, L.H.D.
Founder/CEO
NAVH

* Thorndike Press encompasses the following imprints: Thorndike, Wheeler, Walker and Large Print Press.

CONTENTS

ACKNOWLEDGMENTS

I would like to thank Allen Daviau; Anne Rice; Arthur Sulzberger Jr.; Vicky Wilson, my editor; and Martha Kaplan, my agent, for all their help in getting this book published.

I would like to also thank David Remnick, Dorothy Wickenden, and Cressida Leyshon at *The New Yorker* for their support and for publishing my article "Swimming to Antarctica."

Thank you to my grandfather, Arthur Daviau, M.D., for his support and his great genes.

And thank you to Kenny Hawkins, Dusty Nicol, Linda Halker, and everyone at Knopf for their help in transforming my manuscript into a book. It's been a big dream for so many years, and finally an incredible reality.

Lastly, thank you to all my family and friends who believed in me and in this story for so many years. Thank you all very much!

PROLOGUE

A Cold Day
in August

It is August 7, 1987, and I am swimming across the Bering Sea. I am somewhere near — or across — the U.S.-Soviet border. The water stings. It's icy cold. My face feels as if it has been shot full of novocaine and it's separating from my skull. It's as if I'm swimming naked into a blizzard. My hands are numb, and they ache deep down through the bone. I can't tell if they are pulling any water. They feel as though they are becoming detached from my body. I look down at them through the ash-colored water: they are splotchy and bluish white; they are the hands of a dead person. I take a tight, nervous breath. Suddenly it occurs to me that my life is escaping through my hands.

This frigid and ominous sea is behaving like an enormous vampire slowly sucking

11

the warmth, the life from my body, and I think, *Oh my God, pick up your pace. Swim faster, faster. You've got to go as fast as you can. You've got to create more heat. Or you will die!*

I try to lift my arms over more rapidly. They are sore and sluggish. I am tired. I have been sprinting, swimming as fast as I can go, for more than an hour. But I sense that I am fading, becoming less of myself. *Is my blood sugar dropping? Is that why I feel so strange? Or is my body temperature plunging? Am I hypothermic?* Systematically I check my body. *My lips feel pickled; my throat is parched and raw from the briny water. I want to stop to drink some fresh water and catch my breath. But the water is too cold to allow me to pause for even a moment. If I do, more heat will be drained from my body, heat that I will never regain.*

Through foggy goggles, I continue monitoring my body. I've never pushed myself this far. The coldest water I've ever swum in was thirty-eight degrees in Glacier Bay, Alaska, and that was only for twenty-eight minutes. This swim is five times longer. I am afraid of going beyond the point of no return. The problem is that my brain could cool down without my being aware of it, which would cause a dangerous loss of judgment. I glance at my shoulders and arms:

12

they are as red as lobsters. This is a very good sign. My body is fighting to protect itself from the cold by employing a defense mechanism called vasoconstriction. It is diverting blood flow away from my hands and feet, arms and legs to the core of my body; it is keeping my brain and vital organs warm so they will continue to function normally.

I reach out and pull faster and, through muscle movement, try to create heat more quickly than I am losing it. My breaths are short and rapid, and my chest is heaving. My heart is pounding. I am afraid.

The fog is growing heavier; the air is saturated and raw. It feels as though I am trying to breathe through a wet blanket. With each breath, the chill rolls deeper into my lungs. Now I am cooling down from the inside out. I can't help myself; I think of David Yudovin.

David was a seasoned long-distance swimmer who, during an attempt to swim from Anacapa Island to the California mainland, technically died from hypothermia. His body tried to fight the cold by shunting the blood flow to his brain and vital organs. For a period of time, his core was protected. But at some critical point the blood vessels in his extremities became paralyzed. Blood rushed from his core to his hands and feet, where it was cooled by the fifty-eight-degree water; when it flowed back into his torso, it caused his core temperature to drop. As a result, David became disoriented. His swimming speed dropped, and then his heart went into atrial fibrillation. As he continued to cool down, his heart became less functional, until it suddenly stopped beating altogether.

There had been warning signs: his lips were purple, he was shivering, and his shoulders had turned blue. But his crew didn't recognize the severity of the situation. When they spoke to David, he said he was doing okay, and the decrease in his body temperature was so gradual, they didn't notice his deteriorating condition. Neither did David. His brain had been cooled down so far that he wasn't able to recognize the warning signs. He had no idea he was dying.

At the hospital in Ventura doctors and nurses shot Adrenalin directly into his heart and repeatedly shocked his heart with a defibrillator. They warmed his blood and had him breathe warmed oxygen. An hour and fifty minutes after his initial cardiac arrest, the medical team revived David. He had been lucky.

Will I be that lucky? The water here is twenty degrees colder. Will I be able to recognize if I've gone too far?

Yes. Yes. I will. I can do this. I've broken the world records for the English Channel, I've swum across the frigid waters of the Strait of Magellan, and I've done swims in icy waters where no one else has ever survived.

I can do it.

Thank God (or Ben & Jerry's) for my body fat; it's insulating me from the cold. Still, the cold is moving deep into the marrow of my bones. Chills are curling up my spine and spreading out across my shoulders. My teeth are clenched and my lips are quivering. My muscles are as tight as boards.

I am pushing myself to the limit. But I've got to do this. This swim is not about me. It's about all of us.

It's about doing something that's going to make a positive difference in the world. For eleven years, I have hoped when there was no reason to hope. I have believed when there was little to believe. For the last forty-two years we've been engaged in a Cold War with the Soviets. Somehow it has to be stopped. I believe that this swim will create a thaw in the Cold War. I cannot fail. If I die doing this, the Soviets will regret giving me permission to make this swim. I can't let that happen. *Swim faster! Don't focus on the cold or the pain. Don't give any energy to it. Focus on the finish. Swim faster.*

I think of my parents, brother, and sisters, of friends and of the people who have gotten me this far. I conjure up their faces in my mind's eye. This gives me energy, and I imagine how wonderful it will feel to embrace the people who are waiting for us on Big Diomede Island and to hold their warm hands. This is inspiring. I replay a sentence in my head: *Hand to hand, heart to heart, we can change the world.* This is what I have grown to believe.

With every part of my being I am reaching forward, racing against time and the pervasively cold sea.

I lift my head and look up.

Something is very wrong.

Out in front of me, to the left and to the right, are the two thirty-foot-long walrus-skin boats that are supposed to be guiding and protecting me. On board the one to the right is a group of physicians who are monitoring me during the swim. To the left is a boatful of journalists huddled against the chill. Inuit guides — Eskimos who live on Little Diomede Island — are driving the walrus-skin boats. They are veering away from each other.

The dark fog has grown so thick that our visibility is down to twenty feet. We planned to meet the Soviets at the border so they could guide us to Big Diomede Island, to their shore. Our guides have never ventured across the border. They were afraid that the Soviets would pick them up and jail them in a Siberian prison. This had happened to relatives. They had been imprisoned for fifty-two days.

Pat Omiak, the lead navigator from Little Diomede, asks Dr. Keatinge, one of the doctors, "Which direction do you think we should take?" Keatinge says, "I'm not sure."

Like Omiak, he has never ventured into these waters. But he recommends going straight ahead. I follow them. They are making abrupt turns to the right and left. I am frustrated. Each moment we spend off course diminishes our chances of making it across. It hits me that we are lost somewhere in the middle of the Bering Sea. But I keep swimming and I keep thinking, *Please, God, please let the Soviet boats find us.* I strain to see them through the fog, listen for high-pitched engine sounds in the water, feel for vibrations, and continue praying.

When I turn my head to breathe I notice that the boats are drifting away from me. I shout at the top of my lungs, "Move closer! Move closer!"

They have no idea how frightened I am. They don't know what's happened before. I don't know how long I can last.

1

Beginnings

"Please. Please. Please, Coach, let us out of the pool, we're freezing," pleaded three purple-lipped eight-year-olds in lane two.

Coach Muritt scowled at my teammates clinging to the swimming pool wall. Usually this was all he had to do to motivate them, and they'd continue swimming. But this day was different. Ominous black clouds were crouched on the horizon, and the wind was gusting from all different directions. Even though it was a mid-July morning in Manchester, New Hampshire, it felt like it would snow.

Cupping his large hands against his red face, and covering the wine-colored birthmark on his left cheek, Coach Muritt bellowed, "Get off the wall! Swim!"

"We're too cold," the boys protested.

Coach Muritt did not like to be challenged by anyone, let alone three eight-year-old boys. Irritated, he shouted again at the swimmers to get moving, and when they didn't respond, he jogged across the deck with his fist clenched, his thick shoulders hunched against the wind and his short-chopped brown hair standing on end. Anger flashed in his icy blue eyes, and I thought, *I'd better swim or I'll get in trouble too,* but I wanted to see what was going to happen to the boys.

Coach Muritt shook his head and shouted, "Swim and you'll get warm!"

But the boys weren't budging. They were shaking, their teeth chattering.

"Come on, swim. If you swim, you'll warm up," Coach Muritt coaxed them. He looked up at the sky, then checked his watch, as if trying to decide what to do. In other lanes, swimmers were doing the breaststroke underwater, trying to keep their arms warm. More teammates were stopping at the wall and complaining that they were cold. Laddie and Brooks McQuade, brothers who were always getting into trouble, were breaking rank, climbing out of the pool and doing cannonballs from the deck. Other young boys and girls were joining them.

"Hey, stop it! Someone's going to get hurt — get your butts back in the water!" Coach Muritt yelled. He knew he was losing control, that he had pushed the team as far as we could go, so he waved us in. When all seventy-five of us reached the wall, he motioned for us to move toward a central lane and then he shouted, "Okay, listen up. Listen up. I'll make a deal with you. If I let you get out now, you will all change into something warm and we'll meet in the boys' locker room. Then we will do two hours of calisthenics."

Cheering wildly, my teammates leaped out of the pool, scurried across the deck, grabbed towels slung over the chain-link fence surrounding the pool, and squeezed against one another as they tried to be first through the locker room doors.

Getting out of the water was the last thing in the world I wanted to do. I hated doing calisthenics with the team. Usually we did them five days a week for an hour, after our two-hour swimming workout. A typical workout included five hundred sit-ups, two hundred push-ups, five hundred leg extensions, five hundred half sit-ups, two hundred leg lifts on our backs, and two hundred leg lifts on our stomachs. As we did the exercises, Coach Muritt counted

21

and we had to keep pace with him. Between each set of fifty repetitions, he gave us a one-minute break, but if anyone fell off pace or did the exercises incorrectly, he made us start the set all over again. He wanted to make us tough, teach us discipline and team unity. And I didn't mind that. I liked to work hard, and I liked the challenge of staying on pace, but I detested having to start an exercise all over again because someone else was slacking off or fooling around. Brooks and Laddie McQuade were notorious for that. They were always trying to see how much they could get away with before they got caught. For them, it was a big game. Older boys on the team yelled at them and tossed kickboards at them, but they didn't care; they liked the attention they were getting from the team and the coach. I didn't want to play their game, and I didn't want to do two long hours of calisthenics with them, so I shouted, "Coach Muritt, can I stay in the pool and swim?"

He was wiping his eyes and nose with a handkerchief, and asked incredulously, "Jeez, aren't you freezing?"

"If I keep swimming, I'm okay," I said, and smiled, trying my very best to convince him. I was a chubby nine-year-old, and I was a slow swimmer, so I rarely got a chance to stop and take a rest. But because I just kept going, I managed to constantly create body heat, and that way I stayed warm when all the other swimmers were freezing.

"Is there anyone else who wants to stay in the water?"

"We do," said three of his Harvard swimmers in lane one.

During the college season, Muritt coached the Harvard University Swim Team. He was considered to be one of the best coaches in all of New England; at least a dozen of his college swimmers had qualified for the U.S. Nationals. In the summer, most of his college swimmers worked out with our age groupers on the Manchester Swim Team, and they inspired us by their example. Somehow my parents knew from the start that to become your best, you needed to train with the best. And that's why I think they put my older brother, David, me, and my two younger sisters, Laura and Ruth, into Coach Muritt's swimming program.

Coach Muritt studied the sky, and we followed his gaze. "I still don't like the looks of those clouds," he said pensively.

"Coach, we'll get out immediately if it starts to thunder. I promise," I said, and held my breath, hoping he wouldn't make me do calisthenics.

He considered for a moment, but he was distracted by uproarious laughter, high-pitched hoots, and shouts coming from the locker room.

"Please, Coach Muritt, please can we stay in?" I said.

"Okay, but I'll have to take the pace clock or it's going to blow over — you'll have to swim at your own pace for the next couple of hours."

"Thank you, Coach," I said, and clapped my hands; I was doubly thrilled. I had escaped calisthenics and now I was going to be able to swim for three hours straight. I loved swimming and I loved swimming at my own pace, alone in my own lane, with no one kicking water in my face, and no one behind tapping my toes, telling me I had to swim faster. It was a feeling of buoyant freedom. But swimming into a storm was even better; waves were rushing around me, and lifting me, and tossing me from side to side. The wind was howling, slamming against the chain-link fence so strongly that it sounded like the clanging of a warning bell. I felt the vibrations rattle right through my body, and I wondered if the wind would tear the fence from its hinges. Turning on my side to breathe, I checked the sky. It looked like a tornado was approaching, only without the funnel cloud. I wondered for a second if I should climb out of the water. But I pushed that thought away; I didn't want to get out. I was immersed in unbridled energy and supernatural beauty, and I wanted to see what would happen next.

My world was reduced to the blur of my arms stroking as a cold, driving rain began. The raindrops that hit my lips tasted sweet and cold, and I enjoyed the sensations of every new moment. The pool was no longer a flat, boring rectangle of blue; it was now a place of constant change, a place that I had to continually adjust to as I swam or I'd get big gulps of water instead of air. That day, I realized that nature was strong, beautiful, dramatic, and wonderful, and being out in the water during that storm made me feel somehow a part of it, somehow connected to it.

When the hail began, the connection diminished considerably. I scrambled for the gutters while the college swimmers leaped out of the water and ran as fast as they could into the locker room. One looked back at me and shouted, "Aren't you getting out?"

"No, I don't want to," I said, crawling into the gutter by the stairs. The hail came down so fast and hard that all I heard was the rush and pinging of the stones as they hit the deck and pool. Thankful for the white bathing cap and goggles protecting my head and eyes, I covered my cheeks with my hands. Hailstones the size of frozen peas blasted my hands, neck, and shoulders, and I winced and cringed and tried to squeeze into a tighter ball, hoping that it would be over soon.

When the hail finally changed to a heavy rain, I crawled out of the gutter and started swimming again. As I pulled my arms through the water, I felt as if I were swimming through a giant bowl of icy tapioca. The hailstones floated to the water's surface and rolled around my body as I swam through them. I realized that by putting myself in a situation different from everyone else's, I had experienced something different, beautiful, and amazing.

In the parking lot outside, I saw Mrs. Milligan sitting in her car with her headlights aimed at me. Mrs. Milligan was Joyce's mother, and Joyce was the fastest and nicest girl on the team. Joyce had qualified for nationals a couple of times, and I wanted to be just like her. Once I'd asked her why she was so fast. She'd said that she did what Coach Muritt asked of her. It was such a simple statement, but one that was a revelation for me. If I did what Joyce did, then maybe I could also make it to nationals. I wondered how long Mrs. Milligan had been watching me. When I saw my teammates poking their heads out of the locker room, I knew the workout was over, so I climbed out of the pool.

Mrs. Milligan ran to me; her raincoat was plastered to her body and her short brown hair was standing on end. She was carrying a large towel, and when a gust hit it, the towel spread open like a sail. She wrapped it tightly around me and shouted, "How long have you been swimming in this storm?"

"The whole time," I said.

"Oh, my goodness. Coach Muritt let you swim in this?" she said, guiding me quickly into the girls' locker room and putting my hands between hers to warm them.

"He sure did, and I had a lot of fun." I grinned. It had been one of the most enjoyable workouts of my swimming career.

Rubbing the towel rapidly on my back, she bent over and said in my ear, with absolute certainty, "Someday, Lynne, you're going to swim across the English Channel."

It kind of took my breath away, but from the moment she said it, I believed that it could happen. After all, Mrs. Milligan was Joyce's mother, and I knew how her encouragement had helped Joyce become a fast swimmer. Even though I was only nine years old at the time, I somehow knew that one day I would swim the English Channel.

When I stepped out of the locker room, Coach Muritt turned and looked at me with surprise and said, "Are you just getting out of the pool now?"

"Yes, thank you, Coach Muritt. I had so much fun. You know what? Mrs. Milligan said that someday I'm going to swim the English Channel."

He looked at me for a few moments and said, "Yes, I think you will."

I remember telling my mother, as she drove my siblings and me home from workout in her bright red Buick station wagon, "Mom, Mrs. Milligan said that someday I'm going to swim the English Channel."

Without giving it much consideration, she said, "Well, if you train hard, I'm sure someday you probably will."

I couldn't wait to get home. I ran upstairs, grabbed our National Geographic atlas, and flipped through it until I found the page that featured England and France. Then I began to wonder, How far across is the English Channel? Where do you start to swim? I studied the map and the idea began to take hold in my mind. Maybe someday I would swim the English Channel.

2

Leaving Home

Three years later, when I was twelve years old, my father came home from work one winter evening, opened that same atlas to the pages depicting the United States, and placed the map on the dining room table. He motioned for my brother and sisters and me to look at the map.

"Your mother and I have been discussing moving. We believe that if you want to be successful with your swimming, you need to train with a top-notch coach. We've done our research and found that most of the best swimming programs are in these areas," he said, pointing to Arizona, California, and Hawaii.

We crowded around the table, and my mother said, "We're tired of the long, cold winters, and your father would like to work with a new group of radiologists with more up-to-date radiology equipment."

I had never thought of leaving New Hampshire. I loved it there. I loved exploring the wide-open fields of wild red poppies and bright yellow daylilies, the deep emerald forests. I loved gathering brilliantly colored leaves in fall, and building snow caves in the winter. But I knew that I wanted to be a great swimmer.

My father said, "We need to make this decision as a family. If there is anyone who doesn't want to move, we will stay here."

For the next couple of weeks we discussed the idea and finally decided to move to California. And with each day I grew more excited. I'd never been there before, but I'd seen it on television and I expected to be surrounded by ranches and cowboys, and large orange orchards. When we flew over Los Angeles, I couldn't believe what I saw. Below us in the haze of thin smog was a cement city that filled the entire basin, spread to the mountains, and expanded out along the coast. And I had this sinking feeling inside.

Somehow my father knew that it was important for the family to make an immediate connection with California so we would feel like we belonged. He drove us directly from

31

the airport down the 405 freeway to the Belmont Plaza Olympic swimming pool in Long Beach. This was where we would be training with Don Gambril, the head coach for the United States Olympic Team. Gambril had an age-group club team called Phillips 66, which we planned to join, and he coached a college team at California State University, Long Beach. In coaching circles, Gambril was known as one of the best in the world, and because of that he was able to recruit Olympic swimmers from around the world to swim for his college team.

The Belmont Plaza swimming complex had been built for the 1968 Olympic Trials. It was an enormous modern building of tinted glass and metal, situated on a plot of land four hundred yards from the beach, near the Long Beach pier. We stood outside, just staring at the building. Then my mother said, "Look, it's open. There are people inside."

I pulled the heavy glass door open and stepped into the spectators' area. All at once warm, heavy, humid, chlorine-filled air engulfed me. Off to my right was an enormous rectangular pool fifty meters long and twenty-five yards wide. Only a year old, it was beautiful. The water was crystal blue, and the deep blue tile along the edge of the pool sparkled. From the moment I saw it I knew this was a sea of dreams, almost a sacred place. This was the place where the best in the United States had competed to represent us in the Olympic Games. This was the arena, the stage, where they'd played out their dreams, where they'd given everything they had to be the best. I could almost hear the cheers of the crowd reverberating off the walls and glass windows and skylit ceiling. This building was full of energy, and I was absorbing it. I couldn't wait to jump into that pool, and I couldn't wait to meet Don Gambril.

We drove from the pool to a rental home. Long Beach was just one big city, and I didn't like it. California was not what I had expected it to be. It was a concrete desert with palm trees. A place where all the cities ran together and all the houses looked alike. I felt boxed in, lonely, isolated, and I just wanted to go home. But that wasn't possible. Our house in New Hampshire had been sold. My parents told us that we would have to buy a new one if we returned. I cried through the night. Nothing they did could console me.

A couple of days later, my brother and sisters and I met with Mr. Gambril. He was a

bear of a man, five foot ten, a former football player with a thick neck, a crew cut, and
dark brown eyes. I liked him. He was kind
and had a quick smile and an instant way of
making us feel welcome. He started the
team on their warm-up set and pulled us to
the side and told us what he expected of us.
We had to be at the pool in time for each
workout. If we were late we wouldn't be allowed to get into the water. We would work
out for two hours a day to start with, and if
we did well we could eventually do two
workouts a day, for a total of four hours. He
told us he expected us to work hard, but also
to have fun. He didn't want us on the team if
we didn't want to be there. Then he explained what we could expect of him. He
would coach us for the workouts and prepare us for the swim meets, and he would
keep track of our progress during both. He
also expected us to keep track of our times
during workouts and get our results from
swim meets. He told us he would always be
available to answer our questions. "Do you
understand all of this?" he asked.

We nodded. I glanced at Laura, ten years
old; Ruth, seven; and David, who was fourteen. They were as wide-eyed as I was. We
knew we were now in an entirely different
league. This was serious. And if we didn't

follow these rules, we wouldn't make the team.

We walked along the pool's edge and stopped at each lane so Mr. Gambril could introduce the team members. Squatting down to their level, he told us kids' names, joked with them, teased them a little without using sarcasm, and told us funny anecdotes or habits about some of the kids, making them laugh. It was obvious that they loved and respected him.

Mr. Gambril explained that lane assignments were designated according to a swimmer's speed, race distance, stroke preference, and age. Girls and boys trained together. The first two lanes were for the slowest swimmers. This would be where we started working out; as we improved, we would be moved to the faster lanes. Lanes three and four were for the fast age-group swimmers, five and six were for the Olympic sprinters, and seven and eight were for the Olympic distance swimmers. That was where I wanted to be, in lane eight.

"Do you have any questions?" he asked, willing to answer anything.

Mustering my courage, I said, "Mr. Gambril, how old do you have to be to swim in the Olympic distance lanes?"

There was a flash of recognition in his

eyes. "Please call me Coach," he said. "You don't need to be formal here. You can be any age to swim in lane eight, as long as you are able to do the workout at the pace of the swimmers in that lane." He knew that the difference in speed between the swimmers in lane eight and mine was like the distance between the moon and Neptune, an enormous difference; but Coach Gambril was the master of inspiring dreams. He made a long, high-pitched whistle through his teeth to get the swimmers' attention. They were in the middle of a kicking set. "Hans, Gunnar, come on over here. I want to introduce you to the Cox family."

As they kicked toward the wall, Coach Gambril told us about their amazing background: "Hans is from Germany, and Gunnar is from Sweden. They are on my team at Cal State Long Beach. Both are also training for spots on their Olympic teams. If they keep working hard, they have a great chance. Right now Hans Fassnacht is the fastest man in world in the mile and the fifteen-hundred-meter freestyle, and he has a very good chance of winning the gold medal for Germany at the 1972 Olympic Games. Gunnar Larsson swims the four-hundred medley, all four strokes, four laps each. He's one of the fastest men in the world for that event, and he also has a great chance of winning a gold medal in the 1972 Olympics, for Sweden. If he keeps working hard," Coach added, making sure they heard him.

Sunlight as if from the gods poured down through the skylight in one solid, bright beam, illuminating Hans and Gunnar. As they stood up in the pool, glistening water streamed down their faces, rippled down from their wide shoulders, along their muscular chests, and tapered along their powerful arms. They looked like Greek sculptures of Olympic athletes, only better, for they were alive and they were speaking to me. I could hardly believe it as, in a strong German accent, Hans was saying to me, "Welcome to the team." He extended his hand to each of us. It must have been twice as large as mine and thick with muscles.

Gunnar echoed the welcome: "Glad to have you join us." His voice lilted with his heavy Swedish accent. And he reached up, too, and shook our hands. His hands were bigger than Hans's, like paddles instead of hands.

Getting to talk with them was pretty heady stuff. But somehow I managed to reply, "Thank you. Someday I hope I will be able to swim in your lane." I was a chubby, awkward twelve-year-old girl without any intense training and with no reason to believe I could ever be as good as they were. I was only filled with hope and promise. And they were also so much older than I was, perhaps nineteen or twenty years old. But they recognized that they had once been like me, at the very beginning of their dreams. And they understood what it was like to leave everything they knew behind, in pursuit of their dreams.

Hans smiled at me and there was real kindness in his brown eyes. "If you work very hard, someday you will swim here in lane eight with us."

"And when you make it here, then you will have to work even harder." Gunnar laughed. His light blue eyes shone. He had a pleasing face, oval shaped with a square jaw, light clear skin, and very blond hair.

Adjusting to life in California was difficult. Seventh grade was miserable; I was shy and felt like I didn't fit in. In New Hampshire, students never spoke unless the teacher called on them for an answer. Students never moved out of their chairs. It was so different in California. Classmates blurted out answers, and even turned around in their seats to talk to other students without the teachers disciplining them.

My parents always stressed that first I needed to be an excellent student, and second an athlete. So I paid attention, worked hard, and got good grades, but in my physical education class I was terrible. I was the slowest runner, the worst softball thrower, and during my introduction to gymnastics I broke my foot in two places attempting a back walkover. Worse than that, my physical education teacher, a woman named Miss Larson, disliked me. She thought I wasn't making any effort at all in class. She screamed at me every day to try harder. I did, but how can you do better if no one shows you how? How can you make corrections if someone doesn't show you what you need to correct? I dreaded being in her class and I even had nightmares about her. But in her class I made my first true friend, Cathy Kuhnau. We had spoken a few times in French class, and she had helped me understand French grammar. We were also the worst tennis players in Miss Larson's class. Cathy was petite and I was chubby; no one wanted us, so naturally we became doubles partners. We tried hard, but we were both so unskilled that neither of us could hit the ball over the net. This became an advantage; when Miss Larson came across the court and yelled at us, we got her wrath together.

I was still unhappy in junior high school, but my solace was swimming with the team. Making friends with them wasn't easy. When I swam on the team in New Hampshire, we took time to hang on to the walls and talk. The swimmers on the Phillips 66 team were so much more intense, even in lane two. No one stopped in the middle of a set and talked. No one suddenly did a somersault just for fun. Everyone was serious. Worse than that, I was always the last one to finish in lane two. It was very discouraging, but one day when Coach Gambril came by to check on the swimmers in my lane, he figured out what I was doing wrong. He had us doing a series of thirty one-hundred-meter drills in one minute and forty-five-second intervals. This meant that we were supposed to swim two laps of the pool, check our time, and begin swimming again when the hands of the pace clock at the edge of the pool hit the one-minute-and-forty-five-second mark. Most of the swimmers got ten seconds' rest.

Coach Gambril stopped me and asked, "What was your time for your last one hundred?"

"I don't know," I said.

He looked like he was going to get mad.

"Didn't I tell you that you have to keep track of your times during workouts, so you know how you're doing? Well, then, why didn't you get it?"

"I never have time to stop. I had to keep going so I could stay up with the other kids," I said.

"You mean to say that for the last six months you've been swimming through every one of these workouts without taking any rest?"

I nodded, sure that I was in big trouble.

He shook his head and sighed. "I'm so sorry; I should have been watching you more closely. It's okay for you to stop. You need to take a break between each one hundred or two hundred, whatever we're doing. From now on, I want you to take at least ten seconds' rest."

I looked down at the water, afraid that he wouldn't understand.

"What's wrong?" His voice softened.

"If I do that, I'll be even farther behind the other swimmers." I hated to be behind.

"That's okay; by resting and working each set harder, you'll get stronger. If the kids are doing a set of ten one hundreds or ten two hundreds, just do eight. If you train with more intensity, you will get faster, and I'll bet it won't be long before you are the lead swimmer in the lane," he reassured me.

I could tell he cared about me, and he knew what he was doing, so I followed what he said.

He was right: within a few months, I was the lead swimmer in my lane. Still, it was only lane two. I wanted to continue improving, but I wasn't sure what it took to become faster.

During workouts, Coach Gambril had our top swimmers demonstrate their strokes for us, to show the techniques they used to move through the water. Sometimes we watched films with stroke analysis, but seeing the swimmers in the water with us made it so much easier to understand.

From lane two I began watching Hans and Gunnar, trying to see what they were doing so I could imitate them. It was obvious that they worked out with incredible intensity. Everything they did got their fullest effort. They never cruised through workouts or just got by. It was amazing that they could push themselves so hard. I didn't fully understand it. I didn't know that they were pushing through the pain and fatigue barriers; I was just trying to complete the workouts. But one day I asked one of the top breaststroke swimmers in the nation why she was so fast. She said that she worked hard on every lap, every single day. The message about what it takes to be the best became clearer.

During one workout, Coach Gambril made a "deal" with Hans: if Hans could swim the mile race under a specific time, the whole team could get out of the water early. Hans agreed to the deal. We all moved to lane five, where the water was calmer. Half the team stood in lane four, the other half in lane six, preparing to cheer him on.

Hans climbed out onto the pool deck, walked around, shook his arms, and psyched himself up so much that he hyperventilated and collapsed on the pool deck. He twisted and contorted like a fish out of water, gasping for air. Immediately Coach Gambril grabbed a paper bag from the office, dumped the contents on the pool deck, raced over, and put the bag over Hans's head, so he could get enough carbon dioxide in his blood to stimulate breathing. The bag moved in and out as he sucked in air. In shock, the team stood on deck to watch. It seemed like it took forever before Hans sat up slowly and pulled the bag off his head. He looked dazed and frightened, and he really scared me. I couldn't believe that this was happening to my hero. He got through it, and it made me appreciate Hans even more; it showed me the focus it took to be a champion, the strong connection between the mind and body.

Two weeks later, near the end of the workout, Coach Gambril asked Hans if he wanted to try a "deal" again. The deal was that he would swim the mile in segments: fifteen one hundreds, with a ten-second rest in between each one hundred. This was an exercise that would give him enough rest to go fast, and also enable him to feel the speed he would need to maintain for an Olympic race. When it got closer to the time of the Olympic Games, he repeated this exercise with only a five-second rest in between each one hundred, and then months before the Olympics he would do it again with only a one-second rest.

The whole team stopped what they were doing, lined the wall, and instantly became silent. Hans looked at us and then said, "Okay. I think I can do it."

"All right, Hans. Let's go then! Come on, you can do it," team members encouraged him.

My heart was pounding in my chest when Hans climbed out of the pool. I thought, *I hope he's not going to collapse on the deck again.* Hans curled his toes around the edge of the pool, bent over, and flexed his knees.

As Coach Gambril whistled he circled his arms and sprang into the air. In flight he heard the entire team shouting, "Go, Hans! Go!" And he entered the water like a torpedo. In seconds he was moving like a speedboat across the pool, arms and legs propelling him forward, with a wide bubbling wake behind him.

When he reached the wall after the first hundred, he rested for ten seconds. As he pushed off this time, four of the older girls and boys jumped out of the water, picked up their towels, and waved them in giant circles so Hans could see them as he swam.

He made the second one hundred on time. He pushed off again, and the team began shouting louder. Other swimmers got up on the deck to walk along with him, waving their towels, encouraging him to swim faster. In the background we heard Coach Gambril making a loud piercing whistle, urging Hans to go faster. He made the third, fourth, and fifth times, but by the eleventh he began to slow down. The team went wild, jumped up and down, pushed him with their voices. Finally, after the fifteenth one hundred, when Hans touched the wall at the finish, he looked up, gasping for air, and Coach Gambril broke into a huge smile and said, "You did it. You made the time by three seconds. And all you have to do now is go three seconds faster with an unbroken swim and you'll break the world record."

Hans grinned, and everyone hugged him and patted him on the back. And a few days later, Gunnar made a nearly record-breaking swim in workout in the eight-hundred individual medley.

One day after practice, I swam across the pool and asked them if they would watch me swim and help me with my stroke. They both said, "Sure."

Hans demonstrated the freestyle for me, and Gunnar swam the butterfly, backstroke, and breaststroke. Then they had me swim for them.

"You look really good, but you need to change your breathing if you're going to be a long-distance swimmer," Hans said. "Try breathing every third or fifth stroke — that will help you balance out your stroke. And you could try kicking a bit harder on your freestyle."

And Gunnar added, "When you're pulling the water with your hands, try to accelerate through your stroke, starting out, say, at one mile an hour and speeding up to one hundred miles an hour. You'll get more from your pull."

So I practiced what they told me, listened to Gambril, and worked hard. I enjoyed being a part of the team. And there was nothing as satisfying as seeing myself improving, getting stronger, and even having a few seconds to talk with the kids on the team when we took short rest breaks.

Gradually I began to feel I was accepted. We had been doing long and hard workouts during Christmas vacation and everyone was tired and grouchy. Gambril was about to tell the team what we were going to be doing when I came up from behind him, lifted all 220 pounds of him up, and hung him over the edge of the pool. "How far are we swimming tonight, Coach?" I asked.

The college swimmers broke into cheers. "Drop him in; let him go." And the rest of the team joined in.

Coach Gambril was so shocked, at first he didn't know what to say. When he found his voice he warned, "You better not drop me."

I laughed really hard so he couldn't be sure what I was going to do. The tension in the pool immediately lifted. After that, whenever I sensed that the team was dragging, I'd sneak up behind Gambril and dangle him over the pool, sometimes letting him slip just a little for drama. He would squawk and threaten to make us swim more if I dropped him.

During the course of that first year, Gambril watched over me, gave me pointers, and simply cared. Because of that I was strong enough to move up into lane three. I wanted to improve more quickly, so after a while I asked him if I could start doing double workouts at the college, along with my brother and the college team. I was fourteen years old. He suggested that I wait until I was a year older. He thought it was too soon to start me on four hours a day. All summer long I worked hard, and I moved up to lane four. Finally Gambril agreed to let me start double workouts.

But there was one huge stumbling block: Miss Larson. I had the misfortune to have her for my second year of physical education. And I could only participate in Gambril's morning workouts if I was released from her class. We were learning how to play basketball, and I was doing well, until the day she came by to watch us play.

The game was tied, and we were in the final five seconds of the match. Someone threw the ball to me. Determined to show her that I wasn't a total failure, I leaped up, hit the basket, and collided with three other girls. They landed on top of me on the asphalt. For the first time, Miss Larson said,

"Good job." I held back my tears. I'd hit the ground so hard that I had heard my elbow crack and I felt the pain spread up my arm and start to throb. All I could think was, How is this going to affect my swimming? And I knew Miss Larson was going to be mad at me for hurting myself. But I didn't say a word. That year I didn't enjoy school any more than the previous year, but I wanted to get high grades, and I didn't want to miss any classes. But by the end of the day, I couldn't straighten my arm, so much fluid had accumulated in the joint, and it was hot and throbbing with each heartbeat. Finally I asked to leave school one period early.

My father was working at the hospital, and when he read the X ray he said that I had fractured my elbow. He said that usually a fracture like the one I had was put in a cast in a bent position. But if my elbow healed that way, I would never regain full extension of my arm. So he said he would put my arm in a sling. He told me I could continue working out. I wouldn't be able to swim using my arms; I could just kick with a kickboard. But the water would support my arm and reduce the swelling; gradually I would be able to start using my arm again, and the resistance of the water would strengthen it.

When Miss Larson saw me the next day at school she was furious. She thought I was faking the injury. She demanded that I bring in a doctor's note. I showed her the X rays. She was angry that I had to take an adaptive physical education class. She didn't realize that she was a great motivator: as soon as my arm healed, I asked Coach Gambril again if I could do double workouts. He agreed.

My father set up a meeting with the principal, Mr. Hughes, and Miss Larson. Mr. Hughes was willing to let me out of physical education class, but Miss Larson fought to keep me in. She said that I needed the full range of athletic experience and the social experience. She said I was far too shy. My father argued on my behalf, explaining that I had a talent for swimming; it was both a gift and something I had worked hard for. He was able to convince the principal to let me out of her class, and I was overjoyed.

3

Open Water

After I'd been training with Coach Gambril
for two years, he noticed that my times were
beginning to level off and I was getting frustrated. But Gambril also noticed something
that I wasn't aware of: I was stronger at the
end of the workout than I was at the beginning. Gambril had insight that no one else
had and realized that my problem was that
there weren't any races long enough for me in
a swimming pool. At that time, there wasn't
even a 1500-meter race for women in the
Olympic Games. He recognized that it didn't
make any sense to continue coaching me in
the pool for a race that didn't exist. So after
one workout, Coach Gambril said, "Lynne,
why don't you enter the Seal Beach Rough
Water Swim? There are one-, two-, and
three-mile races. It's an ocean swim, and a

couple of other swimmers have done it and had fun. Why don't you try the three-mile race?"

I loved swimming in open water. That was where I'd first learned to swim, along with my brother and sisters. My grandparents had a camp on a lake in Maine called Snow Pond. It was the place where we spent our summers, learning how to kick and blow bubbles. Our dalmatian, Beth, would jump in and paddle over to us.

My grandfather, Arthur Daviau, had been an excellent swimmer. He had swum across many of the lakes in Maine, and once rescued some college students who had fallen out of their canoe in the Hudson River. He had taught my mother to swim, and she in turn taught us.

Snow Pond was the center of our lives in the summertime; we swam along the edges of the pond, paddled our red canoe to explore the Messalonskee River, to the north, and at night fished with our grandfather near the islands in the middle of the pond. Once my grandfather told me he had swum all the way from our camp to an island and back, about three miles. He showed me the island he had swum to, and I always wanted to swim to it too.

The three-mile race started at six in the

morning. When we checked in we were given numbers to pin to the back of our swimsuits. Mine was lucky 13.

We stood shoulder to shoulder along the shore, an official fired the starting gun, and we ran across the beach and dolphined under the waves. The water was cold, salty, buoyant, smooth, and the deepest blue. And I swam as if I had learned to fly. I raced across the water. My strokes felt powerful, and I felt strong, alive, as if awakened for the first time. Nothing in the swimming pool gave me this pleasure. I was free, moving fast, feeling the waves lifting and embracing me, and I couldn't believe how happy I was. It was like I had gone from a cage into limitless possibilities. With each stroke, my own strength grew; I felt the speed, the wake my body created, just like Hans's did in the pool when he swam freestyle. It was such a tremendous sensation, as if I had found my place, finally, found my niche in the universe. I swam with all my heart, and found myself passing one swimmer after another. *I am really going somewhere. I am really moving forward.* I lifted my head up and I could see the oil rig that represented the halfway point in the distance, about a mile away. I couldn't believe I had swum so fast, but there was nothing holding me back.

There were no walls, no black lines to follow, no lane lines or backstroke flags; I was surrounded by the wide-open sea and the infinite sky filled with puffy white clouds.

Before I knew it, I rounded the large white buoy in front of the oil rig and started my return to shore. I felt currents tugging me first in one direction, then the other, and I wondered with great fascination how the currents moved, how they chose a direction.

Everything was new, fresh, alive, and wonderful. The water played like music around my head, my shoulders shimmered in the sunlight, and I grew stronger, my strokes became more powerful. I went faster and faster, catching more swimmers, delighted with everything. There were white sails on the horizon, slowly drifting toward me; pelicans soared overhead in single file, wings stretched wide, each bird riding the tailwind of the bird ahead. There were fishing boats, with seagulls circling and crying overhead.

I could see the end of the pier and there were people cheering. I saw my mother smiling at me, in a warm, honey-colored coat, and my tall father standing beside her, clapping. They were waving at me. And I was elated. I was flying across the water, stronger, so much stronger than when I'd started. I passed two more male swimmers, saw the beach beneath the water, rode a wave in to shore, ran up the beach, and won the race. For the first time, I'd finished first. It wasn't the age-group race; it was the women's race, and I was thrilled. When the results of the swim were posted, I discovered that I had come in third in the overall standings. That meant that I had raced against not just kids my age but men and women who were much older.

Just an hour later, I entered the two-mile race. It didn't matter that I hadn't had much rest; I felt all warmed up. And this time, I ran across the beach faster, cleared the waves, and won the second race. Then I entered the one-mile race and placed second place. I wanted to do better, but another girl was faster. Still, it was sweetly satisfying to realize that there was something out there for me. All those years of training in the pool had paid off. My parents came over and wrapped a towel around me. "You did a great job," my mother said. Her brown eyes shimmered, and she smiled. My father patted me solidly on the back. "Good job," he said. "How did you feel?"

"I felt great. I wonder if there are other rough-water races. This was so much fun."

Over the P.A. system, Ron Blackledge, the

coach of the Seal Beach Swim Team, was announcing that some of the members of his team were going to be attempting a swim across the Catalina Channel. In a straight line, it was a twenty-one-mile trip from Catalina Island to the California mainland. I don't know why I even thought that it might be possible, but I knew I wanted to do it more than anything I had ever done before.

The next morning at workout I asked Coach Gambril if he would ask Ron Blackledge if I could train with his team and attempt the swim with them.

Ron Blackledge called me that evening. He said he had seen me swim and yes, he would be pleased to have me join them. He explained that I didn't have to commit right away; I could come to some of their workouts and see what they were like. The team was training six days a week, with Sundays off for recovery. Workouts started at five a.m. and went for three to four hours, depending on the distance they were swimming that day. The team had been training for this swim for a year. They planned to make the swim in August, so I would have only six weeks to train with them. "Is this really something you'd be interested in doing? It's a lot different from working out in a pool," Ron cautioned.

"Yes, I really want to do this. I'm so excited that you'll let me try out for the team," I said.

The next morning, my mother drove me to Seal Beach. Beneath the lights of the pier, a group of swimmers were standing in a semicircle around Ron, huddling against the morning chill, while Ron discussed the previous day's workout. He made comments to each swimmer about his or her performance. That was important to me. He saw each swimmer as an individual, and this was how he ensured I would know exactly how I was doing.

"Oh, hello, Lynne." Ron was in his thirties and had a youthful face, wavy dark brown hair, brown eyes, and thin gold-rimmed glasses. He motioned for me to join them, and suggested that my mother join the other mothers on the pier. In a few minutes he would be going up there, where they could watch us swim together.

Ron went around the circle making introductions: "This is Stacey Fresonske, Nancy Dale, Dennis Sullivan, Dale O'Connor, and Andy Taylor. Andy is the youngest one here — he's twelve. Everyone else is the same age as you, fourteen." They each said hello and immediately made me feel welcome.

"This is Lynne's first time working out in the ocean," Ron said, "so I want you to help her, teach her what you have learned. Okay, you're going to start with a mile warm-up. Stretch it out and stay together. Lynne, you swim between Stacey and Dale. Okay, let's get started."

At 5:00 a.m. the Pacific Ocean was onyx black, illuminated only by the small globe lights along the pier.

Stacey led the way into the water, advising, "Make sure to slide your feet along the bottom. There are lots of stingrays here. They look like small bat rays, but they have a long tail with a stinger at the very tip, and they'll zap you if you step on them. It's just a defensive mechanism — they don't attack — but if you get stung, your foot will become as large as a football. If you slide your feet, you'll stir up the bottom sand and scare them away."

We moved under one of the lights on the pier as Stacey tucked her short blond hair into a thick white bathing cap. She was tall and lean. Dale was walking beside me. She was a medium-built girl with long, dark brown hair, brown eyes, and a cheerful face. She showed me how to slide my feet, but the water was pitch-black and I couldn't see a thing. "If you're allergic to the sting you can go into shock," she said.

Something fluttered against my foot, and I instinctively jumped, wondering if it was a fish or a stingray. "What do you do if you get stung?"

"Put your foot in water as hot as you can stand. That draws the venom out," Dale said.

"You're doing fine," Nancy Dale said once we were swimming, her voice high and childlike. Nancy had long blond hair that she wound up and stuffed into her bathing cap. She was a lot thinner than the other girls. "When you dive through the waves make sure to extend your arms over your head; that way if there's a sandbar or something under the water, you won't hit it with your head. You'll want to do the same thing when you come back to shore," Nancy instructed.

A white line of bubbling water surrounded us like skirts of lace. It felt as if we were swimming through New Year's Eve champagne. The bubbles tickled, and the chill made me draw in a breath, and I laughed. This was a great adventure, nothing like swimming back and forth in a heated pool, following a black line and going nowhere. This was so much fun.

When a large wave rose above the horizon Stacey shouted, "We've got to dive under this one or we're going to get crunched."

I dove into the deep black water with my arms extended over my head. And when I surfaced I could hear the others swimming but couldn't see them. Listening for the sound of their hands hitting the water, I swam in that direction. And then I could see just the outlines of their bodies. We were swimming in the early morning because the water was calmer and it would give us a feeling for what it would be like to swim across the Catalina Channel at night.

We lined up side by side, making sure the lifeguard tower on the pier was behind us. We aimed for the flashing green lights on top of the oil islands in Long Beach, using these lights as navigational points, and began swimming toward them. We moved in unison across the water. With Stacey and Dale on either side of me, I felt like a young dolphin protected by older dolphins, riding in their slipstream.

Once we reached the Seal Beach jetty, the half-mile mark, we turned and swam back toward the pier, using the light on top of the lifeguard tower as our reference point. Light was gathering on the horizon as seagulls, pelicans, and sandpipers were rising with the light. Between the rush of breaking waves we heard their plaintive calls overhead.

When we approached the pier, Ron and our mothers were hanging over the railings and shouting, "Good job, kids" and "All right, way to go."

"How are you all feeling?" Ron asked.

"Good," the team chimed, and I said, "Wonderful. Absolutely wonderful."

My teammates didn't think I was being serious, but I was. For the team, open-water swimming was old news. It was hard to drag themselves out of bed at four-thirty in the morning and dive into cold water. It was hard to not just roll over and go back to sleep. They had to want to do this. But they'd been working toward this goal for a year. Somehow Ron understood that having someone new on their team would help rekindle their excitement and revitalize their spirit. And I knew I was lucky to be included.

Ron gave us another set: "I want you to swim five miles. Descending. That means you're going to swim the first mile at a moderate speed, then make each one after that faster. The last mile should be an all-out sprint.

"And Lynne, go at your own speed. Also,

61

you're going to find that the straps of your nylon swimsuit chafe badly. You might want to do like the other girls and tie a string around your waist so you can drop your straps. That keeps your swimsuit from falling off. You can use Vaseline instead on the friction points, but it doesn't work very well."

The orange sun rose slowly above the lip of the sea, creating a river of light that bathed the swimmers in gold. We swam the first three miles together, and then Stacey and Andy broke away with me. We were flying across the sea, arm to arm, breath to breath, pulling deeper into the water, pressing each other forward, moving faster and faster. Inside me there was still so much more energy ready to burst forth. But it was better for me to hold back, and until I had been with them longer, I didn't want to pose a challenge to them; I wanted to fit in and be part of the team.

One of our toughest training swims came a week later. We were supposed to make a ten-mile swim from the Seal Beach Pier to Bolsa Chica State Beach and back. Ron was rowing in front of us in a heavy wooden dory. We were taking short breaks to test our different hot drinks. In 1971, water bottles hadn't been invented yet, so before workout we had filled plastic ketchup bottles with hot tea with sugar, warm orange juice, beef broth, hot apple cider, hot chocolate, and coffee loaded with sugar. We were trying to figure out what we could use on the Catalina crossing to boost our blood sugar and replace lost heat. With salt water in our mouths from swimming in the sea, the orange juice was absolutely disgusting, beef broth was bad, and hot chocolate was a real mistake because it contained milk solids, which were known to make swimmers nauseated. We narrowed our choices to coffee, tea, and hot cider.

That morning, we swam against a slight current, less than half a knot, as we headed south along the California shore, past Surfside and Sunset Beach. The sky was cerulean blue, without a single cloud, and the summer sun was warm on our shoulders. When we made the turn at Bolsa Chica beach, the wind started blowing across the sea, piling the water into half-foot waves. Not only was swimming directly into the chop tiring, it was hard to breathe because we were getting so much spray in our faces and we were swallowing seawater. Nancy began to feel seasick and cold. Ron urged her to stay in the water, and he told us to pick up our pace. The wind increased to fifteen knots. Short, fast waves smashed over our heads. Nancy, who was thinner than the rest of us, was complaining and shivering in the water. Ron recognized that she might be going into the first stage of hypothermia; her body temperature was probably dropping from the prolonged exposure to sixty-eight-degree water. He finally stopped and pulled her out. He was not happy. It was tough work rowing against the waves, and he was disappointed in the team's performance.

I kept working hard, enjoying it, drawing from every experience, learning how to feel the rhythm of the ocean, hear the tempo of the waves, and dance with the water using my balance, my strength, and all my senses. The waves grew louder and stronger. I improvised, adjusted the pitch of my hand, changed the rate of my strokes, and pressed my head deeper into the water so I could move through the waves instead of using more energy to bounce up and over them.

That training swim took us nearly five hours, and by the time we rounded the Seal Beach Pier Ron was so tired and annoyed with us, he said he would wait to discuss what happened the next day at morning workout.

I waited apprehensively until the next morning. At our team meeting, Ron came down hard on us. "How can you expect to swim the Catalina Channel if you can't even make a ten-mile workout in a little chop? What are you going to do, give up? What are you going to do when you hit a current in the channel, swim at the same speed? This swim was nothing compared to what you're going to face in the Catalina Channel. And it wasn't even half the distance. You know that. You're probably going to swim a lot more than twenty-one miles with the current changes. If you're going to do this, you're going to have to work a lot harder. You've got to be more focused, more determined. You've got to be willing to fight for this. You've got to be able to be cold and fight through it. You've got to be able to be tired and push harder. You've just got to change your attitude. If you don't want to do it, tell me now, so I won't waste my time. Is that clear?" His voice boomed and it was filled with underlying anger and exasperation.

No one said a word. Our heads were bowed. I stared at my feet.

Ron continued: "You're only giving a sixty percent effort. You have to give one hundred percent every workout. You need to realize you've only got one month remaining to prepare. I don't want to be the bad guy," he said, softening his tone, "but this is the reality."

We thought he was going to blast us with a hard workout that morning. Instead, he said, "I want you to swim two miles, warm down, and then go home and think about what I've said." Then he turned to me and said, "You're really going to have to do something about those cuts along your neck and, I bet, along your sides or they're going to get infected. I am not going to tell you you have to do this, but I think you'll be doing yourself a favor if you swim without your top."

I no longer cared about modesty. The nylon bathing suit straps had cut deep bloody gashes on either side of my neck and chafed my underarms so badly that I had to keep my arms slightly out at my sides so that the skin under my arms wouldn't touch anything, because it would stick together and then bleed when I pulled the skin apart. The sheer mileage and abrasive salt water had also caused my nylon swimsuit to cut bleeding holes on either side of my chest. Taking a shower had been awful. When I pulled my pajama top over my head, the top stuck to the wounds and I had to rip the skin to get it off.

All of us were pretty glum after the

workout that morning. When we returned the next morning, we were ready to start anew, with more focus than before.

For the next two weeks we intensified our workouts, and since Ron had basically given us the green light to swim at our own speed, I no longer held back. I challenged Stacey, Dennis, and Andy, the faster members on the team. Andy and I would usually break away from the others and race each other to finish first. He had been the fastest swimmer in the group, and now I was faster. Toward the end of the workout I'd leave him behind. On a mile swim, I'd finish two or three minutes ahead of the team. I wanted to make this swim, and I wanted to be prepared, so I gave my best effort every day.

It was understood that we would swim across the Catalina Channel together. That meant we would pace one another and stay with one another from the start to the finish of the crossing. But now that Ron had given me the freedom to go at full speed during workouts, it was as if before I was trotting and now I was galloping across the surface of the sea.

Ron was pleased with our progress, but he was getting a lot of outside interference. People were questioning his rationale. How could he even think of taking six teenage kids across the Catalina Channel? Didn't he realize how far it was? Didn't he recognize how dangerous it could be?

That put some uncertainty into his head, and while he tried to shield us from it, we knew that deep down inside Ron wondered if we would make it. We did too, but that was part of what made this swim so exciting.

Beginning two weeks before the swim, my mother drove me to Seal Beach every night at midnight and stood on the pier with the other mothers, watching me swim. She sometimes stayed for an hour. I could see her under the lamplight, bundled up in a camel-hair coat and red scarf. Sometimes I could smell the coffee in her mug, and I always heard her voice when she was talking with the other mothers or shouting a few encouraging words to me and the team. She didn't stay for the whole workout, though; she had to get home to sleep and take care of the rest of the family.

We swam the same amount of time, from three to four hours a night, doing distances of five to ten miles. But it was very different from swimming in the morning darkness. At midnight the sky and sea were deeper black and a little more eerie, and the golden lights in the homes lining the shores of Seal Beach looked warm and inviting. As the first week passed, sometimes I wished I could go inside one of those homes and just curl up and go to sleep.

Our bodies were tired from the workouts, and we were having difficulty adjusting to the time change. After our workouts we had to force ourselves to stay awake. We'd congregate at Nancy Dale's or Stacey Fresonske's house and have a stay-awake party. We would take showers, play card games and board games, watch old movies and television, eat popcorn and drink hot chocolate.

By six a.m. we would be nudging one another, trying to keep ourselves awake. There were teammates who got cranky, but we didn't care; we were in this together, and we were determined to keep each other awake. We tickled teammates' noses with feathers and put peanut butter on their hands so that when they went to scratch their nose they got peanut butter on their face. We created other gentle forms of torture that kept us laughing and motivated us to avoid being the object of these pranks.

At nine or ten in the morning, we would head home. My mother would pick me up, and once home, I'd immediately slide into bed. With all the normal daily phone calls and family activity it was difficult to sleep during the day. It was also difficult to sleep because with every passing day we were getting closer to the day of the attempt, and our excitement was multiplying exponentially.

Toward the end of the two-week period, we had almost gotten our bodies adjusted to the time change. On that last morning we met at Nancy Dale's home. She opened two bottles of sparkling cider and poured it into some champagne glasses. "I want to make a toast," she said with delight, handing us the glasses.

We raised them high into the air and she said, "We will make this swim across the Catalina Channel as a team. No matter what happens, we will stay together and we will become the first group of kids ever to do this." We drank the sweet cider and broke out into cheers and wide smiles.

4

Twenty-six Miles Across the Sea

We traveled in a forty-foot fishing boat piloted by Dr. Fresonske, Stacey's father, to Catalina Island. On board were members of the Seal Beach and Long Beach lifeguard crews who had volunteered to escort us on the crossing on long paddleboards or in kayaks. John Stockwell and Lyle Johnson, two burly old-time Long Beach lifeguards who had accompanied other swimmers on cross-channel attempts, planned to meet us at Divers Cove on the Isthmus, the westernmost section of the island and the closest point to the mainland.

We reached Catalina Island in late afternoon, a trip that took just two and a half hours. For most of the journey we stayed in the cabin below, not wanting to see the distance we were going to swim, afraid that it

71

would psych us out. We tried to sleep in the bunks, but we were far too excited to do anything other than chatter loudly over the drone of the boat's engines. From the deck above, we heard snatches of conversation, Ron's voice and the crew's discussing how the swim would be coordinated. We knew we were heading into Divers Cove when Dr. Fresonske cut the boat's engine and we heard someone shout, "Drop the anchor." It hit the water with an enormous splash, and all of us raced up the stairs to get to the deck so we could see where we had stopped.

The sun was beating down on the water, the glare so strong that it was hard to see the cove. It appeared to be small and well sheltered by low cliffs covered with shrubs. Except for one small boat, there was no one else in the area. A strong breeze, maybe five knots, was ruffling the water and that intensified our mood. We were not certain whether we would swim that evening; it all depended on having good weather. August was usually a fairly calm time in the Catalina Channel, but anything could happen.

This uncertainty put us a little on edge, and knowing that we had to wait until midnight heightened our anxiousness and excitement. Andy, Dennis, and Nancy decided to put on their swimsuits and paddle over to the island to explore. Stacey and I decided to go back below and try to sleep. We knew we were going to have a very long night. And I didn't want to waste any energy now.

I crawled back into one of the bunks, put a pillow over my head, closed out all sounds, and took my mind away. Time passed — I'm not sure how much — and when I awoke, Mrs. Fresonske was offering us large bowls of chili filled with beans and beef for dinner. It was delicious, but it was not a good choice for a long-distance swim. At that time, carbo-loading and the reasons for it hadn't been discovered.

At about ten p.m. Ron gathered us in the cabin and explained how we would coordinate with the crew.

The boat we were on would be positioned about a half mile ahead of us. We would use the lights on board the boat as navigational guides. While floodlights would have helped us see the boat better, the crew was afraid that a lot of light would attract fish, and decided to use only the cabin light and the small red and green lights on the bow and stern.

We would be swimming in a V formation, like a flock of pelicans. We would swim using the English Channel Association rules. We would wear only bathing suits, bathing caps, and goggles — no thermal swimsuits or thermal hoods or fins. We would tread water or float when we needed to rest. We were not allowed any type of artificial support or flotation. And we could not touch anyone on the boat at any time during the swim or we would be disqualified. That meant that our food and drinks had to be tossed to us; we hoped none of the food spent too long in the salt water before we recovered it.

Ron positioned me at the top of the V, with Andy on one side of me and Stacey on the other. Dennis would swim beside Andy and Nancy would swim on the outside of Stacey. It was strange and sad that Ron didn't mention Dale. She had caught the flu. She and Ron had discussed the option of postponing the swim, but she didn't want to hold us back, and she'd called that morning to wish us the best of luck.

Ron said that Mr. Yeo, one of the Seal Beach team fathers, would be riding a paddleboard beside Dennis and a Seal Beach lifeguard would be paddling a kayak on the outside of Nancy. Every hour or so the lifeguards would trade off with the four

74

lifeguards in the main boat.

The dory rowed by Lyle Johnson and John Stockwell would precede us by about twenty-five yards. They would row the entire distance across the channel and would have a small white light on their stern to guide us. Our paddlers and kayakers would strap small flashlights to their boards and kayak so we could see them during the swim.

At eleven p.m. Stockwell and Johnson began shuttling us ashore in their dory. When I climbed into the boat Stockwell and Johnson began rowing, and with each pull on the oars, I felt my excitement growing. The night was so black we could just see the waves break along the shore. Beyond that it was utter blackness. Guided only by voices, I reached the starting area, where I jumped out into ankle-deep water and searched for my teammates.

"We're over here — come this way!" Stacey shouted, her voice echoing off the invisible cliff walls. Guided by a pinpoint of light from one of the flashlights, I stumbled on some rocks and slid on what I hoped was a clump of kelp.

The light grew brighter, and I saw Mrs. Fresonske holding the flashlight. Stacey, wearing pink Playtex gloves, was grabbing handfuls of Vaseline and slathering them on her neck.

"Here you go." Stacey giggled, picking up one of the five tubs of goo and tossing it to me. "Need some gloves?"

"No, thanks, I'm fine," I said. Using my ring finger and my pinky I dug out a glob of Vaseline, careful not to get any on my other fingers. I would need to keep them clean so I could adjust my goggles. If they were smeared with goo, I wouldn't be able to see anything. I spread the stuff around my neck, armpits, and the leg holes of my swimsuit. Then I checked the wide elastic band around my waist, making sure it was taut so I could drop my straps but not lose my swimsuit during the crossing.

Nancy joined us. She found her jar and covered her arms and legs with the stuff. Andy and Dennis were standing somewhere nearby; we could hear them laughing and slapping handfuls of Vaseline on each other. When they were finished they were covered from their necks to their ankles in slime.

"Here, Nancy, let me give you a hug," Dennis said, opening his arms wide and chasing after her.

Andy grabbed another glob and also took off after her. Someone slimed me on the shoulder and I laughed, then moved out of the light to escape. I didn't want to waste any energy, and I knew that this swim was going to take every bit I had. I also needed to calm down and think. There would be plenty of time to do this during the swim, hours upon hours, but I needed to find my focus.

I looked up at the sky. The moon was distant and less than half full, perfect for the swim. It meant that we would be making the crossing on a neap tide. There would be less water movement between high and low tide, less tidal change, and less current, and this would give us more of a chance of completing the crossing.

Looking more deeply into the sky, I found the North Star and noted our position in relationship to it. I planned to use this as a reference point during the swim. A breeze was stirring the water, and I felt my skin begin to chill. The last thing I wanted to do was start off cold. I told myself to calm down, to take it one mile at a time, and to never look back once I left shore. I knew I was prepared, and I was confident.

Running my hands along the back of my head, I parted my long brown hair, wound one side around my hand and stuffed it into my white cap, then did the same for the other side. The waiting was making me anxious.

Ron finally came ashore. He was speaking on the walkie-talkie with my father, who had come along as the team physician. My father was checking with Ron, asking him where he could find the blankets on the lead boat in case someone went into hypothermia and needed to be bundled up. I could hear the sounds of the paddlers moving their paddleboards into position; it was so black that someone ran into someone else. This all seemed to be taking an incredibly long amount of time. I worried again about cooling off.

Finally, Ron called us over for a last-minute pep talk. "In a few minutes, Stockwell and Johnson, in the dory, are going to turn on a spotlight so they can see you enter the water. Mr. Yeo is going to fire the starting gun, then accompany you on the paddleboard. I want you to stay close together. It is very dark here. Darker than I expected it to be. We don't want to lose any of you in the water. If there is a problem, I don't want you stopping. We won't be able to see you if you stop. You're going to have to keep swimming with your head up and tell us what your problem is. I don't think you're going to have any problems. The water is calm. The forecast is for light and variable winds late in the morning. I don't think we could have a better day for this. You've trained hard. You're ready. Is everyone set?"

"Yes," we said. We turned and wished one another good luck, then we hugged. We walked to the edge of the ocean and Mr. Yeo said, "Okay, take your marks," and then he fired the gun. We saw the white flash and heard the gunshot echoing off the cliff walls.

I walked into the water, dove through the surf, and began swimming. It felt wonderful, exciting, strange, and scary knowing that I had just pushed off Catalina Island and was now swimming across the vast Pacific Ocean to the North American continent. Turning my head and breathing, I saw the universe filled with light from distant constellations. I felt even smaller, and yet somehow powerful.

Swimming was difficult. While we could see the tiny lights on the dory and on the paddleboards, we couldn't see one another. We were on edge. There were deep-water pelagic sharks in this channel: big ones, white ones, man- and woman-eating ones. No long-distance swimmer had been attacked during a crossing, yet we knew that they were down there somewhere and that any moment we could become a midnight snack.

We were swimming erratically — fast, moderate, then faster — and we were unable to settle down and establish a pace. This was using way too much energy. We needed to get into our flow and maintain one speed for efficiency. The truth was that we were excited and scared. We had never swum in such blackness. We couldn't see our own arms or our hands pulling right beneath our bodies. For safety and a sense of security, we were swimming closer than we ever did in workouts. Stacey unintentionally elbowed me in the ribs; I nearly jumped out of my skin. Overcorrecting, she cut too far left and ran into Nancy. Spooked, Nancy let out a series of bloodcurdling screams. That set off a series of chain reactions, and we ran into each other, overcompensated, and ran into someone else.

Sharks are attracted to thrashing and splashing, sounds that resemble sick or injured fish. This is their food source. Using sensors on their snouts, they can detect electrical fields and feel, through their noses, the movement of fish and people in the water. Donald Nelson, a shark expert who did pioneering work in this field, once told me that sharks can detect even minute electrical fields emitted by fish and other animals. I wondered if they could feel the electrical impulses of our hearts. Mine was beating fast and strong. I pushed that thought away. It wouldn't help me at all in my effort to swim across this channel. But I knew the way we were swimming, we sounded more like food than swimmers.

In the distance we could barely see the lead boat. It looked like a star on the water. The paddlers and kayaker were not visible, but I could hear them saying, "You're doing a great job. Keep going."

I lifted my head to find the tiny light on the dory and tried to maintain a constant distance from it, hoping that I could establish a pace this way. After perhaps an hour, it was hard to tell whether this plan was working; there were no reference points to help me determine the distance we had covered or the time it had taken to arrive at that point. Still, it seemed like we were settling into a pace, beginning to stretch out our arm strokes and slow our rapid breathing. Then someone squealed and adrenaline shot through my body, and I felt myself swimming on the upper inches of the water. Worse were those moments of not knowing. There was a delay between the scream and finding out what happened.

"It's okay; it's just seaweed. Don't worry, relax — just reverse your stroke and you'll untangle yourself," one of the paddlers reassured us.

"There's a problem," someone said. There was a discussion, but it was hard to catch the conversation with my head underwater, so I swam with my head up.

"The lights on these boards are fading," one paddler shouted. "So is the one on the dory. Look, it's fading to orange. The batteries are dying. Mine's nearly gone."

"We don't have much time before they both go," said the other paddler.

"Does anyone have extra batteries?" someone shouted.

I heard Stockwell on the walkie-talkie in the dory talking to someone in the lead boat. "They're searching," his deep voice boomed across.

"Have them move closer together."

Then someone whistled loudly and said, "Hey, hold up for a minute." It was Mr. Yeo. "You guys are going to have to stop for a minute. We need to put some new batteries in our flashlights so you can see us."

"Ahhhhh! Shoot!" we said, treading water. "How long are we going to have to wait?" When we stopped swimming, we couldn't hang on to anyone or anything or we would be disqualified.

"This is really dumb. How could they

have forgotten the batteries? Are we going to have to stop the channel swim because of this?" Andy said.

"I'm getting awfully cold just treading water," Nancy said.

When we were swimming, we were generating heat, but once we stopped, our heat production diminished substantially. In a swimming pool, where water temperatures usually ranged from seventy-six to eighty degrees, we wouldn't have lost body heat very quickly, but the cool sixty-five-degree seawater began leaching heat from our bodies. Nancy sucked her teeth, making a shivering sound.

Someone was saying something on the radio. It was garbled. Stockwell translated: "They found them. It will only be a couple more minutes. They're going to turn the lead boat and bring the batteries here. That way you can also have a feeding."

We had the plastic ketchup bottles on the lead boat, along with thermoses filled with warm tea, coffee, and apple cider, and with fresh water.

While the paddlers fixed the flashlights, the crew in the lead boat tossed us the fresh water first. We rinsed the salt water from our mouths, tossed the bottles back onto the deck, and then were thrown our choice of beverage. Floating on our backs, we drank the warm liquids as the crew shouted words of encouragement. I heard my father say, "Good job, sweet." I smiled. I was happy he was with me on the swim. He always seemed to know the right thing to do whenever someone needed to make an important decision.

We tossed our empty bottles to one of the lifeguards and the lead boat pulled ahead, becoming once again a small white light on the black horizon.

"All right, let's get moving," Ron yelled.

In the back of our minds we wondered who would be the first to get out. Who would be the coldest or weakest swimmer? Who would go first or second? None of us thought, *It's going to be me.* And none of us wanted it to happen to anyone. We wanted to complete the crossing as a team. And somehow we sensed that if one of us climbed out of the water, it would diminish the strength of the team. I used that as a motivator and told myself that no matter what, I was not going to be the one to get out. I was going to make this swim.

About two hours into the swim my eyes adjusted to the starlight and I began to relax and stretch my stroke out. I felt as if I were swimming through a black-and-white photograph of the sea at night. Without color, the world I swam through was in stark contrast, reduced to luminous blacks, brilliant whites, and tonal grays. Looking up toward the sky on a breath, I watched the brightest stars travel across the heavens as we moved across the sea. Each time I breathed, I looked deeper into space, seeing stars beyond stars. Suddenly I felt as if I were falling upward. Shaking my head, I searched for a star to fix upon, to help me regain my balance. But I couldn't find one, so I looked down into the deep water. I felt as if I were teetering on the edge of a great abyss. The sky was expanding upward and outward, and I felt I was on the upper inches of the water, and the entire sea was dropping below me.

My mind searched for some stable reference point, but this was so different from swimming along the shores of Seal Beach. There was no pier, no homes, no palm trees — nothing. I had promised myself not to look back, but I had to. Only there was nothing behind us — not even Catalina Island. This made me feel more jumbled. To regain some sense of security, I swam closer to Stacey, and my hand hit her shoulder. We both jumped, but that contact snapped me back to reality, and I marveled once again at the night. Falling stars were arching across the black heavens, leaving long contrails of fiery white light. And in the phosphorescent ocean — the results of a large phytoplankton bloom — silvery bubbles rolled out of my mouth, and as my arms churned the water, they etched a trail of white iridescent light across the shimmering black sea.

We moved together and began to slide into our pace. About an hour passed, and we stopped to feed beside the lead boat. We felt a school of small fish swimming around us, bumping into our legs and feet. Flying fish the size of mockingbirds were leaping out of the water. They'd emerge from the depths and fly across the air, flapping their fins and sailing across the sky. Some flew right into us, and we let out squeals of delight. Some arced over the paddleboards, and a couple landed in the boat. In the phosphorescent light, they were magically turning iridescent pink, blue, purple, rose, and green.

Inspired by the natural light display, we plodded on. Ten miles into the swim, about four hours out, Nancy was having problems. "I'm so cold," she said. Her teeth were chattering.

The crew encouraged her to keep going, and we did the same. But she began stopping every one or two hundred meters. "I'm so cold. I don't think I can do this."

The voices of her teammates surrounded her with encouragement. "Come on, Nancy, just pick up your pace. You'll be fine. If you swim faster you'll get warm. Come on, you can do it."

She swam for another hundred yards. "Ron, I don't think I can keep going. I'm just so cold."

"Pick up the pace, Nancy. You'll be fine," he reassured her.

"But Ron, I don't think I can. I'm so cold," she whined.

Her talk of coldness was making me feel cold. And it was having the same effect on all the team. As long as we sat there treading water, we were undoubtedly getting colder. Every time we stopped, we lost heat. It was heat that we'd never get back. A chill crept into my body, and a shiver rippled through it.

"Let's go, Nancy," Andy said now, impatiently.

"I just can't." She started crying. "I am too cold. I have to get out," she insisted.

"Okay, okay, Nancy. Let's get her into the dory and transfer her to the lead boat," Ron said, his voice filled with urgency.

Slowly she swam over to the dory. Stockwell and Johnson turned on a larger light, and we watched them lift her thin, stiff, pale body out of the water. Her lips were blue, and her voice cracked as she said, "I'm so sorry, you guys. I didn't want to stop. I wanted to stay with you."

"It's okay, Nancy," we reassured her. But my heart was breaking. To have trained so long and so hard for this and to have to get out.

"I think she's going into hypothermia," Stockwell said, and he radioed the lead boat to let my father know what was happening. He would bundle her in blankets and have her sit in a warm area and drink hot fluids to help her get her body temperature back up to normal.

When the lead boat arrived, we watched her being transferred from the dory to the boat. She shouted, "Good luck, you guys. I know you're going to make it. I'll be cheering you on from the larger boat." And then she burst into tears.

It was so hard to see her that way. So hard to know that her dream died at that moment. Silently we wondered who would be next.

Sensing that we needed to push our minds away from what had just happened, Dennis said, "Come on, let's stick together. We can do it."

"Yes, if we stick together, we'll make it," Andy echoed.

"All for one and one for all," Stacey said.

Perhaps four and a half hours into the swim, as the black veil of night was fading to gray, we were swimming strongly. The air temperature was still in the high sixties, as was the water, and I was actually starting to feel relaxed. My stroke was long and deep, and I was beginning to feel myself picking up the pace. For about ten minutes the team stayed with me, but my friends couldn't hold the pace, so I had to drop back. Again, a little while later, I tried to increase the tempo. It didn't work. And at their pace, I was getting cold. I needed to go faster to create heat.

Ron sensed my frustration and told me that he had spoken with Lyle Johnson and John Stockwell. They had suggested that I swim ahead of the group, then wait for them at a feeding stop. It was light enough for the team to easily see the paddlers.

It sounded like a great idea to me, but I asked the team, "Do you mind if I swim ahead of you?"

They didn't care. I had been pushing them too hard.

Thankfully, I began swimming at my own speed. I began to fly across the ocean, like the first time I swam the three-mile race. Everything was working together; everything was in the flow. It felt so wonderful knowing that I could move across the powerful currents of the ocean.

Three times I got up to half a mile ahead of the team and had to tread water and wait for them for ten or twelve minutes. It was awful; sitting there was like sitting in a bathing suit in a refrigerator, but I had no choice; I had agreed to stay with the team. After our feeding, Stockwell and Johnson picked up their rowing pace, and I matched them. They went faster. I increased my speed. I could hear the wooden oars groaning in their locks, and I heard the men breathing heavily. They pushed further, and I followed. Sometime along the way, John Stockwell got on the walkie-talkie, then he shouted to me: "You're halfway across the channel. And you're getting faster with every mile."

I beamed. I was swimming just like Hans Fassnacht, moving like a motorboat across the sea, and I was so excited.

An enormous raspberry-colored sun began rising above the gray Pacific, turning the morning mist to cotton-candy-colored pink and the ocean from slate to bright blue, lavender, rose, and gold. Warm light spread across the water, and now the golden-brown coastal range looked three-dimensional. There was the Palos Verdes Peninsula, and directly in front of us was Point Vicente, our landing spot on the peninsula.

We pulled a couple miles ahead of the team and Stockwell shouted, "Lynne, you're more than an hour ahead of the world-record pace. Not just the women's world record, but also the men's.

"I just spoke with Ron," he added. "He said you don't have to wait for the others. You can go ahead."

More than anything, I wanted to attempt it, and I was confident I could succeed. We were only three miles from shore. It was so possible. But it didn't feel right; I had agreed to stay with the team. From the very beginning, that was what we had decided. They had let me join them. They had helped me. But I wanted to go. How would they feel if I left them to break the world record? Wouldn't that diminish the attention they deserved for their success? How would I feel if they left me behind? I'd be hurt and angry.

The lead boat pulled alongside us, while the crew on board was urging me to go for it. My father was standing quietly near the railing. "You look very good," he said, and smiled.

"Thanks, Dad. How's Nancy?"

"She's warmed up and she's comfortable now."

"Dad, do you think I should go for the record?"

"It's your decision, sweet."

"You'll be the youngest person to hold the world record for the Catalina Channel," Stockwell urged.

Johnson added, "If you wait for the others, you could be in the water for another three or four extra hours."

As I treaded water, others shouted encouragement. "Go for the record!"

"I want to so badly, but I can't. I agreed to stick with the team." I was disappointed, but I knew it was the right decision.

Stockwell saw my expression and said, "Don't worry, you've got plenty of time. You're only fourteen. Sometime you'll come back and break the record. And when you do, we want to be right here with you."

For nearly thirty minutes I treaded water, staring at the California coastline. I wished they were faster. I wished we could break the record together. But when I saw the team slowly staggering toward me, I realized that we didn't have a chance. We had been in the water for at least seven hours. Our skin was splotchy white and gray, our tongues and lips were swollen, and our shoulders were so sore, it hurt to lift our arms. The Vaseline around our arms and necks had clumped up, then melted, and the salt water had acted like sandpaper and chafed portions of our skin away. We looked like we had rope burns around our necks. And despite our goggles, exposure to the salt water had made our eyes painfully bloodshot, and our lids were beginning to swell shut.

Bending over, I grabbed my knees and stretched my back. If I had kept swimming, I don't think I would have had any complaints, but now my sides and my neck ached.

Together we swam at an excruciatingly slow pace. I slipped water with my hands so I could stay with them.

Ron waved me to go ahead. I sprinted forward with Stockwell and Johnson. The cliffs of the Palos Verdes Peninsula towered above us. We waited. We only had eight hundred yards to go, and I just wanted to finish. There were people parking cars on the cliffs, scurrying down a steep embankment to the rocky beach.

Stacey was dropping back. She was about two hundred yards behind the boys, and she looked bad.

When Andy and Dennis reached me, they were too exhausted to talk. Grimly they took long sips of lukewarm tea. We waited for five minutes, but we were getting very cold. Stockwell and Johnson told us to swim four hundred yards and then wait for Stacey.

We crawled slowly forward, and then a current sweeping around Point Vicente slammed into us. The water temperature suddenly dropped to fifty-five degrees. It was so cold every muscle in our bodies stiffened up.

"I'm freezing," Andy said.

"Me too," Dennis said.

"Let's just finish now," Andy urged.

"Look, she's not that far back. She will be here in only a few minutes. Remember, we wanted to do this as a team," I said.

"I can't wait any longer," Andy said, and Dennis joined him.

I waited for Stacey and swam with her to shore.

Dennis and Andy finished the crossing in twelve hours and twenty-six minutes, ten minutes ahead of Stacey and me. We became the youngest group of teenagers to swim across the Catalina Channel. It was a huge achievement, and it awakened a dream that had been sleeping within me: I wanted to swim the English Channel. And now I knew I could make the distance. Both swims were twenty-one miles in a straight line.

While we were rewarming in sleeping bags on the beach in Palos Verdes, I overheard Andy talking with a reporter from the *Los Angeles Times*. He said that he and Dennis were very happy that they'd finished so strongly and that they'd sprinted into shore ten minutes before the girls. That made me angry, but I didn't say anything. At that moment, I decided I was going to swim the English Channel and I wasn't going to wait for anyone. I would try to set a new men's and women's world record.

As soon as I got home that morning I drew a hot bath. I must have sat in it for two hours, and I was so tired I went to bed immediately afterward.

Within a week after the Catalina Channel crossing, I asked my parents if they would support me on a swim across the English Channel to break the world record. They agreed to help. My mother suggested talking with Ron Blackledge to see if he would be willing to coach me.

None of the swimmers who had completed the crossing with me had any desire to make another channel attempt. They returned to pool swimming. If Ron coached me, he would have to do it on an individual basis, and my parents would pay him for his guidance. We discussed the idea over the phone and he asked if he could think about it, talk it over with his wife, and get back to me. Coaching a swimmer for any channel crossing was a huge commitment, and although he immediately said he wanted to do it, he knew that it would impact his time with his wife.

I'm not sure what I would have done if Ron had said no, but when he called and told me that he would coach me, I was excited and happy. Fifteen years old was considered young to attempt to swim the Channel, let alone go for the record. Most of the people who swam it were in their late twenties or thirties. Everyone knew that it took substantial mental and physical maturity. Swimming the English Channel was like climbing Mount Everest. It was the absolute zenith of the sport.

5

English Channel

At first, I didn't know anything about established thought; I was too young to know, too certain that this was something I wanted to do ever since that day in New Hampshire when Mrs. Milligan had planted the original thought in my mind. The day she saw me swimming through the storm. Ever since that day, the dream had been there, just waiting for the right moment to burst forth.

Fortunately, my folks were also able to overlook established thought. They believed age was important, but they also believed that you could achieve almost anything in life with hard work and talent. I was lucky that they were open-minded about this, because I'm not sure what I would have done if they had told me I was too young; I probably would have worked on them until they couldn't stand it any longer and finally gave in. They knew I was determined; my father called it stubborn. Still, they also knew how important it was to have dreams and goals and a path in life. And they instilled this in me.

It seemed, too, that this was exactly the right path for me. Within a week of Ron's commitment to coach me, a cousin introduced me to an Egyptian swimmer who had attempted swimming the English Channel five times. When we met, Fahmy Attallah was in his sixties, although he looked like he was forty. He was a clinical psychologist in Long Beach, California, a humanist, and a gentle-spirited and enlightened man.

Fahmy and his wife, Donna, invited my parents and me to their home to make sure that this goal was something that I — not my parents — wanted to achieve before he decided to serve as a mentor and role model to me.

Fahmy was a short man, only five feet high; this told me that size, like age, didn't really matter unless one let it. His shoulders were broad, as was his chest, and his arms looked powerful.

Still holding my hand in both of his, he led me to the table. There were piles of stuffed grape leaves, triangles of phyllo dough filled with feta cheese, roasted eggplant, and tomato and ground lamb, piles of fluffy rice topped with pine nuts, and wonderful dishes I had never tried until that night.

Fahmy had me sit beside him, and, handing me a platter of rice, he said in a melodious Egyptian accent, "Whatever questions you may have, I will try to answer them for you."

Fahmy had grown up in Cairo and had swum for the Egyptian national team in the 1940s and 1950s. He was one of Egypt's most celebrated athletes, in a country that names streets after long-distance swimmers. In 1941 he made a forty-one-hour long-distance swim in the Mediterranean, establishing a new record for time and distance. Fahmy made this swim at a time before goggles had been invented, or snug-fitting bathing caps, so to protect his eyes and ears from the salt water, he swam breaststroke with his head above the water. The longest swim he accomplished was in the Mediterranean. He swam nonstop for eighty hours. "The way I do this is, I meditate when I swim," he said.

I did too. I knew that we understood each other. I immediately liked him. When my father told him that I was very stubborn, he laughed and tilted his head way back, until tears filled his eyes. "That is a very strong characteristic for a channel swimmer. Perhaps a better word for stubborn would be *determined*," he said, wiping happy tears from his eyes.

During his daily swims, he pondered life's big questions, and I believe that through those daily meditations he had discovered the essence of himself and the answers to his questions. "You know, the ocean is a very, very beautiful place. It is God's gift to us," he said.

I was sure Fahmy was God's gift to me. I think he saw in me a younger version of himself, full of hope, eagerness, and determination. That day I told him that I was very grateful that he was sharing all of his knowledge with me. He said that once there had been someone who had helped him, and one day I would also pass on what I had learned to someone else. That was the way it was meant to be.

He began describing what I should expect. He said, "The English Channel is filled with very cold water, strong tides, and strong currents. But you have already swum across the Catalina Channel, so I know that once you train for it, you can do it. One of the biggest problems is the cold water. It stings; it feels like prickers in your skin. The water temperature in the Channel is usually between fifty and sixty degrees. Many people have problems with the cold water. But you will not have any problem because you are training in the ocean in cold water."

Fahmy's confidence in me made me feel happy, and he made me feel more self-assured. He was not only giving me insights into the physical challenge of the English Channel; Fahmy was beginning to coach my mind. It was so natural for him; he did it without thinking. Everything he said about what I was doing was positive; everything seemed possible.

On the day we first met, Fahmy painted a mental picture of Dover Harbor for me. "The beach at Dover is made of pebbles. You can hear the beautiful waves caressing them. High above the harbor are the beautiful white cliffs, and always there are seagulls, circling overhead. Dover is a very beautiful place. It is well protected, and it is a good place to train."

Fahmy told me that I needed to contact the Channel Swimming Association in Dover and become a member of the organization. They would send an official along on the swim to make sure the crossing was done under English Channel rules. He explained that I could get a list of names of pilots. These were mostly fishermen who knew the tides and currents in the Channel, and, for a fee, they would accompany a swimmer, helping with navigation and ensuring the swimmer's safety during the crossing.

After dinner, we moved into the living room and sat down. I asked Fahmy how long it had taken him to swim the Channel. A pained look quickly crossed his face, and he drew in a deep breath. He said he had attempted the English Channel five times and each time he encountered poor conditions. Swimming breaststroke with his head above water didn't help either. He was a slow swimmer, and the tide was faster than he was, so on his first and second attempts, he was carried with the tide in an enormous circle, not even getting within sight of the English shore.

On his third attempt, his pilot got lost in the fog and guided him in the entirely wrong direction, back toward the Belgian coast. Despite this, Fahmy didn't give up. He swam for twenty-six hours. With a trembling voice he said, "I got within four hundred yards of the English coast. I could see those very beautiful white cliffs of Dover and the pebbles on the beach. The water was very calm, and I rolled over on my back for a moment to rest. King Farouk, the king of Egypt, was standing on the shore. He waved to me. Suddenly two men in the boat put a blanket under me and lifted me out of the water before I could stop them. They thought I had passed out from the cold water. By putting that blanket under me, they disqualified me." He paused.

"King Farouk told me afterward, 'Fahmy, it broke my heart when you did not finish.' And I told him, 'It broke my heart too.' "

After all those years, the pain of not finishing was still apparent. He said that the English Channel had been his greatest disappointment and also the source of his great inner strength. Fahmy believed that long-distance swimming is as much mental as it is physical. He said that you can be physically ready, but if you are not mentally prepared you will not make the swim. He assured me that I had the right mind-set. And he explained that there would be times when I would be tired and cold, when I didn't think I could go any farther, but he knew that I would be able to push myself beyond the cold and the fatigue with my mental strength. Fahmy inspired me and instilled confidence in me, and I knew that when I left for England I would be carrying his dream of swimming the English Channel with me.

Fahmy had stressed the importance of being prepared for the cold. What I needed to do was to condition to the cold on a daily basis, so that my body gradually adjusted to it, and eventually I would be able to tolerate cold temperatures much better than if I had not gone through this process. After workouts I never took hot showers, just warm or lukewarm. At night I slept with my window open to let in the cool night air, and I wore light bedclothes and used only a sheet for warmth.

During the day, I wore sandals, never socks or shoes; that way my feet would always be exposed to the ambient air. Winters in southern California could be cool — temperatures could drop to the low forties — but I never wore a jacket or sweater, usually just a short- or long-sleeved T-shirt with pants or a skirt. Most national and Olympic swimmers shave down before a big race (they shave their entire body, sometimes including their heads) to both reduce drag and create greater sensitivity to the water. But shaving down was the last thing I wanted to do; I didn't want to become more sensitive to the cold. Instead, I didn't shave my legs or arms at all and hoped that this would reduce my sensitivity to the cold.

This cold training diminished my ability to handle heat, not in normal daily settings, but when the air temperature rose above eighty degrees, I would sweat heavily and feel uncomfortable.

The best way to condition to cold water, though, was for me to swim in cold water. Ron offered to coach me in the early morning before school. He suggested that I get released from my morning physical education class to enable me to spend more time in the water. I thought this was a spectacular idea, but there was one major obstacle: Miss Larson, my physical education teacher. Somehow she wound up being my physical education teacher for all three years of junior high school, and her disdain for me had only increased with the years.

My father set up a meeting with Mr. Hughes, the school principal, and Miss Larson. Our goal was to get permission for me to be excused from physical education class so that I could train for the English Channel. My father argued on my behalf that swimming the English Channel took as much preparation as, or perhaps even more than, competing in the Olympic Games. In Miss Larson's class, at the most, I would have one hour of physical education. Out of her class, I would be working for two to five hours a day — two to three hours in the morning in the ocean with Ron Blackledge, and two hours three times a week in the pool with Don Gambril, the Olympic coach.

Mr. Hughes agreed. He had already checked my report cards and said that as long as I kept my grades up at a B average or better, I could be excused from Miss Larson's class. But Miss Larson did not accept this decision, and when Mr. Hughes said it was final, she stormed out of the office and slammed the door so hard the glass window on top shook.

This was a major triumph for me. I was able to have the time I needed to train for the English Channel, and I had escaped Miss Larson's class in the bargain. I had also learned a very important lesson that day: it was possible to go against established thought and not only win but build additional support through the battle.

I continued to build support and to try to find out more about the Channel. I wrote a letter to one of the greatest long-distance swimmers of all time. Her name was Florence Chadwick. She had swum across the Catalina Channel and the English Channel and she had broken the women's world records. She'd made her first Catalina Channel swim during the 1950s at a time when television was first becoming a new form of communication. CBS broadcast her entire swim across the Catalina Channel, and to this day many people remember staying up all night long to watch Florence break the Catalina Channel record. To my happy surprise, Florence Chadwick wrote me a letter wishing me luck, and she asked me for my phone number. A couple of weeks later, she called me, "What kind of workouts are you doing now?" she asked.

"I'm training in the ocean all winter long with Ron Blackledge. The water's in the low fifties. We usually start workout around five a.m. My mom takes me down to the beach and waits for me in the car. Usually we're done by seven, or sometimes eight if it's a long workout," I said.

"Is this something you love doing?" she asked with a cautionary note in her voice. I think she wanted to make sure that this was my idea, not something my parents wanted me to do.

"Oh, I love swimming in the ocean. It's so beautiful, and hard, and fun. Sometimes, though, it's difficult to drag myself out of bed and go work out. Sometimes I'm just really tired. But I know that if I miss any workouts I won't be prepared, and I have to train as hard as I can for the English Channel. I have to be ready for it. It's supposed to be a lot more difficult than the Catalina Channel. Is that true?"

"Yes, the English Channel is colder by nearly ten degrees. And the currents in the English Channel are much stronger. You really have to find a good pilot and pick the best day. Do you have a pilot yet?"

"Not yet, but my mother wrote to the Channel Swimming Association a couple of months ago. Guess it takes the letter a long time to get to England. But we should hear back from them soon.

"Do you remember your swims?" I asked eagerly. "Do you remember if they were really hard? Did you ever get really tired or ever feel like quitting?"

"Funny, yes," she recalled. "I remember some parts of my swims, but it's been so many years ago. My English Channel swim took around fifteen hours, and it was very long and cold. It helps if you have some extra body fat on you. That will help insulate you from the cold. Yes, there were times when I got very tired, but I just kept going — you know, you learn to do that on a long swim. You just keep going and somehow you find more energy from somewhere so that you can do that. I don't think that I ever felt like quitting. I trained hard for that swim. But I think you are training even harder." I'd told her about the types of workouts I'd been doing, and she remarked upon that now. "You're employing a new type of training method, something that was never done in my time. You do interval training in the ocean. You do repeats, and sets of swims. We just used to swim for a certain period of time and then get out of the water. I think you're doing exactly what you need to do for this swim. Yes, I think you're going to be in great shape for it. Here, let me give you my phone number, and please feel free to call me if you ever have any questions. I'd like to help you as much as I can."

From time to time I would call her, asking questions like "Did you coat yourself with Vaseline or lanolin for your swim across the Channel?"

She had used lanolin and told me that I could get it at a chemist's and she explained that in England, a chemist's was the name for a pharmacy. I often thought of Florence and how she too had trained for her swims and how she had wanted to be the best. Sometimes I imagined that I was swimming beside her, staying right with her; although she'd told me that I was much faster than she'd been, I still wanted to swim with her.

During my winter workouts, Ron

Blackledge would meet me at Seal Beach, dressed in a heavy parka with a wool hat and gloves, his eyes and nose running from the cold. He would watch me from the pier and often he'd say, "I really can't believe you're doing this. It's so cold. There was frost on the windshield of my car this morning."

It wasn't easy. Sometimes the beach sand was so cold that I felt as if I were standing in snow. Only half an hour after crawling out of a warm bed, I'd be walking into the water, each shocking cold wave hitting me higher, taking more of my body's sleepy warmth.

For the most part, though, I really enjoyed being in the ocean before the dawn, immersed in the water and bathed in the light of sunrise. It was a great and beautiful adventure. Sure, most people in California were at home sound asleep in their beds, and that was the normal thing to do, but I knew I was doing something really special, having experiences that no one else I knew of was having.

There were days when Ron and I would set off on a long swim; he would row a dory and I would follow close behind. We started from the pier in Seal Beach, and I swam out to the end of the pier, then headed north, toward Long Beach. This first half mile was well sheltered, and in the early morning the water was as flat as black ice. As we passed the river jetty, we altered our course slightly, turning west, toward the man-made oil islands about a mile from Long Beach's shore. The islands were named White, Grissom, and Chaffee, for the astronauts who'd been killed in a launch test preparatory to the inaugural Apollo mission.

As we passed each island, I thought of them, and the intense training and the courage it must have taken to break through the stratosphere and fly into space. Compared to theirs, my goal was very small, but they inspired me, and I thought of them before the tragedy, on other missions, blasting off the launchpad and floating in space, and I wondered if it was the same sensation as floating in the water.

Sometimes as I swam across the black water, I imagined that we were in outer space, traveling to distant planets instead of man-made oil islands. It was fun being out so far from shore, exploring places most people got to see only from boats.

Ron continued to work with me in the mornings in the ocean, and with his help, I got stronger and faster. He seemed very pleased with my progress and had only encouraging things to say. About a month before we were supposed to leave for England for the Channel attempt, Ron called me and said that he didn't think he could go. He said that he couldn't afford to be away from the Seal Beach team for two or three weeks. A lot of people didn't think a fifteen-year-old girl could swim the Channel and had spoken to Ron about it. My father thought that had strongly influenced his decision. It was very tough for me because I had depended on him, and I felt let down. What I had to do was to recognize that Ron had taken me as far as he could, and I needed to continue moving forward.

"Why don't you talk to Coach Gambril?" my mother suggested. "I bet he'll coach you if you ask him. Your father and I have been discussing this situation, and we know that he would not be able to go to England with you, so either Dad or I will."

This made me happy, and I recognized just how much they believed in me. That day I called Coach Gambril, who said that he would be happy to coach me, but he was concerned that he had not coached a long-distance swimmer before. I told him that was okay; I had never swum the English Channel before. Coach Gambril adapted his workouts from the pool to the ocean. He had me doing interval training and pyramids, and he incorporated stroke work into my workouts. This was an entirely new method for long-distance training.

In the mornings I worked out with Coach Gambril and his college team at California State University, Long Beach, but soon we discovered that it was counterproductive for me to swim in the seventy-six-degree pool. It reduced my ability to adjust to cold water. So I started doing all my workouts in the ocean. My mother accompanied me in the morning, and in the afternoon, my father and mother alternated beach-walking days. One would walk with me along the shores of Long Beach, while the other went inside the Belmont Plaza complex to watch my brother and sisters work out. Once in a while, though, they would walk together. Having them with me was very useful. They helped me develop a pace. They walked at a constant speed along the shore, and I had to stay up with them, whether I was hitting currents or swimming into wind and waves. This was challenging, but it taught me how to feel the current and wave-pattern changes and how to adjust my technique accordingly, so that no matter what I faced, I knew what speed I needed to maintain; for the most part, I was able to do so.

There were times, though, during a winter storm, for instance, when I couldn't maintain my speed against the currents, but I kept working at it, day by day, hoping it would be enough to get me across the Channel.

Having my parents with me also boosted my spirits. Knowing that they cared enough about me helped me to pursue this dream. I didn't really know then that not all parents are as supportive, although I did realize that mine had made a large commitment to my dream, and it was one that we really shared. It was great at the end of an especially tough workout to hear my mother or father say, "You did a really good job." They also gave me constructive criticism. Sometimes I was happy to receive it; other times, I didn't want them telling me what I should be doing. For the most part, though, their suggestions helped.

As June 1972 approached, we decided my mother would accompany me to England, while my father would stay home, work, and take care of the family. At the end of June, my mom and I boarded a plane for England.

6

White Cliffs
of Dover

Thoughts about the Channel were always in my conscious mind. They infiltrated my subconscious so that whether I was awake or asleep, I was constantly rehearsing the swim. Working off what Fahmy had told me, I imagined what it would be like when I pushed off the English shore, what the water would be like, the way the current would be moving, and I pictured what it would feel like landing on the French shore. I had never been to England or France, so I studied a map of England and Europe, studied the white space between England and the Continent, and pinpointed the starting place — Shakespeare Beach near Dover — and the finish, in an area called Cape Gris-Nez near Wissant, France.

Fahmy and I spoke often those two weeks

before my mother and I left for England. He fed my mind with descriptions of London, of tall red-brick apartments with small garden plots filled with beautiful roses and multitudes of other flowers. He gave us instructions about catching the train at Victoria Station and what we would see along the way. And as my mother and I rode the train to Dover, his voice played in my head, as we moved through the enormous city of London, past wide expanses of greenbelts, and by tiny villages made mostly of stone, always centered around old stone churches with high pointed steeples.

We arrived in a city called Folkestone, ten miles from Dover. Fahmy had recommended staying in Folkestone because there was an outdoor saltwater swimming pool where I could train when a storm moved through England and the water in Dover Harbour was too rough for swimming. He also recommended Folkestone because every year ten to thirty Channel swimmers from all around the world arrived in Dover with the hope of making the crossing. It could be an intense scene, a place where swimmers were vying for pilots, waiting for favorable tides and weather, and competing to break the record; it could also be a place where swimmers from all over the world met, shared their dreams and hopes with new friends, and enjoyed being with others who understood what it took to arrive at that place at that time. Fahmy wasn't sure what I would face — perhaps a bit of both — and he knew that I would look at all of it as something new and exciting. But he also knew what it was like to be surrounded by this kind of intensity on a daily basis. By staying in Folkestone, I could get away from it whenever I needed a reprieve, or be in Dover when I needed company. It was only a ten-mile bus trip from Folkestone to Dover.

As soon as we checked into the Prince's Hotel in Folkestone, my mother gave me a list of names of pilots that the Channel Swimming Association had sent us, and I chose the first one on the list. Picking up the phone, I felt my excitement and impatience growing as I put my index finger in the hole above a number and dialed, watching and listening to the sound of the disk slowly rotating back into the starting position. Finally the call went through. As I listened to the double ring, waiting for someone to pick up, I anticipated a voice on the end and rapidly rehearsed in my head what I was going to say. But there was no answer.

I selected the second name on the list and

dialed the number. After only the first two rings, I heard a man's voice say, "Hello, this is Reg Brickell."

I had no idea that Reg Brickell was the top pilot for the English Channel. All I knew was that I had finally connected with a real live English Channel swimming pilot, and I was one step closer to realizing my dream.

"Mr. Brickell, my name is Lynne Cox. I got your number from the Channel Swimming Association. I want to swim the English Channel, and I am hoping that you will be my pilot for the swim."

There was a pause. "Oh, you just caught me. I just got 'ome from fishing. Could you speak a bit more slowly, please? Are you from the States?"

"Yes, I am."

"How old are you?" he asked.

"Fifteen."

"Hmmm. That is quite young. Have you ever done a channel swim before?"

"Yes, I swam across the Catalina Channel last year. It's twenty-one miles in a straight line, just like the English Channel, but because of the currents, I swam twenty-seven. It took me twelve hours and thirty-six minutes. I swam it with a group of other kids, and I think I could have swum a lot faster, but we'd agreed to finish the swim together."

"Who is your coach?"

"Don Gambril. He's the U.S. Olympic swimming coach. I've been training with him since I was twelve years old."

"You sound quite serious. Is he with you?"

"No, he's coaching the team for the Olympic Games. My mother came with me to help me on the swim."

"Okay then. Do you think you and your mother could come by my home this afternoon around teatime, say, four o'clock? My home is on the Stade in Folkestone Harbour. If you have any trouble, just ask around — everyone knows me, and you won't have any problem finding it."

From the manager at the hotel my mother and I got detailed directions. He said Folkestone Harbour was about a twenty-minute walk. On that day, I think it took us only ten minutes. Lifting the heavy gold knocker on Reg Brickell's red door, I knocked three times, then held my breath and waited.

Mr. Brickell opened the door; he was about five foot eight, perhaps in his late forties. He had short blond hair, bright blue eyes, and fair skin that had been weathered by sun and wind. His face lit up as he smiled. In the background a teakettle was whistling loudly. "Please 'ave a seat while I get the tea," he said, pointing to the sitting area.

The furniture in the room was cozy, frilly, and feminine — not at all what I expected of him until he introduced his wife, who came out briefly, then retired to a back room. Mr. Brickell poured us tea and offered us short-bread biscuits from a colorful round tin.

For the next hour or so he interviewed me, making sure that I was serious, that I had trained hard, and that this was a swim I wanted to do, not something my parents were pushing me into. At first he just seemed agreeable to being my pilot; when he discovered that my average speed was two and a half miles an hour, he grew more enthusiastic. And when I explained that my goal was to break the men's and women's world records, he got excited about escorting me on the attempt.

I asked him if he had taken many swimmers across the Channel. Had he taken any world-record-breaking swimmers? How much did he charge? How did he select the day for the swim, and how did he inform us about it? What kind of boat did he use: a wet stack, which discharged engine fumes into the water, or a dry stack, which discharged its fumes into the air? What was the size of his boat, and how large was his crew? Did he have a small boat for backup in case anything disabled his engine? What navigational systems did he use? And when would he be available to escort me on the swim?

Brickell seemed rather surprised that I would ask him such detailed questions. Usually he was the one who conducted the interview. From my questions, however, he gathered that I was serious about the swim, and he gave me an overview of navigating through the English Channel.

He went into another room for a moment and came back with a chart. Unfurling it on the table and anchoring it with teacups, he explained the process of a swim from start to finish. The day for a swim is first selected based on the tide. Back then, English Channel swims were always done on a neap tide. Neap tides last for four to five days. They happen when the moon is half full, as well as two days before and two days after the half moon. They are the tides when there is the least movement between high and low water. Spring tides are those that occur when the moon is full. During this time there is a great deal of water movement through the Channel, meaning that the currents are much stronger.

For a very fast swimmer, these currents could be an advantage: if they are caught at just the right time, they could help push a swimmer across faster. Brickell said that because I was such a fast swimmer, he would think about having me on a spring tide, but he wasn't sure if he wanted to take that risk. If our timing was off, I might wind up too far off course to complete the swim. He would consider it, but he favored the tried-and-true neaps.

Brickell used a Loran navigational system, which today has been outdated by GPS (global positioning system) systems. He used the Loran to plot latitude and longitude navigational points that would get us within a half mile of our target (today a GPS would get a swimmer within a few meters of the desired course and finishing point). Brickell also used radar, as well as a compass, and he navigated by dead reckoning and by sight. As a fisherman, as well as the son of a fisherman, Brickell knew the English Channel intimately. He'd spent more of his life on the water than he had on shore. From being out at sea every day he'd developed an ability to read the currents and tides, and could also read a forecast and predict which direction the wind would blow and how strong it would become. The ocean has a certain rhythm to it and follows certain patterns, much like a human being. He could look at a stretch of water, see a slight change in color from light to dark, and know that the wind was increasing and which direction it was moving.

Weather played as significant a role in selecting a day for a Channel crossing as the tide did. The wind must be light and variable or less for an attempt to occur. Anything above that, Brickell said, and the ocean would be covered with white horses — whitecaps. Once that happened, he explained, conditions in the Channel would deteriorate before they improved.

"Which direction would you like to swim?" he asked.

"Either from England to France, or France to England. Does it make any real difference?" I asked.

"Yes, it does make quite a bit of difference," he said, and picked up a pen to use as a pointer. "The straight-line distance from England to France, or vice versa, is twenty-one miles. Because of the tidal changes in and out of the Channel, you will swim an inverted-S course. The tide will carry you north this way, toward the North Sea, or this way, south toward the Atlantic Ocean. It will also push you backward and forward. Sometimes you will even find yourself swimming right in place. How much you move depends on current strength and, somewhat, on wind speed. The more current, the bigger the S, the more distance you swim." He looked up at my mother and me to make sure we understood what he was saying.

He continued, "You can swim in either direction. There are pluses and minuses for both. If you swim from England to France, you don't have to travel to France a day ahead of the day you may be swimming and wait it out over there if you don't go due to poor weather. If you leave from England, you know that you are starting the swim. There is quite a disadvantage, swimming from England to France, however. See how Cape Gris-Nez projects into the Channel? It's a peninsula, and there are very strong currents off the point. There have been many swimmers, perhaps thirty, who have gotten within a mile or even half a mile of shore but couldn't break through the current to reach the land. Sometimes they've been swept up to Belgium, or south to Brittany. The land falls back if you don't hit Cape Gris-Nez, five miles on either side. And even if you have to keep swimming, there's no guarantee that you'll get in. It's quite a heartbreaker, that is." He didn't say anything further for a moment, but his expression conveyed that he had some disappointing memories.

He pointed at Cape Gris-Nez again. "If you swim from France to England, you can face the current when you are fresh, and you may even be able to use it to your advantage. Also, if you look at the English coast, you can see how even it is — there are no big projections like you see with the coast of France, so the currents along shore aren't as strong, and you have a large landing area. If you miss Dover, you really have the whole British coast upon which to land.

"You also have to consider the record. If you swim from England to France, you have to break a faster time than if you go in the other direction. Let me get out my book and check the time. It was set by a Canadian named Helge Jensen twelve years ago. I was his pilot. His time was ten hours and twenty-three minutes. That record's stood for twelve years. Corrie Ebbelaar, a Dutch swimmer, set the women's world record. Her time was ten hours and forty-three minutes. Since you're going for the record," Brickell said, "you may want to swim from France to England."

I shook my head. "I don't want to sound like I'm bragging or anything, but I just want to do the fastest time. That's really my goal. Mr. Brickell, which direction do you recommend?"

He gave it some thought and said, "I think it would be better for you to swim from England to France. That way you can start out fresh, you don't have to worry about getting seasick in a boat traveling to France, and you don't have to spend a lot of time waiting around there. Also I think you're strong enough to break through the current off Cape Gris-Nez if it's running fast on the day you swim, and I think it would be a feather in our cap if you could do the fastest time."

In order to select the best weather conditions, Brickell monitored the weather every night when out in the Channel fishing. He also watched the weather forecast on television every afternoon. He didn't say this, but I gathered from talking to him that he was an expert at both selecting the best day and piloting for a swimmer. He took pride in what he did. And he had honed his skills until he was the best. He had taken the greatest number of world-record-breaking swimmers across the English Channel, but he said he had never taken a swimmer who was so young who wanted to break the world record. That intrigued him, and I could tell by that flicker of light in his blue eyes that he was very interested in working with me. He never said it, because he was very humble, but he knew better than anyone how important a role the pilot played in getting a swimmer across the Channel. With an ordinary pilot, all that could be expected was an ordinary swim. Pilot and swimmer work in many ways like a mountain climber climbing Mount Everest and a Sherpa; one could not succeed without the technical ability of the other. Brickell believed he had the knowledge and expertise to get me across in world-record time if I could swim fast enough, and he understood that he would have to draw on everything he knew to give me that opportunity. He loved that challenge, and he made it clear that he wanted to pilot me.

We stepped outside his home and he showed us the *Helen Anne Marie 137*, his forty-five-foot-long fishing boat, anchored in Dover Harbour. It was an old boat, and its chains and lines were rusted, but it had been freshly painted and was clean and inviting. He would have taken us on board, but the tide was out and the boat was too low in the harbor for us to climb aboard. The *Helen Anne Marie* had a wet stack. This wasn't good; it meant that engine fumes were released into the water. The fumes could make a swimmer sick or cause headaches. The exhaust area was on the left side of the boat, so his solution was to have me swim on the right side and forward, near the bow. If he had his choice, he liked to have a swimmer there or beside the pilot's cabin, so that he could keep track of the swimmer throughout the crossing.

On every Channel crossing he had at least one deckhand. On my crossing he wanted to have the best, his fourteen-year-old son, Reg Brickell Jr. Brickell asked if we had spoken with the Channel Swimming Association and if they had lined up an official for me, a man named Mickey Moreford. When I told him yes, Brickell lit up and said Mickey was the best.

The fee for the swim would be roughly one thousand dollars. The agreement was that once a swimmer set off, the pilot would be paid, whether the swimmer swam only one hundred meters or the entire distance across the Channel. There was no negotiating on this point. The Channel Swimming Association also got paid a fee, for supplying an official to monitor the swim and the condition of the swimmer and to ensure that the swim was achieved under English Channel swimming rules. The swim began as soon as the swimmer's foot touched the water and finished when the swimmer fully cleared the water on the other side. The swimmer couldn't touch anyone or anything during the swim and could not use any type of flotation equipment, fins, or paddles. The swim had to be done under the swimmer's own powers of endurance. A swimmer could eat during the crossing; in fact, it was the swimmer's responsibility to provide food for the entire crew as well. The only thing a swimmer had to keep in mind was that during the feeding time, he or she could float on his or her back and feed but could not touch any of the crew or hold on to the boat. Food was tossed to the swimmer much the way a seal is fed.

While some swimmers crossed the Channel during the day, Brickell preferred night. The wind was less strong; the water was calmer. Would I be okay with swimming at night? he asked. I had no problem with it at all. In fact, I told him, I loved the serenity of being on the water at night. He smiled. We liked each other. I had a very good feeling about him. He was confident in himself and in his abilities, and I think he felt the same way about me. I was so eager to swim.

The first tides that Brickell would have

available would be in two weeks, at the beginning of July. I was thrilled that I might be able to swim across the English Channel on the Fourth of July. But if the weather wasn't favorable on July 4th or during that week, an Australian swimmer named Des Renford had the next set of tides booked with Brickell, so I would have to wait until after the end of the month for another chance. I didn't like the idea of having to wait at all. I was already set to go, and it was hard for me to think that I was going to have to wait around two weeks for my attempt. If I didn't get to swim then, all my training would be thrown off, and somehow I'd have to stay in shape but be rested.

Brickell asked me if there was anything else I needed to know. For the time, I told him, I had run out of questions. He suggested that I meet with Mickey Moreford in the next couple of days, just so we would get to know each other. I'm sure Brickell wanted me to meet Mickey because he was so enthusiastic. He was a complete English Channel swimming fan.

The next day my mother and I were invited to Mickey Moreford's home in Folkestone. Mickey was an older man, perhaps in his sixties; he was thin and slightly stooped over. He also had a wife who retired to another room, as well as a blue-eyed blind dalmatian named Buster that he loved beyond words.

Mickey was excited about my goal. He told us stories of all the successful swims he had been on as the official observer. He opened a scrapbook and showed us the signed black-and-white photos of swimmers from twenty years before. He said that he would hold a page in his scrapbook for me. When he turned the page, he said, "Oh, this is the Greek swimmer." Tears came to Mickey's eyes, and his voice tightened.

The Greek swimmer had been swimming from England to France. He was a young man in his late twenties or early thirties, and he was a strong swimmer. He made good progress until he reached the French coast and the tide changed. He fought it but couldn't get across. He kept swimming, although he complained of feeling cold. Then he passed out in the water. It was as if the entire scene were replaying in Mickey's mind: "The pilot and I jumped into the skiff and rowed over to 'im. 'E was facedown in the water, so I jumped in with my clothes on and rolled 'im over. 'E wasn't breathing. Somehow, the pilot grabbed 'im by the hair and we lifted him into the skiff and then into the boat. We 'ad a doctor on board, and 'e listened to the Greek swimmer's 'eart with a stethoscope. He couldn't hear a 'eartbeat, so 'e tried doing a 'eart massage. That didn't work, so the doctor cut 'is chest open with a knife and tried to massage 'is 'eart by pumping it with 'is 'and. Ah, it was terrible, love. The doctor wasn't able to save 'im.

"Oh, don't you worry, missus. Your daughter will be fine. She has more body fat than the Greek did, and it will help her stay warm. She's also a much faster swimmer than 'e was. Don't you worry," he said, wiping his eyes with the back of his hand.

"Does this happen often — do people go into hypothermia?" my mother asked.

"Ah, yes, love, swimmers get very cold in the Channel. Sometimes they 'ave to get out because of the cold. But I've never been on any other swim when someone died. I hope I never do. Now let's get back to more 'appy things," he said. He showed us other pictures of successful swimmers and then explained what we should expect. He suggested that we stay in touch with him and urged us to call him if we had any questions at all. Then he gave us both a big hug and told me, "I'm sure you're going to do this, love. From the moment I saw you, I knew; you are strong and able to break that record."

132

The next day my mother and I rode the bus to Dover and I began swimming in Dover Harbour.

It was even more beautiful than Fahmy had described: the white cliffs were higher, more magnificent, and brighter white than I'd ever imagined. The water in the harbor was a clear, vibrant gray-blue. And when I listened to the waves, I heard Fahmy say, "You can hear the waves caressing the little pebbles. It is a very beautiful place."

I imagined how it must have been for him the first time he stepped into the water and started swimming. I felt that he was very near me as I started my own workout, and I was excited to finally be training in Dover Harbour. Just outside the harbor walls was the English Channel, the place I had been dreaming about for what seemed like forever.

When I got into the water, I was glad I was conditioned to the cold. The water temperature was in the high fifties, and I had to swim fast to stay warm. First I headed toward the white cliffs for half a mile, then back toward the pier. As I swam, my mom walked along the beach with me, but with a lot of difficulty. The beach tilted at a sharp angle, so after the first lap I suggested that she sit and watch me from the beach.

While I was swimming, I saw another swimmer enter the water. He swam over to me and introduced himself. He said that his name was Des Renford, he was from Australia, and he was training to swim the Channel both ways. He told me he had been watching me and I looked pretty fast. He asked me my name and if I wanted to pace — to swim at the same speed as him. I was thrilled to meet him, and I told him that Reg Brickell had told me about him. Des asked if Brickell was my pilot too. He said that he had had other pilots for the crossing, but Reg Brickell was the finest. He explained that there were a few pilots who didn't care about the swimmer and were just into Channel swimming for the money. They would take swimmers out on an attempt knowing that the weather was going to be bad; the swimmer would fail and they would be able to collect their money in a short amount of time.

We had a very good workout together. Des said that I was faster than he was. But I wasn't by much, so I really enjoyed swimming with him. He told me about some of the other swimmers he thought I'd like. A swimmer from New Zealand named Sandy Blewett would be attempting the Channel for the first time. It wasn't unusual, Des recounted, for swimmers to attempt the Channel four or five times. Sandy was just a few years older than I was. There was also another unusual swimmer from Florida named Stella Taylor. She was in her forties and had been a nun for many years in a convent in England.

A few days later, during a training session, I met both Sandy and Stella. They had been working out together when my mother and I arrived. Sandy was from Auckland, New Zealand, from the North Island, and for years she had dreamed of swimming the English Channel and then, one day, perhaps becoming the first woman to swim between the North and South Islands of New Zealand. This swim was only ten miles, but the currents between the two islands were fierce. Only three men had achieved the crossing.

As we treaded water in the harbor, Stella spoke about her years in the convent, how she was so happy to be free and how she had once been invited to Bahrain by a sheikh, to swim in the Persian Gulf. She said the sheikh had fallen in love with her. He'd especially loved her blond hair, but he could not marry a Christian, so she'd returned to England and decided to swim the English Channel. Stella was a very slow swimmer but she was very determined, and I enjoyed meeting with her and Sandy and listening to stories of the convent and New Zealand. There was a real sense of camaraderie between us, and with the other swimmers we met during our training swims. There was a large team from Egypt, a swimmer from India, three or four English swimmers, and a man from Texas.

After the first week of workouts, the tides became favorable for me. Every night after the weather forecast I called Reg Brickell, and every night Brickell said that a storm front had stalled off the English coast and the sea was too rough for us to go. It was hard being on standby for five days straight, and even worse when July 6, the last possible day for my set of tides, passed. Now I would have to continue training and wait to see if Des got favorable weather for a double.

Des and I continued working out each day in the harbor. We pushed each other when we worked out, applauded each other, and kept each other motivated. He was a good friend.

After workouts my mother and I took small trips to explore England and take a mental break from the Channel. We needed to get away, to think about something else, and to learn something. We took bus trips to Canterbury Cathedral and to a butterfly farm in Wye; we explored the small seaside town of Deal and climbed to the top of the white cliffs to explore Dover Castle. We also explored English cuisine and decided that England not only had fantastic fish and chips, but excellent ethnic cuisine, especially Chinese and Indian.

When Des's tides arrived, at the end of July, the low-pressure region finally started to move. The weather through the first and second days of Des's tides wasn't calm enough for Des to attempt the swim. But by the third afternoon, the British flag in the center of the harbor, which we had been watching every single day, was not even wavering. I thought that Des must have been given the green light to go ahead with his swim that evening. We hadn't seen him, so I assumed he was preparing his bags, getting the food together, and taking some extra rest.

In late afternoon Mickey Moreford arrived at our hotel in Folkestone. He was completely out of breath, bent over and gasping for air. We waited, concerned that he was going to have a heart attack. Ages passed, it seemed, before he caught his breath. Then he said, "Brickell's been trying to reach you all day long. He's rung you up a dozen times. And he sent me to find you."

Conditions would not be good enough for a double, so Des had stepped aside to let me have his tides, exchanging his tides for mine, if I agreed. Sure, I told Mickey, leaping into the air, wanting to race off and thank Des and get my swim bag packed, all at once. Mickey said that Des could have held on to the tides until the very last minute, hoping the conditions would improve, but he wanted to release them now to allow me to prepare. He was a real class act.

Mickey had further instructions: "Take a cab to Shakespeare Beach, Dover. Be there by eleven p.m. to grease up, and be ready for a midnight start. I will be coming round with Brickell. Reg Junior will row me ashore in the launch so I can see you begin and start the watch. Then we'll 'ave your mother climb into the launch with us, and we'll take her out to the *Helen Anne Marie*."

I tried to rest that afternoon in my hotel room, but there was just no way I could relax. Hours dragged by. Finally my mother and I had dinner, watched some television, and caught a cab at ten-thirty. The cab driver was surprised when my mother asked him to take us to Shakespeare Beach.

"Are you a Channel swimmer?" he asked

looking in the rearview mirror.

"Yes, she is," my mother said proudly.

"Well, you don't look like a Channel swimmer to me. You're too fat to be one," he said.

That hurt, and it made me angry. How would he know what a Channel swimmer looked like anyway? "Well, I am one," I said, wanting to explain that my body fat would help keep me warm; that is why dolphins, seals, and whales have extra insulation.

When the cab reached the cliffs overlooking Shakespeare Beach, the driver let us out and then said, "Well, good luck to you anyway — but you certainly don't look like a Channel swimmer."

We crossed an old railroad bridge and walked down at least a hundred tiny steps to the beach. It reminded me of the cove at Catalina, but the white cliff walls of Shakespeare Beach reflected the moonlight, and it was a lot easier to see. We walked across the pebbles and huge clumps of brown kelp to the edge of the shore, where I pulled off my sweats and placed them in my swim bag.

After my mother opened two large jars of lanolin, oil residue from sheep's wool that is used by Channel swimmers for insulation, she pulled on gloves and smeared handfuls of it on my neck, shoulders, and underarms and around the bottom of my swimsuit. The lanolin was nasty stuff, worse than Vaseline. Pale yellow and as sticky as marshmallow cream, it smelled worse than a dead sheep.

Then we waited. A cool breeze circled the cove, waves slid into shore along the pebbles, and I smiled as I thought of Fahmy. We had phoned home to let the family know the swim was on. My father had promised to tell Fahmy and Coach Gambril. They would be waiting by the radio for news.

We first heard Mickey's excited voice: "We're 'ere, love. We're 'ere." He was standing up in the boat, trying to climb out before Reg Junior had landed.

Mickey jumped out into ankle-deep water, jogged up the beach to us, and said, "Are you ready, love?"

"Yes, Mickey, I am very ready."

"This is very exciting," my mother said. She handed the gear to Reg Junior, and he helped her into the launch. Mickey followed her, then said, "Let me 'ave a look at my watch. You too, Reg Junior. Let's synchronize our watches so we get these two times plus the stopwatch. Right, you ready, love? Okay, go."

I jogged into the water, dove under the waves, and began sprinting. No doubt I would be swimming for hours, but there was always a coastal current, and I wanted to get through it quickly. I didn't want to take the coastal tour of England. Besides that, my body was flowing with adrenaline. This time I was going for the record and I didn't have to wait for anyone; I could swim at my own pace, flat out, or go slower whenever I wanted to or needed to.

It took me only a few minutes to reach the *Helen Anne Marie* and Brickell. The night was clear, and while the crew maneuvered from the launch to the boat, I continued swimming, not wanting to wait for anything. Every minute mattered; I was going for the record. So much could happen during this swim, as Fahmy had told me and Des had warned me; I had to keep moving forward, keep the pressure on, keep pulling strongly, so I could get across before something happened.

For the first three hours, we flew across the sea. Mickey and my mother were sitting near the bow, and every hour Mickey would count my strokes for a minute, making sure I maintained my pace. They did not take their eyes off of me, and I felt as if they were propelling me along with their thoughts. I was so happy they were beside me. Brickell, too, was the complete professional. He would stand at the pilot's cabin, move inside to check his navigational system and continually update our course, then step outside to check on me. When I turned my head to breathe, I heard the ship's radio, someone talking on it, and the weather forecast. I couldn't quite hear it and wondered what it was saying.

Maybe around four in the morning I started running into round balls. It was too dark to see anything, and it was strange to feel them rolling off my body. I had never felt kelp like that before; I couldn't imagine what it was. Finally, the curiosity overwhelmed me, and I shouted, "Mr. Brickell, what's in the water?"

"Lettuce. Someone dumped a shipload of old lettuce," he said, and laughed.

Somehow I'd never expected to be swimming through a sea of lettuce.

The current carried us north as expected, and we quickly completed the bottom of the loop of the inverted S. I could tell that Brickell was pleased. That made me feel stronger, knowing that I was swimming right on pace and we were right in sync.

By five hours into the swim, I was starting to feel fatigued; I had been working at 80 percent of my maximum speed, nearly sprinting across. I tried to think of Hans, how he kept swimming with intensity for each one hundred; this was the same thing, only I was thinking in terms of one mile at a time. "Mom, could I have some apple juice?"

She tossed me a bottle of fresh water, and I rinsed my mouth; then she threw a bottle of warm apple juice to me. Floating on my back, I took a couple of sips while Brickell explained the situation. "You're right on course and you're three hours ahead of world-record time. I can't believe it. You're the fastest swimmer I've ever seen," he said.

"You picked a great night," I said.

"The wind's supposed to increase five knots. But you should have no problems," he said with absolute confidence.

Not wanting to waste time or to get cold and have my muscles grow stiff, I began swimming fast again. The juice boosted my blood sugar and I felt a lot stronger. My father had recommended that I stop to feed every hour to maintain my blood-sugar levels, but I hadn't wanted to stop at all. I just wanted to keep going. Now, looking back on it, I knew he was right; it would have helped significantly. But I was still on pace, swimming better than I had imagined.

About an hour later, Brickell came out of the pilot's house and waved at me to lift my head up and listen. He asked, "Do you think you can sprint for a mile?"

I had been swimming hard already, and the thought of sprinting — well, it would be harder. But yes, I told him, I could do it.

"Good, because there's an oil tanker coming down the Channel at nine knots. He cannot stop for you. You're either going to have to wait here and tread water for thirty minutes or cross the tanker lane before he gets there," Brickell explained. He didn't mention that once we had committed we could not hesitate or we could be crushed by the oil tanker. Somehow I already knew how serious this was.

"Okay, I'll sprint," I said quickly, putting my head down and taking off, moving as fast as I could for about twenty minutes, until I saw Brickell wave to me again and point. The tanker passed us like a whale cruising past a minnow, with the bow waves surging toward us, lifting us high into the air, maybe fifteen feet, and we surfed the waves toward France.

By seven a.m. my arms were burning. They felt like I had been lifting twenty-five-pound dumbbells for hours. My neck was sore, as I had been raising my head up to see the French coast, now a dark outline on the horizon. And my lower back ached and I was getting tired. Stopping to stretch my back by grabbing my ankles, I asked for an oatmeal cookie. I was so hungry. For hours I had been dreaming about eating a real American hamburger and a chocolate milkshake. My mother tossed me a cookie. My coordination was off, and I completely missed it. She threw a second. I picked the slightly mushy snack out of the sea and ate it quickly.

"Can you see Cape Gris-Nez yet, Mickey?" I asked.

"See that point? The one with the little light'ouse?" Mickey yelled.

"Yes, I see it!"

"That's Cape Gris-Nez, Gray-Nose," Mickey said.

"Lynne, this is going to be the most difficult part of the swim. There's a current around that point. You're going to have to hold your pace if you're going to break the record," Brickell said.

"But I thought I was hours ahead of record time," I said, somewhat confused.

"You are, but the current's already pushing you north, slightly off course. You've already lost half an hour," he said.

"Okay," I said with determination, "this is where all those sprints at the end of workout are going to pay off."

My mom and Mickey cheered, "You can

do it." "Come on, love. Let's go."

Brickell turned the *Helen Anne Marie* slightly into the current to compensate for the northward drift and I began sprinting, trying to break across the current. For nearly an hour I swam harder than I could remember, and I was tiring.

Stopping to stretch my back, I asked for a drink of water and heard Brickell: "Lynne, you've got to go faster — you're not through the current yet."

My sides were starting to ache from breathing, and I didn't feel good. I swam faster, but after another half an hour or so Cape Gris-Nez didn't appear to be any closer. And the stench of the lanolin combined with the smell of diesel and dead fish from the boat was making me queasy. The wind was blowing the fumes into my face. "Mr. Brickell, could I move to the other side of the boat? The fumes are bugging me."

"Certainly. Lynne, you're caught in the tidal change now. You're going to have to swim faster. I know you're getting tired, but if you don't get through this, you're not going to get the record," he said.

"You can do it. Come on, honey," my mother said, and Mickey cheered as well.

This time I started swimming like I was at the end of a workout, doing the last mile, giving it everything I had. It was painful, but I pushed on. For more than an hour I didn't look up at shore. When I did, we had drifted farther north, and Cape Gris-Nez had slid more to the south. This was hell, liquid hell.

I began reaching for more energy I'd never known I had. It was from all those cold mornings when I didn't want to get in and work out, but did anyway. It was from all those years of training when I was tired but pushed myself through the workout. It was from all those people who believed in me. I pictured the faces of my family, my friends, my neighbors, my teammates, everyone who said, *You can do this,* and I sprinted. My breath burned in my throat. My arms were on fire, moving faster than they ever had. I lifted my head. We were making progress. We were directly in front of Cape Gris-Nez.

"You're a mile from shore," Brickell called to me. "This is where it gets tough. This is where a lot of swimmers give up." His voice sounded tired, and he should have sounded happy.

"What's wrong?" I asked.

"The tide's increasing. It's pushing you south now. You're going to have to sprint or you're going to miss it entirely. The next landfall will be Wissant, five miles south," he said.

Now I understood his fatigue and wished I didn't. Sprint, he said. Sprint. *Oh, man. Okay. Okay. You've got to do it now. You've really got to do it. You're only a mile from shore. It's only a mile. You can do it. Come on.*

Again I put my head down and sprinted, and when I looked up I thought we'd be a half mile from shore; but the cape was far to the north. "How much farther, Mr. Brickell?"

"Five miles. You've missed the point and you're heading toward Wissant."

My brain couldn't register it for a minute. Five miles? How could I have lost it that fast?

"Do you think you can pick up your pace? If you can, we're going to cut at a very sharp angle. You're going to feel it pushing right against your face," Brickell said, drawing in a tense breath.

"How come we're not heading directly for the point?" I asked.

"You'd have to land on the rocks, and you could get a bit cut up," Brickell said.

"They're closer than the beach, aren't they?"

"By half a mile," he said.

My mom didn't like the idea; I could see it

in her face. She was almost in tears.

"Mickey, can I still break the record?"

"Yes, love, you can."

"Okay, then, let's go for the rocks. I want to finish this swim now," I said.

Everyone broke into smiles, even my mother — she couldn't help herself. Taking a deep breath, I began sprinting again, counting my strokes, telling myself that I wouldn't look up again until I'd swum one thousand strokes. Slowly I gained a foot, then a few hundred yards. Now I realized why the English Channel was the Mount Everest of swimming: we had climbed the mountain and all we had to do was reach the summit. But the summit was where the air grew thinner, where everything became challenging.

Don't look up for five hundred strokes. Go as fast as you can go. Push it. Pull your arms with everything you have. Kick. Yes. Kick those legs. Pull deeper. Faster. Come on. Pull.

In the background my mother and Mickey were shouting, "Come on!" "Go, love!" They weren't letting up. I heard Brickell shouting. For the first time, he was cheering too. And then I saw the excitement in his face.

We were almost there. But I couldn't look yet. I had three hundred more strokes before I could look up. Brickell was turning the boat; I had to look up. Was there another problem? No, there wasn't. We were almost there. The rocks were bigger than before.

Mickey and Reg Junior jumped into the launch and followed me. I swam faster, lifting my head to pick a landing spot. Waves were breaking on the rocks. I could see the surge and the white water. High above from the cliffs overhead, I heard voices. They were shouting in French. I was excited; I had never been to France before.

For over a year I had rehearsed this in my mind, but nothing could compare with the experience of actually being there and finishing the swim across the English Channel.

Searching for a space between the waves, I sprinted, hoping that a surge wouldn't catch me and smash me into the rocks. I started moving in, and suddenly felt myself being lifted; I was moving too fast, right into a big sharp rock covered with mussels and barnacles. My knees struck the barnacles; then the wave tore me back out toward sea. Another wave, larger than the last, was breaking. Swim forward or back? Oh, no. I had no control. I could see it. I was going to get bashed. My other knee was sliced by the mussels. There was blood squirting out, but I couldn't feel it much. My legs were numb from the cold. Another wave was surging toward me. *Maybe this wasn't such a good idea after all. No: find a spot. You can't turn back. The watch is still ticking. You've got to clear the water for the swim to be completed. Come on, use the wave, let it lift you up, don't fight it, let it carry you into the rocks, don't back down. If you hit the rock, grab ahold of it and climb out of the water now.*

The wave lifted me and I smashed into another rock. It hurt a lot. I grabbed for the rock and missed, then leaned forward and grabbed a handhold. I pulled myself up. The rock was sharp; it cut my feet, and the barnacles shredded my skin. But I wasn't thinking about it, just trying to find another handhold and pull myself out. *Got it.* I pushed up with my feet, clung with my fingers, reached another handhold, and hauled myself onto a rock, clear of the water.

The crew cheered wildly. We had made it.

"Vous avez nagée La Manche?" someone shouted from the Cliffs. You swam the Channel?

"Oui, j'ai nagée La Manche," I said. Yes, I swam the Channel. I did it. I just stood there for a moment and looked around. My legs were wobbly, but I had to see France. The cliffs above us looked like the white cliffs of Dover. And I thought of Fahmy and smiled.

He would be so happy too.

"Over 'ere, love! 'Urry. 'Urry, love. Step on that rock." Mickey pointed and shouted.

I looked at the rocks. The waves seemed larger, and I didn't want to go back down that way. One knee was bleeding. I was scared. If I messed up this time, I was really going to get scraped. I looked around. "I can't get down there," I yelled. The waves were too big. But I couldn't walk along the point either; it was at least half a mile to the beach. "Can you move over there, around the point a little?" The waves didn't seem as big there. I stepped down, then glanced back at the lighthouse one more time. We did it, I thought, and I felt a deep, warm sense of satisfaction spread through my body. My father and brother and sisters would be so happy too. A wave lifted me, tossing me back up; I fought it and swam out to the launch.

Mickey had me face him, then slid a towel under my arms. He and Reg Junior dragged me on board like a netful of fish. Mickey held my head in his hands and kissed my cheeks. "You made it, love. You made it. Congratulations."

Reg Junior said, "Congratulations, great job." He was laughing at Mickey. He was very happy too.

"Did I break the world record?" I asked.

Mickey had started to cry. "I get very emotional sometimes," he said, wiping the tears off his face. "Yes, love, you did. On July 20, 1972, you set a new world record. The fastest time anyone has ever swum the Channel. Nine hours and fifty-seven minutes. That record's going to last a very long time."

When I saw my mother in the boat, she said, "I'm sorry. I didn't want to push you so hard. I knew you were tired." She burst into tears.

"I'm glad you pushed me, Mom. I needed your help. Thank you."

She hugged me tightly. And then Mr. Brickell came over to me. He was absolutely beaming. He grabbed my hand and hugged me. "You did it! Congratulations. What courage."

"*We* did it, Mr. Brickell. We did it. Thank you," I said, and I hugged him again.

I was so cold and tired. Mickey and my mother wrapped me in blankets and I sat down, leaned against the pilot's house, and fell asleep. When I woke up we were entering Dover Harbour, and I saw those beautiful white cliffs. I couldn't wait to phone home.

There was no way I could have anticipated the crowd of reporters waiting for us on the dock. They were from the *Manchester Post*, the *Telegram*, even the BBC. Each of them asked about the swim. They were thrilled. When my mother and I got back to the hotel there were radio stations calling from New York, Boston, Los Angeles, Bangkok, and even Australia. And there were so many requests to have pictures taken the next day.

The next day, before I did anything, I had to call Brickell, to thank him for all he had done and to include him in the photos, but he wasn't in. He had taken Des out on his attempt to do a double crossing of the Channel. All day long I thought about Des, wondering if he would make it. Finally the news came back; he'd made it one direction, but the weather hadn't held, so he'd pulled out. Somehow I knew that wouldn't stop Des. He would try again. That was part of a long-distance swimmer's nature.

When my mother and I boarded the flight home, my spirits felt higher than the plane after takeoff. At age fifteen I had reached my highest goal in life.

7

Homecoming

A couple days after I got home, I went to the Belmont Plaza pool to detrain, stretch out, and just get back into the water. There was a banner at the pool, and all my teammates cheered when I walked onto the deck. It was a wonderful feeling to receive their recognition, and when Coach Gambril took my hand and shook it, then hugged me, I thought it couldn't get any better than this. But it did. Hans came over to shake my hand, and he said, "You did such a fantastic job. I can't believe it. You were so fast."

Then Gunnar walked over, shook my hand, rumpled my hair, and smiled. "Yes, you did a great job."

It was nearly too much to have my two heroes telling me that I did great. And I nearly lost it when Hans said, "We talked with Coach and he said that you'll warm up with us in lane eight today."

What an honor, to swim with them.

That day I worked out with them, and for the first time I was able to see them up close, to see the power and beauty of their bodies as they moved seemingly effortlessly through the water. This time I could hear their breathing, and see the expressions on their faces, and watch their flip turns underwater, and feel the power they released when they pushed off the wall. I asked them if they would watch my stroke and help correct it. They did. Both gave me some pointers: kick harder, keep my head down.

It had been over a year since I'd swum in the same pool as they swam in, and they looked so much better than ever before. They were beginning to taper, reducing their mileage and getting more rest. In a couple of months they would swim in the Olympic Games. Hans would win the silver medal on the German freestyle relay team, and Gunnar would swim the four-hundred-meter individual medley to win the gold medal and establish an Olympic record.

What do you do at fifteen when you've achieved your highest goal in life? What can you ever do to surpass that? Coach Gambril left California to coach the Harvard University team, and I was sad about that; I knew he was not only the best coach I would have but one of my best friends too. I also knew he had taken me as far as he could, and he had to move on his own life's path.

My brother, who had been competing at the national level in long-distance events in the swimming pool, swam across the Catalina Channel from the island to the mainland. He established a new overall record of eight hours and fifty minutes.

My younger sisters, Laura and Ruth, were still swimming for the team, but they were starting to become interested in playing water polo. My brother had started playing in high school, and I had played some on a club team in the evenings after my ocean-swimming workouts, with girls who would become members of the U.S. National Team. I loved the game, but I was only adequate at it. From the moment Laura and Ruth picked up the yellow ball, they were naturals. And there was no doubt that someday they would be great water polo players.

I was still trying to figure out what to do next when my folks suggested that I take a complete break and visit old friends in New Hampshire. It was a great idea, and I enjoyed being back, being free of thoughts of swimming, world records, and competitions. It was wonderful until a former neighbor handed me the morning paper with tears in her eyes. She was too choked up to talk and just pointed to the story. Davis Hart from Springfield, Massachusetts, had broken my time across the English Channel by thirteen minutes. It took a few minutes to absorb the news. There had been some controversy surrounding the time. One official said Hart had finished three minutes slower than my time; later, reports came in that that time had been a mistake; he in fact had swum thirteen minutes faster than me. This made me think about returning to swim the Channel again, but I knew I needed a break. Besides, if I decided to do it again, I'd have to ask for support from my mother and father, and for them to underwrite the cost of the trip.

Entering high school at Los Alamitos helped me return to an almost normal teenage life. Studies were just as important to me as swimming.

It was water polo season when I entered high school, but there was no such thing as a girls' water polo team. The boys' swimming and water polo coaches, George Devina and Dennis Ploessel, knew about my background. My brother swam and played water polo on their teams during the school year. The coaches knew that I had played water polo on a girls' club team that was a feeder program for the U.S. Women's National Team. Mr. Devina and Mr. Ploessel recruited me for the boys' high school team. I was excited about joining the team. I loved water polo; it was a lot of fun, and hard work, and it allowed me to be on a team where I played as a team member.

Coach Devina suggested that I try out for the boys' team. Not everyone thought this was a good idea, especially some of the parents of the boys on the team. Coach Devina decided to hold a team vote. The outcome was close, sixty to forty. Fortunately, the boys voted me on. Coach Devina was delighted. He said it was a major triumph for me to become the first girl on a boys' high school water polo team in the state of California, perhaps in the nation.

Playing on the boys' team was fantastic. It was fun working out on a tight-knit team, and, like the boys, I had to prove myself every day at workout. My first year of high school, sophomore year, I was a starter, and I lettered that season. But it wasn't always easy being on the boys' team. There were a couple of guys who didn't like having me on the team, and it was certainly surprising to the other high school teams to suddenly play against a girl.

One time, swimming down the pool, I heard a boy yell, "I got this boy" — he stopped in mid-sentence — "girl covered?" Someone on my team passed me the ball, and he was in such shock that I scored off him. His father was in the stands and he angrily shouted, "You let that girl score off you?" It seemed strange that sometimes the parents had more of a problem with me being on the team than the boys did. Eventually, I was accepted, and I became close friends with four of the boys. It was difficult, though; at various times, each of them asked me to go out, but I couldn't because I felt like I would have been showing favorites and it just wouldn't have worked, being on an all-boy team. A couple of boys really persisted, and I did want to date them, but I told them it would be better to just be friends. Besides, between schoolwork and workouts, I had very little free time for dating, and by nighttime I was exhausted.

The first time I got hit in the face — on purpose or by mistake, I'm not sure — two of the players on my team saw it and swam after the other player. Fortunately, the referee saw what was happening and broke things up before there was a fight. But the referee had been a national player himself and knew that the other players were letting the player on the other team know that he couldn't get away with anything. There was a clean way to play the sport and a dirty way, and the dirty way wasn't acceptable. The referee was able to gain control of the situation before anything happened, and I was pleased that the boys cared about me enough to stand up for me. It made me feel I had been accepted, especially when there were many times in high school that I felt very isolated.

Everyone in high school knew me simply as "the swimmer." This bothered me because I felt there was so much more to me than just being a swimmer. I was a serious student too, and like everyone else, I wanted to be accepted for who I was. That was probably why my handful of close friends weren't athletes.

By the end of the school year, I'd decided that I wanted to go back to England and try to break the world record. Expectations for my second attempt were much higher than before. Since Coach Gambril had moved on to Harvard, my brother coached me in the ocean. We trained together off the shores of Long Beach and Seal Beach. It was difficult at times having my brother for my coach, but for the most part, I listened to him — not all the time, though, because I didn't think he knew more than I did. But I understood that this time I would have to train more intensely, and stronger and faster. My commitment was deeper than before. Missing one workout or just going through the motions would make the difference between breaking the world record and failing.

My mother and I traveled again to England, and we went through the same preparations as the first time. Just as before, waiting for the right day was exasperating, and the pressure was so much greater because the expectations were so much higher. Completing the thirty-mile swim was no longer enough; if I finished the crossing without breaking the world record, I would fail.

With the same crew as the year before, I set out to cross the English Channel. We started from Shakespeare Beach, which looked just as it had on my last crossing. But the current was a lot stronger this time and our inverted S became much wider. The year before I had had to maintain my pace and increase my speed to cut across the currents. This time I had to crank everything up a couple of notches. I constantly wondered, *Am I going to make it in time?* I'm not sure why I wanted to put that kind of pressure on myself or why I felt the need to go back to swim the English Channel. Some people explained it by saying that swimmers get "Channel fever." It's as if the Channel lures swimmers back to Dover like a siren. It's the place, the history, the friendships, the successes, and the heartbreaks. The Channel has a strange pull on swimmers, even if they've succeeded before. And some swimmers return to England year after year to pit themselves against the Channel again and again.

For me, I think it was that I needed another goal, something to focus my energy. I knew that one of my reasons for returning was to prove that I had not just been lucky on my first crossing. Some people had dismissed my previous swim by saying that I had had perfect conditions, though that wasn't true. The currents had been changeable and very tough.

This year, no one could say I had it easy. By the middle of the night the wind had increased to ten knots and the chop on the sea surface to just before whitecaps. The tides were a lot stronger too. When we reached Cape Gris-Nez, the tide was so strong that for every stroke I was taking, the current was pushing me back four or five. For over an hour I fought a losing battle, with time slipping away and the lighthouse receding into the cliffs.

Brickell made many course changes, but nothing seemed to work. Finally he decided to turn south so we could cut across the current and hopefully find ourselves in a second current that would circle back and carry us toward the point. Brickell wasn't sure it would work, and after we started, he was even less sure; we weren't making progress. The crew — Mickey, my mother, and Reg Junior — cheered me on. Brickell made three or four more course changes, and finally we started moving forward. But then we hit another current, and it started to pull us out into the mid-Channel again. There was nothing more discouraging than almost touching shore, almost climbing out of the water, only to be dragged back toward mid-Channel.

Again Brickell made more course changes, and I swam with all I had. Finally, we broached the current, swung around, and fought our way in to shore. In total I swam thirty-three miles, three miles farther than the year before, and I broke Davis Hart's world record with a time of nine hours and thirty-six minutes. It was a great moment, being able to repeat an English Channel success, and I felt a great sense of satisfaction. But after that I decided I had had enough of swimming the English Channel; I wanted to do something else.

8

Invitation to Egypt

Later that year I received, because of my world-record Channel swim, an invitation from the Egyptian government to join a group of long-distance swimmers for a race in the Nile River. When Fahmy Attallah heard about the invitation, he encouraged me to go, and to have David accompany me as my coach. Fahmy told us that in Egypt long-distance swimmers are more revered than NFL quarterbacks. Streets are named for them, and parades are conducted in their honor throughout the city of Cairo. He said we would have a wonderful experience, and he romantically described how beautiful Cairo would be, and how well we would be taken care of. He said that Egyptians were very gracious and generous people; they would welcome us into their homes and would take good care of us. Fahmy gave us the names of his brothers and a cousin who lived in Cairo, in case we needed any help with anything.

A few months later, during spring vacation in 1974, when Dave and I stepped off the United Arab Airlines plane onto the unlit tarmac at Cairo airport, submachine guns were trained on us by Egyptian army troops. The Yom Kippur War between Egypt and Israel, which I had intently studied in my current affairs class, trying to figure out why they'd had to go to war at all, had recently ended, and we were witnessing its aftermath. We'd never expected to see so much devastation in Cairo.

As we fumbled through a black corridor lit only by handheld flashlights into the arrival area, dust clouds rose around us, illuminated by moonlight streaming through the mortar holes in the airport ceiling. The moonbeams spread out, and as people passed us to stand in line for customs, they cast ghostly shadows against the bullet-pocked walls.

On the way in the United Arab Airlines plane had nearly crashed twice, during landings in Zurich and Cairo. Somehow, the first time, the pilot misjudged our distance to the ground, and we bounced down the runway with so much force that the over-head compartments sprang open and the contents flew across the plane; one woman got banged on the head by a silver platter. The second time, as we landed in Cairo, the brakes failed. We overran the runway, stopping moments before we crashed into a metal fence.

Now a customs official who hadn't taken a shower for days, and was wearing an old, torn, and faded uniform, was studying our passports. He leaned in close to Dave and whispered something that sounded like "baksheesh."

At first, neither Dave nor I understood what he was saying, and then it occurred to us that he was demanding a bribe and wasn't about to let us go unless we paid him off. He turned Dave's bag over and dumped his clothes onto a table. Then he picked up each article of clothing piece by piece, opening the shirts, inspecting the seams, and turning the pants and underwear inside out. When he didn't find anything of any value, he unzipped my travel bag, pushed my street clothes aside, and began fingering my underwear and leering at me.

"Jeez, I can't believe this guy," Dave said loudly enough for everyone in the room to hear us. The army officer who had led us into the terminal came into the room. He said something in Arabic to the customs official, who tried to wave the officer away. But the officer conferred with his men posted nearby and he turned to the customs officer and started shouting at him. Abruptly the customs official turned to us, his entire demeanor softening. "So sorry for the delay. Welcome to Cairo. I hope you enjoy your stay in our beautiful city."

He led us into the lobby, where we were supposed to meet with an official from the Egyptian Swimming Federation. It was three a.m., and the arrival area was completely deserted. We didn't know what to do; we didn't know where we were supposed to stay. We couldn't speak Arabic so we couldn't talk to anyone outside the terminal, and we couldn't exchange our travelers' checks, since the bank was closed.

We had been traveling for thirty-six hours, with a brief stopover in London. Not only was I exhausted, but I suddenly felt very far from home, in a place I didn't think I wanted to be. Sinking down onto the floor, I tried to hold back the tears. I knew crying wouldn't help, but this seemed like a strange and scary place, and I had no idea what to do.

"Don't worry, they'll find us here in a

couple of days," Dave joked to make light of our predicament. He had no better idea of what to do. He was only nineteen, and he had never traveled outside the States. So we sat for a couple hours and waited.

Fortunately, a man who owned a car-rental agency saw us looking very forlorn. He spoke a little English, and he offered to call Fahmy's brother Nassief. I felt bad that we were calling him at five in the morning, but we didn't know what else to do.

Nassief immediately offered to put us up in his apartment until everything was sorted out. The car-rental-agency man told us to wait for a minute while he called us a cab. The cab that pulled up a few minutes later had barely survived the war: the hood was tied to the bumper, the tires were completely bald, and the trunk had been so smashed forward that we would have to hold our luggage on our laps.

Reaching through broken windows, we opened the doors and climbed in. There were no seat belts, but that didn't matter, since there really weren't seats. The driver turned the ignition key at least a couple of times before the engine started, and then he stomped on the accelerator. He drove like an Indy race-car driver on an obstacle course. Dave and I held on to whatever we could, laughing uncontrollably as we sped around corners, tires squealing, the car launching over innumerable bumps and potholes.

We flew through the sleeping city, tears streaming down our cheeks, past stark concrete buildings, going the wrong way down ancient one-way cobblestoned streets and through a city that was unlit except for the stoplights, which, to our driver, were mere decorations. At one police checkpoint, he sped through without hesitation even as the policemen blew their whistles and waved angrily at him to stop. A few minutes later, we arrived at an apartment complex.

Nassief Attallah, a tall, broad-shouldered man in his sixties, trotted downstairs wearing long striped pajamas and a red nightcap over his thick silver hair. Phillippe, his younger brother, followed, walking with a limp. Phillippe looked very much like Fahmy. He said, "Welcome, welcome, welcome." It was Fahmy's voice. One phrase connected the families a world away, and everything suddenly seemed so much better.

Lena, Nassief's wife, led us to our room, where Dave and I slept deeply on mattresses filled with sweet straw. In the midafternoon, I awoke to the exotic sounds of donkeys braying, car horns blaring, and a muezzin in a minaret calling Muslims to prayer over a loudspeaker. Still exhausted, I tried to turn over and fall back to sleep, but searing white desert light was streaming through sheer curtains beside my bed, so I got up and looked outside.

The world below was swirling with humanity. The men were dressed in Western-style clothes and long cotton shirts that looked like pajamas; some of the women were dressed in Western clothes too, but many wore long, heavy black chadors. Immediately below the window, women and children were selling pita bread stacked in open wagons, the children shooing off the flies with a straw brush. Cars were everywhere, completely disregarding traffic signals and people attempting to cross the street.

While we ate a delicious breakfast of warm, chewy pita bread, salty feta cheese, and homemade sweet date jam, Phillippe arrived and told us he had phoned the Egyptian Swimming Federation. There had been a mistake in our telex, and we had arrived a day earlier than expected. We were instructed to take a cab to the Continental Hotel, where we would be staying with the other foreign swimmers for twelve days. This would give us time to get over the jet lag and prepare for the race.

At the hotel, a throng of journalists and television crews greeted Dave and me as if we were rock stars. The press thought we had been avoiding them, and one journalist in particular was annoyed at me. He was a short man with a thick black mustache and greasy black hair plastered to his head. He said his name was William Amen and he was a journalist for the largest newspaper in Egypt. He started following me around, asking me a number of questions over and over again. At first I thought he didn't understand English very well, and since I was the only American who had been invited to the race, I wanted to represent my country to the best of my ability. I wanted to make sure that he understood me, so I politely answered his questions over and over again. Finally, I broke away to deposit my luggage in the room Dave and I would be sharing.

A few minutes later, Fahmy's cousin Morad Luca, a very wide, bald, and friendly man, arrived. He was one of the top defense attorneys in Egypt and he spoke a little English. Phillippe had called him and told him that we needed his help, so he'd arrived to take us to the Egyptian Swimming Federation's old steamboat, anchored on the Nile River. It doubled as the federation's offices and sports club. While I went back to the room to change into my swimsuit and sweats, Morad phoned ahead and organized a guide and a rowboat for us. While Dave, Morad, and the boat captain discussed the Nile River currents, I took off my sweatsuit apprehensively and looked across the river. Fahmy had described the Nile as the river of life and the birthplace of the world's ancient civilization. With dreamy eyes, he had said, "The Nile is very, very beautiful. It has its very own shade of blue." Sixteen years had passed since Fahmy had lived in Egypt, and much had changed. The river was not any shade of blue; it was dark brown, thick, and opaque, and it stank like something old and dying.

Stalling, trying to psych myself up to dive into the water, I slowly pushed my short, chlorine-bleached blond hair into my yellow swim cap. I wondered if I was going to get sick if I swam in that water. Never had I swum in any water as filthy.

From the steamboat's deck, I watched Dave, Morad, and the rowboat captain discuss the positioning of the boat. Morad explained that the racecourse would be around two islands in the middle of the river, in the center of Cairo. The swimmers would travel a figure-eight course twice;

each figure eight would be ten miles long. And there were to be two races held concurrently: an amateur race for men and women (the race I had entered because I wanted to maintain my amateur status in case I decided to swim in college) and a professional race for men and women.

The steamboat and the start of the race were located in the Big Nile; on the other side of the two islands was an area known as the Little Nile. Later that day another swimmer would tell me that the Big Nile was where all the chemical sewage was discharged, and the Little Nile was where all the raw sewage was dumped.

Dave motioned for me to get into the water. Holding my hand over my face so water wouldn't shoot up my nose and possibly infect my sinuses, I jumped in. The water smelled like a sewer, and the stench was so strong I felt my stomach turn.

Once you start swimming, I told myself, *you'll feel better. You always do.* But this time I didn't.

Swimming with my head up, I moved toward the boat through an oil slick about a hundred yards wide. My swimsuit filled with goo. It never occurred to me that I was the only swimmer training in the Nile River; I just kept swimming until my right hand hit something rubbery. It was a dead Nile perch, floating belly-up. I shuddered and kept swimming.

Some four hundred yards down river my hand hit something else. Instinctively, I turned to see what it was: it was a dead rat with one eye missing. A sudden current had carried it down, and soon there were a dozen dead rats bobbing around me, eyes missing, heads gnawed away. This river of life that Fahmy remembered was a river of death, and I wanted to run out of the water. But I couldn't; I had to train, so I forced myself to stay focused. I sprinted forward, leery of what lay ahead.

Off to my left was a large drain the width of a truck. Here the water became warmer and thicker, and the upper inches were covered with a crust of frothy brown scum. Trying to avoid smelling it, I breathed late and was suddenly choking on a mouthful. I felt my resolve begin to crumble. Dave was just as disgusted with the water conditions as I was, and so after only an hour of training, I climbed out, back onto the steamboat. I wasn't keen about ever getting into the Nile again. But I knew that I had to, to be in the race.

Dave and I discussed it on the deck. He thought I needed to work out at least twice more in the river so we could figure out our best course. I was wiping brown slime off my face when I noticed a group of male swimmers — mostly teenagers and some that looked as if they were college age. They were wearing the Egyptian team's green-and-white sweats and were listening to one of the older swimmers, who had his back turned to me. He was taller than his team-mates and had dark, wavy hair and the perfect V shape of a swimmer in top condition. Speaking excitedly in Arabic, using animated gestures, he held the entire group's attention. A boy sprang up, grabbed his hand, and held on to it, and he laughed so delightedly that I started laughing too. The young man spun around. He had large, dark brown eyes and a wonderful smile. He extended his hand and said his name was Monir. He was the captain of the Egyptian team. I introduced myself, but he already knew who I was. He had heard that I was training in the Nile. He introduced me to his team, and the young boys stared at me as if I had just arrived from another planet.

"They are surprised to see that you are not a man. They didn't believe me when I told them that you held the record for the English Channel. They expected only a man could swim that fast. I told them to come and see you for themselves," Monir said.

I said hello to them and shook hands. Monir told me that there was a better place to train. It was called the Gizara Club. The club had once catered to the British elite, but now it was where the Egyptians trained, with an American coach named Rick Field. Monir said that he thought the girls on the team would like to meet me too, and perhaps I could come by during the afternoon workout and encourage them. I said I'd be very happy to meet them.

That afternoon I convinced Dave to accompany me to the Gizara Club instead of returning to the Nile. By the time we arrived, Monir was already in the pool, so we introduced ourselves to Rick Field. I watched Monir train. He was a strong swimmer, and each time he took a stroke, the water flowed down his biceps and deltoids, then rippled past his lats and along his streamlined bronze torso. He looked as if he was about the same speed as me. I was eager to get into the pool and have someone to pace with, but Rick asked if I would talk to the girls on the team. He made a point of telling me that there was an equal number of girls and boys on the team. Only two girls had qualified for the Nile race, though. Most Middle Eastern teams, he explained, had few female swimmers. Rick had me talk to the girls about my swims and training. And they shyly told me a little about themselves.

After the workout was over, Rick invited Dave and me for a tour of the city. I wasn't feeling very well, so I decided to return to the hotel. Just as I was about to fall asleep, there was a knock on my door. It was William Amen, the reporter who had been following me. He asked if he could come into the room and interview me. He opened his writing tablet, sat on the bed opposite mine, and pretended to read old notes. Patiently I answered him, until he suddenly got up and shut the door, saying that with all the noise in the hall, he couldn't hear me. Feeling uncomfortable with this arrangement, I got up and opened the door halfway, making an excuse that Dave would be back shortly and didn't have a key.

"Do you like Egypt?" William asked.

"Yes, it is a very exotic country," I said.

He reached out and touched my arm. "Your muscles are tight," he said.

"They're just fine," I said.

"You know the Dutch swimmer, I give her massage. I give you one?"

"No, thank you," I said, sensing that something weird was going on and it wasn't just cultural differences.

William unbuttoned his shirtsleeve and rolled it up, and pointed to his forearm showing a large blue tattoo on his biceps. "I am Christian," he said.

"That's nice," I said.

He reached over and grabbed my hand and declared, "I come to see your father in three years."

"What for?"

"To marry you," he said.

"No, thank you," I said, and thought, *You've got to be out of your mind.*

He looked dumbfounded. "You must marry me."

"You had better leave," I said, slipping free.

"You will change your mind," he said angrily.

"Not in this lifetime."

Dave and I were so sick that in the morning Morad drove us to see a physician who worked for the swimming federation. The doctor, a plump man in his late forties, let us into his office.

Pickled frogs, unidentifiable organs, animal embryos in jars, and medical books lined the shelves of his office. We sat around his desk while Morad described our symptoms. The doctor said confidently in broken English, "Yes, I have pills. They will cure you. Don't worry."

He turned to a counter covered with large bottles of unmarked pills, located one containing blue pills, unscrewed the lid, counted out eight, and dropped them into an envelope. Then he found another containing pink pills and counted out eight more. He handed David the blue pills — presumably because he was a boy — and me the pink ones, because I was a girl. He instructed us to take one every day for the next eight days. Neither David nor I had any confidence in the medication. Instead we decided not to eat anything and to give our stomachs a rest. But it was Easter Sunday and, as a surprise, Morad had arranged for us to celebrate with his wife, daughter, and extended family.

Morad welcomed us into his home, where we met the family, and we moved into the dining area. We had never seen so much food. Platters were piled two feet high with kabobs, pilaf, a ham, Easter eggs, and countless holiday specialties. The last thing we felt like doing was eating, but we were guests and didn't want to hurt our hosts' feelings. The feasting lasted from noon to midnight, and by the time we'd finished we felt like we would explode.

When we returned to the hotel, the Sudanese swimmer hurried over to talk with me. They had forgotten to tell us that all the swimmers in the race were supposed to participate in a demonstration race. While we were out, everyone else had completed the race, and then the swimmers had been taken through the streets of Cairo in open horse-drawn carriages. Thousands of cheering spectators had lined the parade course to get a glimpse of them, throw flowers and streamers, and shout good wishes.

When the parade finished, the race organizers had tried to find me for television interviews; when they couldn't, they'd had a swimmer from the Netherlands impersonate me on the air. It seemed very bizarre. But Dave and I were beginning to understand that we had entered a very different culture, and we weren't sure how to handle it.

The Sudanese swimmer was very angry, too. He said that the journalist who had been following me around had written a very bad story about me, and it had been on the front page of the Cairo paper. The gist of the story was that Dave and I had been out partying all night long and had been ever since we arrived in Egypt. The reporter was waiting in the lobby for me, so I went with the Sudanese swimmer and we talked. The reporter said that he was sorry but he'd had to make up a story to explain why I wasn't available for the parade and the interviews. I explained to him that I understood, and I would not be speaking to him ever again.

For the next seven days I trained in the swimming pool at the Gizara Club. Both David and I grew increasingly ill. In an attempt to replace all the body fluids we were losing, we drank large amounts of bottled water. One morning, though, I discovered a waiter in the hallway standing over a sink, refilling the bottles with tap water and resealing them. The water wasn't purified, and it no doubt was contributing to our problem.

Two days before the race, the Egyptian team and all the guest swimmers were bused out to a restaurant near the Pyramids for dinner. Monir was sitting with a friend on the bus, and I managed to get a seat behind him with Dave.

Monir was a pharmacy student at Cairo University. He said that he understood that we were both sick. Dave explained the symptoms, and Monir diagnosed the problem as dysentery. When Dave showed him our pills, Monir shook his head in disbelief. They were placebos, just sugar pills. Dave told him that we had been given them from the Egyptian Swimming Federation doctor. Monir grimaced with disgust. He said he had friends at the university who were physicians and he would get some real medication for us.

"How quickly do you think it will work?" I asked.

"It depends upon your condition, the strength of the medication, and how fast your body responds. It could take effect within twenty-four hours," he added optimistically.

"That would be great," I said, hoping it would be soon enough.

A Sahara wind was gusting around the Nile River, unfurling the flags of the twenty-five nations whose swimmers were about to compete in the twenty-mile race. This race had been held since before Fahmy was a boy, always in spring, and had always been regarded in the Arab world as a swim of great honor and prestige.

Monir was standing on a hill above the Egyptian Swimming Federation's boat, studying the river below, ablaze with brilliantly colored flags with interesting crests and insignias and designs. There were over one hundred rowboats on the water, and there would be at least a dozen swimmers from the Egyptian team competing in the race. Monir was having a difficult time locating his boat.

Below was a scene of chaos; with the strong south-flowing current, none of the boats could hold their positions. They were slamming into each other, jockeying for position. Tempers were flaring, crews were screaming, and everyone was using expressive hand gestures. Finally Monir found his boat.

I had no difficulty finding mine. It was the only one with the American flag, positioned a hundred yards ahead of the starting line.

Monir noticed me and hurried over. He wanted to know how I was feeling. I told him much better, but it wasn't true. I had lost nearly twenty pounds in ten days, most of it from dehydration, and my stomach was cramping and killing me, but I didn't want to tell him that. "Are you okay?" I asked.

"Just a bit nervous," he said.

"Oh, don't worry — so much can happen in eight or nine hours. Just take it as it comes. Sometimes it seems like a lifetime can pass in eight or nine hours," I said to exaggerate the point.

That was exactly what Monir needed to hear, and he repeated it and visibly relaxed.

Thousands of people lined the race-course, many waving small Egyptian flags and shouting the names of their favorite swimmers. A loudspeaker was blaring; an announcer was introducing the athletes' names as if a horse race were about to start. More people kept arriving.

A few moments later I lined up with the other swimmers, and the announcer shouted something in Arabic. It must have been "Go!" because all the swimmers were running into the water except me. Pulling on my cap and goggles, I dove into the river.

The pack was already heading north, toward a buoy in the center of the Nile. All one hundred swimmers were trying to squeeze around that buoy and locate their crew. It was more crowded than Times Square at rush hour, and more competitive. Someone kicked me in the stomach. Someone else elbowed me in the ribs. I felt as if I were back on the water polo team. Looking up, I found a hole in the pack and zigzagged toward it, then crossed to the opposite shore, where the current was weaker. Dave was calling me, and when I looked up I saw the American flag, the beautiful white stars and red stripes reflected in the wavering brown water. "You're right on pace and in first place. Good job!" he shouted so I could hear him above the cheering crowd.

We rounded the northern tip of the north island, then turned south. There we moved into the middle of the river to take full advantage of the current. The city, the crowds — people washing clothes, fishing, and defecating in the water — flew past like a video on fast forward.

We cut back across the center of the eight and entered an area where I had not practiced before. Dave had tried to convince me to swim there, but the stench had made me gag. The water was stagnant, hot, and as thick as engine oil, and it was filled with chunks of brown sewage. It got worse. We came to an area about two hundred yards long where large metal barrels had been strung together and placed parallel to the shore. During the war, the Egyptians had placed the barrels in the Nile in an area where the current slowed so that if the Israelis mined the river, the mines would collect in this area and unexploded mines wouldn't explode on shore. The Egyptians admitted that the chances of this happening were remote, but the barrels were still in place. They also believed that the mines would drift into the barrel area and this would help protect ships from exploding mines.

Two men were standing thigh deep in the water, pushing the barrels aside so we could swim through a narrow opening. Here the water was so shallow that every time I took a stroke my arm sank down into the heavy, thick brown muck, to my shoulder. Waste swelled in clouds around my face and filled my swimsuit with putrid water. On my next stroke my hand sank more deeply into the goo, and I cut my fingertips on some broken glass. Knowing the water was like a test tube filled with virulent bacteria, I just about lost it. I didn't realize at the time that the other swimmers had built up a resistance to the microbes in the water, or that those who hadn't had stayed clear of the river until the day of the race.

Finally we cleared the barrels and moved offshore. Rounding the bottom loop of the figure eight, we turned directly into the current. Here my speed was cut in half. I was feeling weak and dizzy, but I was still in first place.

Stroking along at seventy strokes per minute, faster than my normal speed, I tried to compensate for the current and push ahead. Something large hit my arm. Then my hand hit it. It felt soft, spongy, and bony.

The smell made my head spin.

"What was that?" I shouted to Dave.

"You don't want to know," he said, having turned away in disgust.

"What was it?"

"A dead dog. Your hand punched through its rib cage."

Dave kept talking to me, encouraging me, saying that I was doing really well, that I was strong, that I'd never looked better, but I knew he wasn't telling me the truth, and I knew he knew it too. I told him I was having a rough time. I didn't feel good. I felt really cold in the water, and I was starting to shake. That made no sense at all, since the water temperature was in the high seventies. Dave urged me to continue. He suggested that I drink some canned apple juice. I tried it, but I had to fight to keep it down. Good coaches know when to push a swimmer and when to back off. David knew, and he understood that I was almost at my limit. "You've got an Egyptian swimmer about one hundred yards behind you," he said.

I turned to breathe, and on that breath I could see it was Monir. Putting my head down, I tried to snap into gear, but he continued gaining on me. I pulled faster and deeper, but my arm strokes had no power behind them. When I glanced back, Monir had closed the space between us. He pulled alongside me so quickly that I felt as if I were going backward. Then I understood that he had the strength to fly right by me, but instead he slowed down and moved closer so I could ride on his slipstream. Matching my strokes with his, I paced with him. His arm strokes were long, smooth, powerful, and beautiful. Water flowed over him like a second skin and magnified the smooth contours of his body as he glided across the water's surface. He grinned at me reassuringly and I smiled back at him. Finally this was fun. Pulling a little more strongly, he egged me on, and I met his strength, quickening my pace by a notch. He increased his pace, extended his arms out farther, dug deeper, and pulled more water. I tried to snap into my next gear, but I couldn't. I tried again, but it wasn't there. He waited and moved closer so that our arms were nearly touching. We breathed at the same moment and he smiled, letting me ride more of his slipstream.

From the boat Monir's coach was shouting at him, but Monir was breathing only in my direction so that he didn't have to look at his coach. But I could see the coach, and he was going nuts.

"I can't hold this speed," I said, lifting my

head so he could hear me.

"Just try," Monir said, and eased back.

When I turned to breathe, there was a Syrian swimmer gaining on us.

"Come on, pick it up," Monir said.

My arms weren't responding.

Monir slowed down. His coach was screaming at the top of his lungs. He was pointing at the Syrian swimmer, trying to get Monir's attention to let him know that the Syrian was moving in.

"You've got to go now; you've got a guy right behind you," I said.

"Try harder," he coaxed. He knew, as all long-distance swimmers do, that if you keep going you can usually break through the wall. You get a second, a third, and even a tenth wind.

Every part of me wanted to stay with him. "You've got to go now or you'll lose this race."

He glanced back. "Okay, I'll see you at the finish," he said.

"Don't worry — I'll come up from behind and catch you before that," I joked, knowing there was no way I would ever catch him that day.

"See you soon," he said, cranking up his speed and leaving me in his wake. When he rounded the top of the figure eight, I lost sight of him. Stopping, I drank some apple juice. My stomach cramped. I tossed the juice bottle back into the rowboat and wearily I put my head down. I was so cold I was shivering hard in the water. Slowly we rounded the top of the figure eight.

I tried to use whatever I could to motivate myself: *You're the only American in the race. You've got to do this. Keep going.*

An Italian and a Greek swimmer passed; I could tell by their flags. I tried to reach down within myself, but there was nothing there. "Dave, I can't do this," I said, surprised I had uttered those words.

He tried to convince me to keep swimming, and I did, for another few hundred yards. Then I started to slow down, but there were some kids on the riverbank and they began throwing rocks at us. It seemed unbelievable at first, but it became very clear that they were aiming for us when they hit Dave in the shoulder and the pilot on the head. A shower of rocks hit the water. Dave told me to me to sprint, and I did, but we continued to be pelted. Fortunately, a couple of army officers who were on the shore for crowd control saw what was happening and grabbed the kids by their shirts and hauled them away.

My stomach cramped so hard that I

started crying. "I can't do this. I don't feel good."

"Okay, okay, swim over to the boat. You can get out," he said.

I looked at him leaning over, reaching for me, and I couldn't do it. I couldn't disqualify myself, couldn't give up. "I'm okay now. I can keep going," I said as my stomach cramped again and I lost all sense of balance in the water. I was listing to one side as I swam.

Dave stopped me and insisted that I drink some juice to boost my blood-sugar levels. Floating on my back, I squeezed the liquid into my mouth and watched a couple of girls from Egypt pass me. I didn't care anymore.

I managed to hold on for another quarter of a mile, but my stomach started cramping again, so hard I couldn't breathe. I cried into the water so no one would see me. What was wrong with me? Why couldn't I do this? My stomach cramped again and I felt the world shut down inside, and I got scared. "Dave, I don't feel good; I can't go any farther. I can't, I can't, I can't," I said, and I slapped the water in frustration. I'd never slapped the water before; I'd never cried in the water; and I'd never felt so bad.

"Okay, get out, okay, come here, let me help you out," he said.

"Just a little more. I'll try just a little more," I said, and took some strokes. I couldn't feel my arms. The cramps were coming one right after the other now, and I couldn't focus. I was falling over, going down.

"Here, take my hand," Dave said urgently.

There was that moment, that horrible, terrible moment, when I knew I had to touch his hand and disqualify myself. Even then, I didn't want to do it. I didn't want to give up. It was so strange. I could feel myself slipping away. I reached up for his hand and let him grab my wrist. Somehow it seemed better that way, letting him disqualify me, rather than me doing it to myself. There was something so awful in giving up. But once he held my wrist, I just let go of myself. I let my face fall into the water, felt myself being dragged toward the boat. I was choking on that thick water, and then they were lifting me into the boat. I shut my eyes. I didn't want to see where I was or what was happening. I could feel Dave holding my head in the boat. He was talking to me. I couldn't understand what he was saying. My stomach hurt so much. I couldn't open my eyes. Everything hurt so much.

Dave and some other people dragged me from the boat, loaded me onto a stretcher and then into an ambulance that he later said looked like a milk truck. As we sped to the hospital I faded in and out of consciousness. It was hot outside, but I was so cold, I was shaking hard.

Sirens blared as we raced through Cairo's streets, and Dave held on to me so I wouldn't flip over in the back of the ambulance. I pressed my fists into my stomach to block the cramping, clenched my jaw so I wouldn't scream, and squeezed my eyes shut. Somehow I pushed my mind away, detached myself, found comfort in the gray space, the netherworld between consciousness and unconsciousness. I wanted to remain there — not think, not feel, not know anything.

"Is she allergic to any medication?" The doctor was speaking to Dave.

"No, nothing," he said.

"When did she last eat?"

"Ten days ago."

"Ten days?"

"She's had dysentery for that time. She's had some apple and some orange juice."

"Is she taking medication for it?"

"Yes, but she only started yesterday." Dave's voice sounded small and scared. I was sorry to put him through this, sorry I had not finished, and sorry I failed. I wanted to tell him I would be okay, but I didn't think I would ever be okay again. I couldn't control my body or my emotions.

"We're going to give her some muscle relaxers, some glucose and electrolytes, and see how she does with that. Then we will start her on some medication for the gastrointestinal infection," the doctor said, adding something in Arabic for the emergency team.

Someone stuck a needle into my vein, and I slid blissfully away into the gray space. Time passed, I don't know how much, but after a while I heard Rick Field talking to Dave: "The doctor gave her three injections for the abdominal cramps and a strong sedative. He's replacing her fluids now. She's lucky he used new needles. They usually have to reuse old ones."

The doctor said, "She was dangerously dehydrated and her heart rate was over two hundred. She was hypothermic from her condition. The electric blanket is helping her get back to a normal temperature. She seems to be relaxing now, but we will keep her overnight for observation." He patted me gently on the cheek.

"Thank you very much," I said to him, and saw him smile. Then I turned to Dave and asked, "How far did I swim?"

"A little more than fifteen miles," he said.

Tears welled up in my eyes. I hated not finishing.

The doctor leaned over the table, touched me on the cheek again, and wiped away the tears. "What did she say?"

Rick told him, and with utter exasperation the doctor said, "Doesn't she realize she was in a life-threatening situation? Doesn't she realize she went too far, way too far?" He shook his head with disbelief.

While we were in the hospital, Monir finished the Nile race. For the last five miles he held the Syrian swimmer off, and he won. The crowd carried him around the finish line on their shoulders. They were jubilant: the hometown favorite, the captain of the Egyptian team, had won. He was very happy, but when he discovered that I was in the hospital, he jumped into a cab, still in his wet swimsuit, to find me. But I had convinced the doctor to release me from the hospital and was back at the hotel resting.

I saw Monir the next evening at a celebration dinner. He was talking with his teammates, and when he saw me, he immediately excused himself. He said he was glad to see me and had been afraid that I wouldn't come to the party. He invited me to have

197

dinner with him at a table with a group of men who were in their late seventies and eighties. It seemed strange to me that Monir chose to sit with them rather than the younger swimmers, but it was his way of paying homage to the older men, because he had learned from them, and by winning the Nile race he had joined their ranks. Monir had asked me to join him there because he knew they would welcome me too, for my swims across the English Channel.

I discovered the other reason why Monir had selected this particular table: here, we could talk without being overheard, and he wanted to hold my hand under the table. He did it very slowly, touching my fingers gently, asking me if it was okay for him to touch my hand. My every nerve ending seemed to feel his hand and respond to it. Ever so slowly I traced the outline of his hand with my fingertips, and then we simply held hands and felt the beating of our hearts within our hands. I had never held some-one's hand like that before.

Candlelight danced in his eyes, and when he smiled, I was so happy.

"Will you come back to race in the Nile next year?" he asked.

"No, I don't think I ever want to swim in the Nile again," I said, flinching.

"Then I don't think I will see you again," he said, his voice heavy.

"Don't worry, I'm sure someday we will meet at an ocean or a swimming pool," I said.

We sat beside each other on the bus back to the hotel. I was very close to him, leaning against his side. I still felt so fragile. Somehow Monir understood it all, and he held my hand again.

"You know, during the race I thought about what you said and it really helped me. You will always be a champion; you will always do your best. Nothing more than that can ever be expected. I learned that myself. But you can't learn everything at once. It takes time," he said gently.

I slid my arm around his back and hugged him. It was not acceptable behavior in a public place like a bus, but fortunately, the bus was dark. He turned and faced me and we just hugged.

It didn't make any sense, but my feelings for him were deep, unlike anything I'd ever felt before.

I think I had fallen in love with him. And I think he had the same feelings for me. There were big smiles on our faces and tears in our eyes when we parted.

9

Lost in the Fog

Within my first couple weeks of being home, I got my first letter from Monir. I was so happy to hear from him. In barely a week and a half, he had made an enormous impression on my life. I thought about him all the time and wondered how he was, what he was doing. Until that point, I had never been that caught up in someone else, but from what I'd seen, I knew he was someone special. So I wrote and told him how happy I was to hear from him, that I had recovered physically from my experience, that I had returned to high school and finished out the year with my studies and swimming for the girls' swim team. Then I explained to him that I wanted to continue with my long-distance swimming. It had always bothered me that I could have broken the Catalina record, so I'd decided that I wanted to attempt it again.

A month passed. It was the summer of 1974, and nothing had really changed in a big way. I was still seventeen, living the same life: getting up, going to work out, seeing friends in the neighborhood, working out again in the afternoon, going to movies. But when Monir's second letter arrived from Egypt, and I opened it, the whole world seemed suddenly to be cast in a new, warm, vibrant light. Everything around me was blooming, awakening, and intensely beautiful. I read his letter at least five times, then put it away in my desk drawer with the first one, so I could read them again sometime.

He said he had decided to take a coaching position and he was very excited about that choice. I told him that I was about to swim the Catalina Channel. With Coach Gambril at Harvard and Dave on his way to college, for a brief time I had continued swimming for what had been Gambril's team. The name had been changed to the Long Beach Team. I'd swum for the new coach, Dick Jochums, but we did not mesh at all. So I'd changed teams and started training with Jim Montrella at the Lakewood Aquatic Club.

At midnight, my support crew assembled: my father and mother, Fahmy; John Stockwell and Lyle Johnson, the veteran lifeguards who had accompanied the Seal Beach Swim Team crew three years earlier; Mickey Pitman, who would pilot the *Bandito*; John Sonnichsen, who had worked with other channel swimmers and had volunteered to help with this swim; Mr. Yeo, who had also been along on the previous crossing; Jim Montrella; Lynn Simross from the *Los Angeles Times*; and a combination of Seal Beach and Long Beach lifeguards. At the last minute Pat, a local pool swimming coach and a friend of one of the lifeguards, volunteered to help paddle. He was a surfer but had no experience in open-water swims. We pushed off from Santa Catalina Island and headed for the California coast.

The wind was down, the sea was calmly reflecting the heavens, and I was swimming very strongly, gliding with each stroke, like a skater sliding across the ice. Everything seemed to be just right.

After four hours of swimming, fog began slowly drifting into the channel. Clouds connected into long bands so that at times the lead boat was completely obscured. It made me feel a little uneasy, and Stockwell and Johnson, in the dory, felt that way too. Stockwell got on the walkie-talkie and suggested that Mickey move the *Bandito* closer.

It took him just a couple of minutes to

turn the *Bandito* around, but the fog had become so thick that we couldn't see him at all. Instinctively I moved closer to Pat, on the paddleboard. Stockwell continued talking on the walkie-talkie, giving Mickey our compass heading. When I turned my head to breathe, the dory suddenly disappeared into the fog. Pat and I tried calling to Stockwell and Johnson, but they couldn't hear us. Pat pulled the flashlight off his paddleboard and shone it into the clouds. To our horror, the light only reflected back at us. There was no way anyone anywhere would see it, except for us. At that moment it became very clear that we were lost in the fog, in the middle of the night, in the center of the Catalina Channel.

Foghorns bellowed around us, their deep voices coming from all different directions and distances; some were louder, others softer, punctuating the darkness with deep, rumbling moans. And as the fog descended into the channel, the moaning grew louder and more frequent, until we were encircled by phantom voices, so that we became disoriented by the sounds.

A few minutes earlier I had seen light beams from a lighthouse somewhere out there, but the flashes had dimmed, and now there was nothing at all. I was doing everything I could to remain calm, to be optimistic, until the bow waves from the tankers and freighters started hitting us. They came out of nowhere, and some were ten or twelve feet high. We could hear the ships' horns blaring, sending out warnings; they were so close they hurt our ears. But there was nothing we could do. There would be a pause between the warning and the wave, and then suddenly we'd be lifted up off the surface of the earth, it seemed, into the clouds. Scrambling to stay beside Pat, I'd fight back the feeling of panic. I was so afraid that I would lose Pat on a wave in the black fog or be crushed by a tanker. The tanker waves kept hitting us from different directions, so it was hard to tell which way to move, where to go so we wouldn't be run over. We tried to move in one direction only to be hit by another set of waves. Then Pat got caught on the crest of a wave; he was lifted into the fog, and I was in the trough, so I couldn't see him or the board. On the verge of panic, he shouted to me at the top of his lungs, though his voice was muffled by the clouds: "Stay with me. I'm here. Right here. Move this way."

The wave lifted me up and I looked down into the black cloud, terrified beyond anything ever before. "I'm here. Right here," I said, feeling my fear rise as the wave lifted me higher, straining to see him through the black drape of fog. There was nothing that I could use as a reference point, nothing to connect me to earth — no lights on the water, no moonlight, no starlight, nothing. Everything had been smothered by fog. Even my breaths were short and labored. I felt like I was trying to breathe through a cold, wet towel.

Pat was somewhere down there, in the wave trough, still shouting, although I couldn't make out his words anymore. The clarity was gone — all I could hear were muffled sounds. Then I heard a ship's engine. It was deep, close. Putting my head well into a wave, I listened intently for the engine sounds, hoping I could figure out which way the ship was moving, hoping I could move out of the way in time so I wouldn't be sucked in by the ship's engines, hoping I wouldn't be cut in half by the huge propellers, hoping that Pat would choose the right direction, hoping that I would find him again. So much time passed in those moments.

Then it happened so fast: I felt a deep, powerful stream of cold bubbles and a current churning around me, dragging me toward it, pulling me down. It was the slipstream of the tanker. I tried to pull away, to sprint, but there was nothing I could do to match the force of that current. It dragged me backward and then released me.

With the passing of the ship, there was a pause in the waves. All the while, Pat and I had been shouting off and on to each other. Somehow we found each other. That in itself was a miracle. Now the question was what to do next. We couldn't sit in the shipping lane and be run over by a tanker, but we couldn't swim off into the fog either. Pat wanted to keep going, but I didn't think that was a good idea. He had no nautical experience, and I tried to explain that when people were lost in the fog, they tended to make a huge circle, and perhaps become more lost. I thought we should stay put. He didn't agree. He told me that I had to continue swimming, that I needed to keep going so I could break the record. But that seemed so unimportant now.

Then something began to happen underwater, and I was barely able to hold it together. There were fish, very large ones, moving below me. They might have been seals, dolphins, or sharks — I couldn't tell. I couldn't see anything below. The water was as black as the inside of a coffin. But I knew they were big: I could feel the water suddenly become hollow, and I could feel myself dropping down into the hole when they swam below me. It felt like I was being pulled down into an abyss, and fear rose again in me. Something big ran into my legs; I felt a thud and was spun halfway around. I couldn't help myself — I screamed, a blood-curdling scream.

A school of fish — maybe grunion or anchovies — ricocheted off my body. Then some larger ones moved below. I shuddered.

Pat suddenly let out a long, heart-stopping scream. A school of fish, maybe one hundred or more, attracted to the flashlight on his paddleboard, were flying out of the water like invisible torpedoes, smacking into his chest, flapping into his arms, and snapping against his hands.

"It's okay, they're just flying fish. They won't hurt you," I said.

"Come on, let's go. If you stay there you're going to get cold," he said.

He was right. I was freezing. I wasn't generating any heat at all, and my fear seemed to exaggerate the effect of the cold. Still, I argued with him: "We've got to stay where we are. Weren't you ever a Boy Scout? Don't you know that when you get lost you're supposed to remain in one place?"

The crew was searching for us. They started by making a wide circle around where they had last seen us, then, accounting for time and drift, extending that circle. They were facing many of the same problems we were experiencing with the ships and the disorientation caused by the fog. Fortunately, the crew was very experienced. They had put out a call to the coast guard, informing them of our situation and requesting that they broadcast a warning to all shipping. The coast guard did just that and offered to help in the search if we weren't found in the next hour.

Meanwhile, Pat had decided that if he started paddling, I would follow him. "Come on, stay with me," he yelled as he paddled into the blackness.

I treaded water and watched him go. In a moment he'd disappeared. All I heard was the sound of his hands paddling. He shouted again at me. I didn't respond. He turned the board around. "Where are you?"

He was going to get us lost. Maybe forever.

"Where are you?" His voice was becoming muffled.

I felt fear surging in me. I started shaking. I don't know if it was because I was scared or because I was cold.

I didn't want to follow him. But I didn't want to lose him either. I couldn't let him vanish. Something could happen to him.

"I'm over here!" I was really afraid, more afraid than I've ever been in my life. He just didn't get it. He didn't understand what he was doing. He was endangering both of us. I guided him back to me with my voice.

"Okay, now will you follow me?" Pat asked. "You've got to keep going if you're going to get across the channel. I'm sure we have to go in this direction," he added with certainty.

"No, I will not follow you. You don't know where you are. You don't know where you're going."

"Come with me. Stop arguing. Just follow me," he said, and he started to paddle.

If we were going to survive, I had to keep him from paddling in a circle, from making it more difficult for the crew in the boats to find us. My words weren't working. I reached up quickly and touched the board, disqualifying myself. As I did, everything in me felt like it was falling apart again. I didn't want to stop. I didn't want to quit. I didn't want to fail. But I had to stop him.

Pat looked at me with complete astonishment. "How could you do that?"

"I don't want to swim anymore. I don't," I

said. I could feel myself choking up, all those horrible feelings I'd had in the Nile River rushing back, but I had to push them away.

"It's okay. Let's pretend that you didn't touch the board. You didn't hang on or anything. Come on. Just swim with me," he pleaded.

There was no sign that the fog would lift, no sign of the *Bandito* or the dory. Nothing to indicate that they were going to find us anytime soon. So I reached up and grabbed the nose of his board and held on tight. I hated doing it. "I'm too cold to go any farther. I think I have hypothermia," I said, not knowing if I did or didn't, just trying to hold him in one place.

"Okay, you can get on the board with me. Here, I'll hold it — climb on," he said.

It took me a couple attempts to pull myself onto the board. When he got back on, I asked him to move beside me so we could keep each other warm. With both of us on the board, there was no room for him to paddle. We shouted into the fog, "We're here! Over here!"

Only foghorns and ship horns answered.

Maybe it was only half an hour that we were lost, I don't know exactly how long, but it seemed as if we were gone for a very long time. Before we could see them, we heard Stockwell's booming voice and Johnson's little one, and then they emerged from the fog. They had turned on every single light they had on board, and in the fog, they were surrounded by a halo of pure light.

"Are you okay?" Stockwell asked.

"Yes," we both said.

"We just spoke with Mickey. He thinks he knows where we are. It's a good thing you stayed put or we'd never have found you. The *Bandito* is closing in on the circle, and they should be here soon," Stockwell said, pulling alongside us. Johnson reached for my hand and hoisted me into the center of the dory, and Pat stayed on the board. This brought back memories of Egypt again. Wrapping my arms around my knees, I put my head down and closed my eyes, trying to stay warm.

It was only half an hour or so later that the *Bandito* broke through the fog. When the crew helped me onto the boat, I completely lost it. I started crying really hard. My father and mother tried to soothe me. I felt so bad to be sobbing in front of Montrella, in front of the reporter for the *Los Angeles Times* and all the lifeguards. It got even worse when I saw Fahmy's face. He knew exactly what I was feeling. I started crying even harder. I had been so scared. I didn't realize it until we were safe, but then I'd let my defenses down. My father tapped me on the cheek with his hand, first gently, then harder, trying to snap me back to reality. He was afraid that I would become hysterical. I hated this scene. Hated giving up. Hated failing. Still, I wasn't fully comprehending the lesson that I should have learned in Egypt: no swim, no athletic venture was worth dying over. There were times when you had to quit. Times when it was too dangerous to continue. Times when you should walk away and try again another day.

That was exactly what my parents wanted me to do. That was what Fahmy urged me to do, and Stockwell and Johnson, and the entire crew. But I didn't want to. I wanted to hang up my swimsuit forever. I had had enough.

During the next week they worked on me. My folks said that I was in great shape and I had a great chance to break the record — why would I pass all that up? Fahmy called me and met with me a handful of times and told me that I really needed to go back again, that I was mentally tough, and that if I didn't go back now, I would wonder all my life what I could have done. Stockwell and Johnson called to say they would go with me again, that they hadn't been able to fulfill their promise to me. Montrella also encouraged me. He said that he knew I could make the swim. I was more prepared than ever before.

There had been things about swimming from Catalina Island to the mainland that had bothered me. One major concern was my brother's world record: I didn't really want to break it. I knew how hard he had worked for it, and I knew how I felt when I had my English Channel record broken. I also wasn't excited about having to cross the Catalina Channel again and then swim the distance we had just covered. So I discussed this with my parents and the crew and we decided that I would start at Point Vicente, near San Pedro.

Two weeks after my initial attempt, we set out. The night was perfectly calm, and the sky was filled with stars. We moved quickly offshore, and I broke through the current easily. My pace was a little faster than two and a half miles per hour. The two weeks of tapering had revived me, and I felt very strong. But something happened about halfway across the channel; I lost all motivation and bottomed out. John Sonnichsen, who had been on my previous attempt and had been on other people's swims, said it was due to low blood sugar, and that I needed to stop to drink some juice.

Calmly I told the crew, "I don't want to do this."

"We've talked all about this, sweet. I thought you worked through it. Come on, you can do it," my father said.

"I don't want to do it anymore. I don't care," I said, taking off my goggles.

"You're just going through a bad period right now. Put your goggles back on and keep swimming," John Sonnichsen said, tossing me a red plastic bottle filled with apple juice. "You'll feel better once you drink it," he urged.

I started swimming again, but three more times, I had my doubts about what I was doing out there.

With the crew's encouragement, however, I finally managed to pull my head together. After I'd been swimming for six hours, Sonnichsen told me that I was on record pace. And then it came back to me: I wanted to do this because I wanted to be good at something, and because I loved swimming. I loved being out on the open ocean with them, doing something so beautiful, risky, and tough.

I pulled harder, laughed, joked with the crew. The crossing took me eight hours and forty-eight minutes, and I broke the men's and women's world records. I thought it was so cool my brother had the record in the other direction! I had succeeded and failed, and I had learned things that would become valuable later in my life. And so I began dreaming again, looking for swims that had never been done before.

10

Cook Strait, New Zealand

After five hours of swimming between the North and South Islands of New Zealand, across the mighty Cook Strait, I was farther from the finish than when we'd started. The weather was deteriorating; it had been ever since I'd entered the water, although the weather forecasters had promised winds that would only be light and variable, with no surf at all. They were wrong: the waves were four feet high, crashing headfirst into us; the wind was already up to fifteen knots, churning the strait into chop; and I was physically and mentally exhausted. I had made an enormous mistake. From the onset of the swim, I'd thought this twelve-mile swim would take five hours, at most, to complete.

Months before the channel crossing, I had spoken with Sandy Blewett, the swimmer from New Zealand I had met in Dover while preparing for the English Channel. I knew that one day she had wanted to swim Cook Strait and I knew it was her idea to be the first woman across. But she had attempted the English Channel and had had very poor conditions; she hadn't been able to complete the swim. Phoning her, I'd asked her if she minded if I attempted the crossing before she had a go at it. She had no problem with that at all, and even offered to help. Sandy provided me with background information, and, based on my speed in the English Channel, I had thought Cook Strait would be a piece of cake.

For more than four hours, John Sonnichsen had been shouting at me, using a bullhorn pressed against his mouth. Sonnichsen had offered to come to New Zealand as my adviser. I was getting into new territory now, and in this case, I was attempting a swim that a dozen people had tried but only three men from New Zealand had completed. Because Sonnichsen had experience setting up swims in areas that had rarely been swum, figuring out tides and currents, my folks had agreed to pay him and to send him with me to help on the swim, and also to be my chaperon. By profession, Sonnichsen was a physical education teacher in Rancho Palos Verdes, California, and he had a wife and three daughters. He was a good guy, but that bullhorn was driving me crazy. He had been shouting at me all morning long. I wanted to tear that bullhorn out of his hands and throw it into the ocean.

Sonnichsen had just informed me that the tide had swept us back around the tip of the North Island and we had been steadily going backward for the past two hours. He hadn't wanted to tell me because he'd thought I would be discouraged. Oh, he was right; I was.

When I looked up to breathe, to confirm what he had just told me, off to my right side was the North Island, and I could see our starting point, jutting out ahead of us by three or four miles. When I lifted my head straight up, to see where the South Island should have been, all I saw in the distance was haze, and a sea of waves and heavy winds. It was impossible to think of continuing through it; I was exhausted. So was the crew.

Accompanying me on paddleboards were lifeguards from the Island Bay Surf Lifesaving Club. They had been battling against the sea with me all morning long. And on the two boats ahead of us were Sam Moses, a journalist from *Sports Illustrated*; Keith Hancox, a radio announcer and one of the three men who had swum the strait; Sandy Blewett; John Cataldo, the head pilot; and his fishing crew. Some of the crew were getting seasick and were having difficulty standing without tumbling over.

For more than five hours, I thought, *I've been swimming across Cook Strait and no one told me I've been going backward most of this time?* It occurred to me that something might be wrong, but I had no idea how wrong.

Most of New Zealand knew what obstacles we would have to overcome; Keith Hancox had been broadcasting our progress — and lack of it — hourly over Radio Wellington, a local station on the North Island. More than anyone, Hancox knew what Cook Strait was all about. He knew how incredibly tough the crossing could be from a swimmer's perspective, and he informed his listeners that I was really struggling. His listeners understood and related to it. Because Cook Strait separates the North and South Islands of New Zealand, most residents had crossed the strait by ferry.

New Zealanders knew how terribly rough Cook Strait could be, and they got caught up in the story. Every hour they stopped whatever they were doing for an update. They told Hancox over the ship's radio that they were as caught up in listening to the broadcast as they had been the day Neil Armstrong had walked on the moon. It was as if, one by one, people lit a million candles. Throughout New Zealand people turned on their radios, and interest grew so quickly that Radio Wellington canceled its normal programming and went to live national coverage. News stations from around the world had their reporters tune in.

New Zealand was, after all, the land of Sir Edmund Hillary, the first man to climb Mount Everest, and there was a certain national pride and character that was infused within them, too, a can-do attitude. People throughout the country began calling the boat. Mothers, fathers, sheep farmers, fishermen, Girl Scouts, Boy Scouts, bee farmers, people from the most remote farms and villages called. When I started getting really discouraged, the paddler had me swim close to the lead boat so Keith Hancox could tell me what was happening. He was elated. "A Girl Scout just called in from Nelson. She said to tell you to keep going; she thinks you will make it. A farmer called a minute ago from Christchurch; he said to send you his best wishes. So many people are calling, Lynne, to wish you their best. You've got the entire country of New Zealand pulling for you," he said.

Cataldo had watched the weather reports on television the night before. A typhoon was hitting the Cook Islands, nearly fifteen hundred miles north of Cook Strait, and an Antarctic storm was raging about one thousand miles to the south. None of the forecasters thought the storms would affect us. But they did. Both storms were converging on Cook Strait, and we were sandwiched between them. That explained why the tides were so different from their normal pattern. It explained why we had been swept so far around the North Island. Although the storms were hundreds of miles from us, they were still affecting us. Without any landmasses to act as buffers, we were beginning to feel their effects as they continued their approach.

I felt as if I were swimming through a washing machine on spin cycle. Breathing was nearly impossible. I tried breathing later than normal, delaying my inhalation, letting my arms shield my face from the waves. But then my arms obscured my vision. That was dangerous. The skiff was becoming a real hazard. Cataldo was fighting to keep it on course, but the waves were lifting him four or five feet into the air, then tossing him sideways, right at me. I heard him shout, "Watch out, Lynne."

Out of the corner of my eye I saw the skiff smashing down into a trough. Cutting quickly left, I felt the propeller graze my leg. Cataldo pulled hard to the right, knowing now that he had to, opening the space between us. This made navigation even more challenging for both of us. There were periods of time, ten or twenty seconds, when we couldn't see each other at all. It was nuts. I felt as if I were swimming all over the ocean.

Sensing my frustration, a lifeguard from the support crew pulled his board closer to me. That made me feel better. There were sharks in Cook Strait, white pointers. A number of surfers had been killed by these sharks. We thought if there was any sign of a problem, such as a shark circling, I would get out. *When in doubt, get out* was always my axiom, but in this case, I don't think we could really see anything.

Lifting my head again — it was becoming a very bad habit — I looked toward the South Island. The sea was a mass of white waves breaking helter-skelter, without even the outline of the island on the horizon. I made a decision. Calmly, I pulled off my cap and goggles and shouted to Sonnichsen, "I don't think I can go any farther. I want to get out."

"Just swim another half mile," Sonnichsen coaxed through the megaphone.

I wanted to drown that megaphone.

"You're going through a bad period," he said.

You're not kidding, I thought.

"Here, have some apple juice," he said.

I wished I had a cork. If I had a cork, I could stick it into that megaphone, and then I wouldn't have to hear him.

The apple juice tasted sweet, delicious. I grabbed my knees to stretch out my back. The crew in the boat waved, cheered, and shouted encouraging words. Keith Hancox told me I was doing an incredible job. He said he had never seen a swimmer persevere through conditions like this. He was very impressed. That gave me a real lift. I respected him — now more than ever since I understood what he had achieved — and his encouragement helped me find my resolve.

For the next half an hour we made progress, but the seas were relentless. They were cresting at five feet, and when I lifted my head and looked at the size of the space between us and the horizon, I pulled off my cap again and said, "I really can't go any farther." Memories of the Nile River flooded my mind; that level of exhaustion was something I never wanted to repeat. I was so tired.

Sandy Blewett jumped into the water and swam over to me. "Come on, let's see some of that Cox courage," she said, which got me moving again. She swam for half an hour with me, then had to climb out. She had had a back injury before this attempt, and she was in pain. I knew she was the one who had courage. For a while after she got out, I continued, but I felt discouraged.

Captain Brown, the pilot for the *Aritaka*, a cross-channel passenger ferry, changed the course of his ship and raced over to us. It was against the rules of his company, but in his mind I was a ship in distress, and he was determined to help. He pulled the ship alongside us and raised the American flag, while hundreds of passengers climbed out on deck. They waved and cheered and stayed beside us for ten or twenty minutes.

When they left, Keith Hancox shouted, "I spoke with Captain Brown on the radio. He told me that all of New Zealand is following your progress. All the boats that pass between the islands and all the planes that fly overhead have been watching you all day long." His voice was filled with both excitement and fatigue.

I was overwhelmed. It didn't matter to them that I wasn't from their country.

The waves in Cook Strait were up to seven feet high now. I could just make out the outline of the South Island. *How am I ever going to do this?* I wondered. *Keep going. Just keep going,* and for a while I did, but my attitude was quickly turning for the worse.

Keith Hancox waved me over to the boat and suggested that I stop and drink some apple juice. He told me, "All day long, local yachtsmen and fishermen have been radioing us, and giving us updates on the water condition out ahead. Air New Zealand has been following our progress too; they've been radioing our boats, giving us weather updates." Then he pointed. "Look up there in the sky."

An Air New Zealand jet was circling overhead, and it dipped its wing to salute us.

Hancox turned to pick up the radio, listened, then turned to me and said excitedly, "The prime minister of New Zealand, Prime Minister Rowling, just called. He said to tell you, 'We believe you can cross the mighty Cook Strait. You can do it. You have the entire nation of New Zealand behind you.' "

I looked at the ocean. The waves were now eight feet high, too big to take in all at once; I had to tip my head back to see an entire wave. I prayed, "Please, God, I can't do this without your help. I need the waves to go down. I need you to make something happen. I can't do this." I put my head down and started swimming again. The winds were shifting all around, blasting us from one direction, then the other, and they had increased to thirty-five knots. When I reached the crest of a wave I looked across the sea, and there was the South Island. It was getting larger, sharper.

I put my head down. My arms felt like they were on fire. Everything ached. I buried my head, hoping to get lower in the water so I wouldn't become airborne, so I could let the waves wash over me, so I could go through the heart of them and continue to move forward.

"Robbie, what was that?" I shouted to a lifeguard on the paddleboard.

A large, dark streak had brushed beneath me, and it had moved quickly.

Robbie peered down into the water. "It's probably the reflection of the boat," he said, but he continued looking down.

"There it is!" I shouted with my head up, feeling myself swimming rapidly on the upper inches of the water.

Robbie's eyes got as large as saucers, and he shouted to the crew, "Check below!"

Before they could say or do anything, five large black forms broke the water's surface.

"They're dolphins," Cataldo shouted gleefully, making a dolphin move with his hand.

Two black-and-white dolphins that looked like they were wearing tuxedos swam right beneath us. In unison, they rolled over on their backs and looked up at us. I could see their big brown eyes as they rolled over simultaneously. Suddenly three more leaped out of the water in front of us.

"Those are the scouts. They're having a good look at us," Cataldo shouted. He was laughing, knowing what was going to happen next.

Moments later the sea was filled with the voices of dolphins chattering, squeaking, clicking, whistling, calling. Their voices were fast and excited. Pods of dolphins arrived. There were twenty, then thirty, and when I looked down through the crystal-clear water, I saw dolphins below, and dolphins below them, and yet more dolphins. They were threading their way between one another, moving in close, rotating onto their sides so they could look up and see us better. It seemed as if they were happy, as if they somehow knew we needed them. It was inspiring. Maybe they were the answer to my prayer.

In unison, two dolphins swimming snout to snout rolled over and gazed up at me. They held that position on their sides for maybe an entire minute, as if they were checking me out. They were clicking and whistling back and forth, communicating with each other and with others nearby. When they rolled back over, I wanted to reach down and just touch them. Extending my arm, I tried to get closer, but they maintained a distance of at least a couple of arm's lengths. The wind died slightly, too, and the sea grew flatter.

More dolphins, perhaps fifty in total, arrived en masse and completely circled our flotilla. Then, as if someone had given a signal, a dozen tuxedoed dolphins began dancing on their tails across the bright blue sea. Some were leaping high out of the water over lacy white waves, while others pirouetted in the air and dove beak-first deep into the sea. They popped up around us chattering, as if they were laughing at their antics.

Mesmerized, we watched them put on a display unlike anything we had ever seen. The dolphins entertained us for more than an hour, and then they departed as suddenly as they had arrived.

We had made progress; the South Island was now coming clearly into view. We could distinguish mountains in the foreground and in back, and what was once only black in the distance was now becoming shades of green, brown, and gold. Patterns and the coarse textures of trees, grass, shrubs, and rock were taking shape.

Right then, Sonnichsen leaned over the bow of the *San Antonio* and gave me the bad news over the megaphone. "You're caught in a rip. It's carrying you back out toward the middle of the strait. You're going to have to start sprinting now if you're going to get in."

Nodding, I put my head down and started counting my strokes from one to one thousand, five times over. And I focused on just moving forward. On a breath, I saw Sonnichsen giving me the thumbs-up sign. We had made it across. Ten hours of swimming. Somehow the dolphins must have sensed it, because a pod of twenty or so returned, and this time they moved in closer to me, a hand's distance away. Every part of me wished I could hold on to their fins and just ride in to shore. I tried again to touch them, but they moved away. Maybe they knew the channel swimming rules. They stayed with us for about half an hour and then swam on.

The waves had grown to nine feet high. The wind, funneled into the pass between the North and South Islands, was roaring through the strait, moving at gale force and gusting up to forty-five knots. Now, though, the waves were behind us. We were surfing mid-channel as the Beach Boys' song "Catch a Wave" played in my head. I felt as if I were in fact sitting on top of the world as we rode one wave after the other, surfing toward the South Island.

As we moved into the lee of the land, the waves flattened to two feet, the wind continued to gust, and a rip current grabbed us. Once again, it started pushing us back out into the strait. Sonnichsen and the crew cheered me on, and Cataldo and Sonnichsen conferred. Cataldo had the crew call up a friend, a fellow fisherman who lived on the South Island. The friend had positioned his boat near shore, and he was giving Cataldo minute-by-minute updates about the tides and currents, helping him select a landing spot. Cataldo asked if he could check with others in the fishing fleet, to gather more information and make the best decision, but the weather was so poor that none of them dared leave the harbor.

Somehow, realizing that once again I had hit a brick wall, the dolphins reappeared. A dozen or so this time, they moved in closer to me and let me ride their slipstreams. We quickly cut across the rip, and then they disappeared.

As the sun began to set behind the South Island, ten dolphins swam over to the paddlers and me, in a tight formation. Their voices were higher pitched now, their squeaks more frequent, and they were no longer chattering happily. It was as if they had become very serious.

When we got to within a half mile from shore, the sun set and the dolphins moved in closer, as if to protect us. This was the area Cataldo was worried about. Here the ocean floor dropped and the Antarctic Current welled up. The water suddenly dropped to fifty-four degrees and took my breath away. It wasn't the cold, though, that was the real danger. With this current change came an increase in plant and animal life. Cataldo knew this was a favorite feeding area for large predatory sharks.

We were five hundred yards from shore and had a choice of entering one bay or the other. Cataldo chose the one to the left; it was about a hundred yards closer. The dolphins turned to the right. I turned left to follow Cataldo. The dolphins began chattering excitedly, moving erratically. Within a moment I knew why the dolphins had turned the other way; there was a current to the left, one I didn't have the energy to cross.

Cataldo and I turned right, following the dolphins. Here the current was sweeping north, and Cataldo urged me to hurry. If I didn't, I would be swept out of Picton Sound. But the dolphins were inches from my fingers, and I knew they were guiding us in to shore. As I grabbed long strands of thick, brown bull kelp and pulled myself onto some rocks to clear the water, I heard the dolphins and crew chattering and cheering. We had made it across Cook Strait. In twelve hours and two and a half minutes, we had completed the crossing, with the help of so many from New Zealand, and I became the first woman to make that swim. It was the roughest swim I had ever finished.

After I climbed down from the rocks and slid back into the sea, Cataldo again told me to hurry. I thought he was joking, but he was adamant. Once he conveyed why he was concerned — he was afraid a shark would attack me, especially in this bay, where sharks frequently fed — I sprinted to the boat. He and Robbie quickly helped me into the skiff.

That evening we motored back to the North Island through gale-force winds. At one point, our boats nearly sank from taking on so much water, but I had no idea; I was asleep. Church bells had rung throughout the country when we'd finished the swim, and the following day at noon, church bells once again rang at the same time, to celebrate the crossing.

More than anything I now understood that no one achieves great goals alone. It didn't matter to New Zealanders that I wasn't from their country. It only mattered that I was trying to swim their strait. They had cheered me on for hours, and in doing so, they had cheered the same human spirit within themselves. Through the Cook Strait crossing, I realized that a swim can be far more than an athletic adventure. It can become a way to bridge the distance between peoples and nations. During the Cook Strait swim, we were united in a human endurance struggle that surpassed national borders.

11

Human
Research Subject

Despite traveling to the far-off reaches of the world, taking on challenges, I actually had a very normal life. After graduating from high school, I was admitted to the University of California, Santa Barbara. When I arrived there, I knew my focus would be on my studies.

As in high school, I decided to join the women's swim team and water polo team. This would give me a sense of stability and belonging, and it would be a way to have fun and train for other goals outside the pool. After Cook Strait my father had pulled out a map of the world. He knew that once again I was searching for what to do next; I really wanted to do something more, but I wasn't sure what it was.

He pointed to the Bering Strait. There

were two islands in the center of the strait: one on the American side, called Little Diomede, and the other, Big Diomede, in the Soviet Union. In a straight line, the distance between the two islands — from the United States to the Soviet Union — was only 2.7 miles.

My first thought was, *There have got to be icebergs in those waters; there's no way I could do that.* But my father suggested that I do some research to find out more about the area and, if it looked like a swim was possible, start contacting officials to get a visa to the Soviet Union. Obtaining permission to land in the Soviet Union didn't seem very likely. It was fall of 1975 and the United States and the Soviet Union were in the midst of the Cold War, locked in a power struggle, distrusting and fearful that the other would start a nuclear war. But as early as age sixteen, I'd known that one of my life's goals was to make a positive difference in the world. I wanted to somehow make it count, to do more than just live a life from day to day. So I began to think about how this swim could be done. I wrote letters to the Alaska Fish and Game Department to find out information about water temperatures in the Bering Strait, and I wrote to my local congressman, Jerry Patterson, asking if he could contact the Soviets for me for a visa.

Meanwhile, I began college, and in May 1976 Dave volunteered to travel to Alaska to investigate the Bering Strait. Naively we thought that if he gathered enough information that spring, in the summer of 1976 I could make an attempt.

When Dave called us from Wales, Alaska, on the radiophone, he sounded like he was calling from Mars.

On the map, Wales looked nearly as remote. It was a small Inuit village of perhaps 150 people, about an hour's flight north of Nome. Dave's voice was filled with excitement. He had flown from Nome to Wales in a small plane, and they'd landed in a blizzard. By dogsled, the chief magistrate had taken him home and offered to let him stay with his family and to help him. When Dave had explained the reason for his trip — his younger sister wanted to swim across the Bering Strait — the chief magistrate thought he was either joking or just crazy. It was the middle of May, and the Bering Strait was frozen from the mainland of Alaska to Siberia. The strait could be ice-clogged until mid-July.

The chief magistrate in the village told Dave there had once been a natural land bridge between the two continents and that about fifteen hundred years ago, his ancestors had probably walked across. The water had risen over the centuries and the bridge was submerged. Swimming the Bering Strait was not possible: the water was far too cold; no one survived. More to the point, the villagers did not trust the Soviets. They had removed some of the villagers' family members from Big Diomede and several of them had been put in prison camps in Siberia. The villagers didn't want to have anything to do with the Soviets.

Dave decided to travel to Tin City, an air force base — a concrete blockhouse north of Wales — set up as a distant early-warning station for tracking Soviet aircraft and missiles. It took a big effort on Dave's part to convince the officer that he was seriously trying to gather information for a swim. The officer told Dave the idea was not possible — most people die within twenty minutes of falling into the water — but it was also militarily and politically dangerous.

While there had been brief periods of thaw in the Cold War, in 1976 there was a lingering chill in the air. Mutual distrust had escalated over our granting the Soviets most-favored-nation trade status contingent upon their increasing the quota of Soviet Jews allowed to emigrate to Israel. Neither side would accommodate the other, and tensions were rising between the two superpowers. While most people thought of U.S.-Soviet relations in terms of Washington and Moscow, two capitals five thousand miles apart, Tin City was less than one hundred miles from Siberia. This was the front line of the Cold War.

Sporadic incidents had also been occurring along the Bering Sea border — incidents that didn't make the evening news. The United States and Soviet armed forces were playing war games, finding where they could breach the border as a way of testing their respective security systems and response times. Given the current political situation, the officer doubted that the Soviets would permit anyone to enter their waters.

Even more significantly, Big Diomede Island, in the Soviet Union, the place I wanted to swim to, was a listening post — a military installation equipped with sophisticated devices that monitored our ships' and submarines' movements in the Bering Strait and beyond, as well as a state-of-the-art tracking system for spying on our aircraft and missiles. It was unlikely that the Soviets would allow any American to land on their spy island.

Meanwhile, we pondered the logistics anyway. The Bering Strait usually thawed by July. The water temperatures were between thirty and forty degrees, and after the thaw, the only way to reach Little Diomede from Wales was by helicopter. We now had something to go on. But the question was: How could I ever prepare to swim in water that cold?

Anne Loucks, a UCSB swim-team friend of mine who was a physiology student, asked if I would be willing to be a research subject. Annie was doing research on campus at the Institute of Environmental Stress, with Dr. Barbara Drinkwater and Dr. William McCafferty. Dr. Drinkwater was one of the most respected research physiologists in the world. She had done pioneering work on women's physiology. Dr. McCafferty was working on postdoctoral studies on the way surfers acclimate to the cold.

The research team was doing physiological studies on body type and athletic performance, as well as acclimatization to cold. They had just completed a series of tests on Jacqueline Hansen, the women's world-record holder in the marathon, and they wanted to run some comparison tests on me.

Dr. Drinkwater suspected that because of my background in long-distance cold-water swimming, I might somehow respond differently to the cold than the average person. She explained that when most people enter a cold environment without adequate clothing, they eventually go into hypothermia — their internal, or "core," temperature drops. Cold water leaches the heat from the body twenty-five to thirty times faster than cold air. People keep their bodies warm through a variety of defense mechanisms. As a first line of defense, the body narrows the blood vessels under the skin, forcing warm blood into the brain and the core of the body to protect the vital organs. Also, the skin temperature drops to reflect the surrounding environment. Second, the body attempts to generate heat by shivering. If the body temperature drops too low, the cold blood becomes acidic from lack of oxygen. This results in arrhythmia; the heart doesn't beat effectively, and cardiac arrest can occur.

From the onset, Dr. Drinkwater explained that by participating in these studies I could help them better understand how the human body functioned. It could help them figure out basic human responses to the cold, and maybe increase people's survival rates. It was also basic research and what they discovered might not be directly applicable for years. Dr. Drinkwater also told me that whatever they learned, they would share with me, so that I would be able to better understand what my body was doing on my long swims. I was excited about participating, and a little scared, but I agreed to be part of the study.

The scientists began by running a number of underwater weighing tests to determine my percentage of body fat. Healthy men have a low percentage of body fat, and that fat is usually distributed around the abdomen. This generally makes them negatively buoyant, which means they tend to sink. Most women, on the other hand, have a higher percentage of body fat that is well distributed throughout their bodies, making them positively buoyant, which means they float.

Dr. Drinkwater told me, "You're different. You have neutral buoyancy. That means your body density is exactly the same as seawater. Your proportion of fat to muscle is perfectly balanced so you don't float or sink in the water; you're at one with the water. We've never seen anything like this before."

Her Zen-like finding meant that I didn't

have to use energy to either fight against sinking or pull myself down into the water to counteract buoyancy. This enabled me to swim more efficiently, and it helped me conserve energy — energy that I could use for propelling myself forward.

Researchers began observing my workout sessions along the Santa Barbara coast. In the early morning, just before sunrise, Dr. McCafferty, and sometimes his wife and their small dog, Sunshine, walked along the beach below the university dorms as I swam from Coal Oil Point to the pier and back. Before and after these workouts, I'd hide behind a bush and take my core temperature using a rectal thermometer, the only way to get an accurate reading after immersion in cold water. I always made a point of telling Dr. McCafferty my temperature just as joggers were passing; they'd give him quizzical looks, since it appeared to them that he was talking to the bushes.

Through the course of these observations, as well as countless others, Dr. McCafferty discovered that my body temperature before a workout was usually a degree below what was considered normal. By the end of a two-hour workout, after swimming in water between fifty and sixty-five degrees, my temperature had risen to a degree or two above normal. Dr. McCafferty explained that the human body has a natural thermostat that strives to keep its temperature at a set point. What my body did was to lower that set point so it didn't have to work as hard to stay warm. This was all new and exciting information for the scientists and for me.

Dr. Drinkwater and Anne Loucks also made some interesting findings. They were thrilled when they discovered that I reacted completely differently than the average person when I swam in cold water. Most people who swim in fifty-degree water lose body heat more rapidly than they can create it, and so they go into hypothermia in a relatively short amount of time, depending on their conditioning, body fat, and many other factors. But the scientists discovered that I was different. After I'd been swimming for four hours in fifty-degree water, working out at a fast pace, Dr. Drinkwater and Anne Loucks measured my core temperature and found that it was up to 101 degrees. They hypothesized that I was working at such a high rate I was creating more heat than I was losing, I was able to reduce blood flow to my extremities efficiently, and my well-distributed body fat acted like an internal wet suit that kept me warm.

What I decided I needed to do was to

swim in water temperatures that would simulate those in the Bering Strait or the Strait of Magellan. It was apparent that obtaining permission for the Bering Strait was not going to happen quickly, so I'd decided to shift my goals and set my sights on the Strait of Magellan. No one had ever attempted this swim. I thought it would be exciting and romantic to attempt a swim across a waterway where ships had difficulty navigating. It seemed like a big challenge, but I also thought that I could collect research information, core-temperature measurements and the like, that might be useful to the doctors.

I asked Dr. Drinkwater and Dr. McCafferty if it might be possible for me to swim in the cold-water research tank at the institute while they gradually lowered the water temperature over a two- to three-week period. Both Dr. Drinkwater and Dr. McCafferty were excited about the proposal, but when they approached the director of the institute, Dr. Steven Horvath, he said he would not permit it. Dr. Horvath was afraid that I would endanger myself if I attempted swimming the Strait of Magellan, but Dr. Drinkwater and Dr. McCafferty helped me convince him that this was my next goal whether or not I had his support.

It would be better, the doctors argued on my behalf, if we got a chance to see what the effects of forty-two-degree water would be like in the lab, in a controlled environment, rather than out in the wilds of the Strait of Magellan. And, the doctors added, they would obtain valuable research data otherwise unattainable.

Dr. Horvath begrudgingly relented, although he didn't go along with the idea of gradually lowering the water temperature and doing daily studies. He told us he would give me a onetime deal only: the water temperature in the cold tank would be dropped to forty-two degrees, and he would let me swim while being supervised by his research team. A cardiologist and an internist would also be present in case we ran into any problems.

Brigette, the nurse at the Institute of Environmental Stress, led me to a tiny white cubicle and had me take off my sweat-suit jacket. Sitting down facing me, she picked up a piece of fine-grit sandpaper, leaned over, and began sanding my chest as if it were a coarse two-by-four. After rubbing two quarter-sized bright pink spots on my upper chest, she had me take off my swim-suit top so she could sand three more spots around my left breast. The skin there was very tender, and she quickly reached the nerves. I held tightly to the chair arm.

Brigette explained that she needed to sand the skin away to ensure good contact with the EKG leads. An accurate reading was critical. Based on normal responses of human beings, the experiment could put an enormous stress on my heart. No one was sure how I would respond, so the cardiologist present in the lab would be watching the EKG monitor throughout the test.

To prevent water from getting into the EKG circuitry and shorting out the system while I was in the water, Brigette attached twelve long wire leads to the electrodes and then covered the electrodes with airplane glue and a thin layer of plastic. Then she broke out a fresh piece of sandpaper and lightly sanded my big toes, fingertips, and a couple of spots on my forehead. To these areas she attached thermocouples that held the electrodes on my skin; the electrodes would measure my skin temperature during the experiment. Using waterproof tape, she taped more leads to my big toes, fingers, and forehead. By the time she finished I looked like Medusa.

She collected the leads, held them while I pulled up my suit, and then draped them over my right shoulder. She gathered the thermocouple wires and let them rest in a pile on the floor. Just before we left the cubicle she handed me a tube of K-Y Jelly and a lead that was at least twenty feet long. She explained that the lead was called a rectal probe; it was a thermometer that would measure my core temperature during the experiment. I needed to insert it so they could get the necessary readings. She left me standing there with the jelly in one hand and the twenty-foot-long probe in the other. I was completely baffled. The whole thing? I wondered. Too embarrassed to ask, I stood there wondering what I should do. Thankfully, Anne Loucks came by to check on me and explained that all I needed to insert was four inches; then the lead would be taped to my upper thigh so it wouldn't slide out during the test.

Once we secured the probe, Anne untangled the leads and held on to the cluster of EKG leads with one hand and the thermocouples with the other. Following her into the lab, filing past the researchers and lab assistants, I felt very self-conscious, especially with a twenty-foot-long tail wagging behind me.

When we entered the cold-tank area, it looked like NASA's mission control. Dr. Drinkwater, Dr. McCafferty, Dr. Horvath, and two other physiologists, as well as Dr. Reyburn, an internist, and Dr. Borjia, a cardiologist, were standing around the tank, all wearing white lab coats, checking their equipment, and calibrating it to ensure that the measurements would be accurate. Some were making notes on their clipboards, others rehearsing the test.

Lab assistants, computer experts, and the man in charge of the lab's technical equipment were wheeling equipment in on dollies. Printers were buzzing, the tank was gurgling, and Dr. Reyburn and Dr. Borjia were on the phone with their colleagues at Cottage Hospital, alerting them to the experiment and asking them to be prepared if there was an emergency. This, they assured me, was just to make sure that nothing got out of hand.

A lab assistant wheeled a dolly to the doorway and left it outside the room.

"Anne, are those defibrillating paddles?" I asked.

She nodded. "We're placing them within reach of the tank in case your heart stops during the experiment. We won't need them unless something really goes wrong," she reassured me.

"Why aren't they placed closer to the tank?" I asked, feeling a little apprehensive.

"We don't want them too close to the tank. The defibrillator could accidentally discharge while you're in the water and electrocute you. If we need to use them, we have to make sure you're clear of the tank."

"If that happens, I'm going to be deadweight," I said, starting to worry.

Dr. McCafferty, who overheard our conversation, ripped his lab coat open like Superman and said, "That's why I'm wearing a wet suit, so I can jump into the water and pull you out if I need to." Dr. McCafferty was a tall, strawberry-blond, blue-eyed, fit surfer boy and a vegetarian. In a short time, he had become one of my best friends and supporters. He had also become a mentor to me, teaching me about human physiology, as well as life philosophy. He looked at what we were doing as a great adventure, an exploration into the limits of human endurance, and he was just really a great guy.

Dr. McCafferty explained that he would be getting into the tank with me. He would tie a rope around my waist like a surfboard leash in case they needed to drag me out of the water. They would also have me wear an army belt that would have a long piece of surgical cord attached to the belt and to the tank wall, so that I could swim tethered.

The water in the tank was radiating so

much cold that some of the technicians had to leave to get coats and sweaters. Dr. Drinkwater handed me a nose plug and asked me to put it on so that I could get used to breathing through my mouth. As I started climbing down a ladder into the tank, Dr. McCafferty handed me a mouthpiece that resembled a diver's regulator. He instructed me to clamp down on the mouthpiece with my teeth. The mouthpiece was connected to two long plastic tubes, devices that would allow them to capture gases during the experiment to measure my oxygen intake, which would enable them to see how hard my body was working.

Dr. McCafferty gathered some of the leads while Anne took the remaining ones, and they plugged them into their respective monitoring devices.

Dr. McCafferty asked me how long I intended to swim. I told him an hour, and he raised an eyebrow. He said that since this was the first time anyone he knew of would be swimming in forty-two-degree water, perhaps it would be wise to reconsider. He said that in a wet suit, before the experiment, when he was setting up the devices in the tank, he had only been able to stay in the water for five minutes. I told him I understood, but I really wanted to see how far I could go in the controlled setting.

Dr. Drinkwater completely understood, although she cautioned me. She said if I started feeling very cold in the water, I should get out. I promised her that I would.

The noise in the room had dulled to a low-pitched buzz. The doctors and lab techs went to their stations. My heart began beating faster.

The tank was about half the size of a backyard swimming pool and that, coupled with the surgical-tubing leash, wouldn't allow for much movement. I looked around the room. Dr. Horvath was just entering the lab; he asked some questions, checked the equipment, and made sure I was okay. He was about to turn and leave but I stopped him. I was afraid that at the end of the experiment I would be so cold that I wouldn't be able to talk, so I said, "Dr. Horvath, I just want to thank you for letting me do this, and I want everyone here to know how much I appreciate their help."

It took him by surprise, but he smiled, and so did the entire research team.

"We're ready when you are," Dr. Drinkwater said, smiling confidently at me.

Nodding and focusing inward, I climbed down the steps into the tank. In seconds my feet went numb, then my calves, and my entire body tightened. It was so cold it hurt. Pushing myself, I took another step down. Now I was immersed to my waist, and my breathing was rapid, my eyes wide open. Remembering to pull my goggles down over my eyes, I stopped and looked at the water. Forty-two degrees was a lot colder than anything I'd ever swum in before; it took my breath away. My legs were aching. Stepping down onto the next rung, I was immersed to my shoulders and focusing hard to bring my breathing back to normal. "Lynne, you doing okay?" Dr. McCafferty asked.

I knew that once I put my face in the water, my heart would slow down and in a minute or two I would gain control over my breathing and get back into a natural rhythm.

Dr. McCafferty followed me down the stairs to make sure all the lines remained untangled. He winced when the water reached his waist, and I wanted to laugh. He smiled at me and reminded me, "Take your time. Remember that you're accustomed to walking into the water slowly. Let your body gradually adjust to the temperature change."

Dipping my chin in the water, I let it go numb, then immersed my lips. I told myself to put my nose in very slowly. There is a nerve in the nose called the vagus nerve. It's what triggers a response called the diver's reflex. When someone falls suddenly into extremely cold water, this nerve is stimulated and can cause the heart to suddenly stop beating. So I dipped in the tip of my nose, then ever so slowly placed my face in the water. It was like pressing my face against a block of ice.

My goggles were fogging up. Dr. McCafferty took them off and licked them for me — the protein in saliva inhibits fogging — and then put them back over my eyes. "You okay?" he asked again.

I nodded and he climbed out of the tank; then I started swimming. Tethered on every side by leads, probes, a mouthpiece, and the army belt, I felt as if I were trapped inside a spider's web. Batting the leads away with my hands, I tried to make room for my arms to move, but I couldn't turn them over as quickly as normal.

"Five minutes," Dr. McCafferty shouted, looking at his stopwatch.

It had seemed like fifteen; it had seemed like forever. And I was feeling a little claustrophobic.

The water was so cold that my arms were completely numb. When I pulled, I couldn't feel anything. I was so frustrated. I knew then that there was no way I could swim for an hour. But I told myself to break it down into smaller pieces, to think not in terms of an hour, but of five-minute blocks. In theory, that should have worked, but I didn't know if I could last for even another five minutes. I was discouraged. How could I even consider swimming the Strait of Magellan if I couldn't last more than five minutes in forty-two-degree water? *Focus. Keep going. Count your strokes to one thousand. Okay, again.*

Lifting my head, I heard Dr. McCafferty say, "You've been in for twenty minutes."

That was all I could stand. Putting my hand up, I knew I couldn't go any further. I was just too cold. Dr. McCafferty and Dr. Drinkwater grabbed me under the arms when I reached the top of the stairs; Anne held on to all the leads. Someone threw a towel over my shoulders, and Dr. Drinkwater asked me if I could stay in the room for a bit while they finished gathering all the gases and data. Unable to talk with the mouthpiece still in, I nodded. I was so disappointed. My time in the water had been brief.

Dr. McCafferty was right beside me. "You did a great job. Really amazing," he said.

I was shaking very hard as Anne walked

with me to the shower. She turned on only the cold water first because it felt warm to me, and because there was no feeling in my hands. Gradually, as I warmed up, she added more warm water. Maybe twenty minutes later, she helped me take off all the gear.

Later that day, Dr. McCafferty met me outside the lab, at an overlook above Goleta Bay near Santa Cruz Dorm. He was tremendously excited about the preliminary data the research team had gathered. From it, he saw that my body performed differently than those of all the other research subjects he had worked with in the past. My core temperature had increased by a degree at first; ten minutes or so into the experiment, it had dropped only a couple degrees, then stabilized. All the other subjects he had worked with were in water temperatures in the sixties, but they had continuously lost body heat. Dr. McCafferty was fascinated that, in forty-two-degree water without any training, I had been able to stabilize my core temperature.

I didn't understand why he was so excited, so he explained that by training in cold temperatures, there was a good chance that I could adjust enough to stay in the water for a longer time period and maintain a normal body temperature.

This meant that there was a good chance that I could swim across the Strait of Magellan, and he, Dr. Drinkwater, and Anne Loucks offered to accompany me off and on during the training program and to continue gathering data. For two months, I trained in fifty-four-degree water. During one workout in fifty-degree water, Dr. Drinkwater took my core temperature. It was 101°. None of us knew what would happen to me in the Strait of Magellan if the water temperature was in the forties, but I decided I had to try.

12

The Strait of Magellan

When John Sonnichsen and I arrived in Punta Arenas, Chile, we were welcomed into local people's homes and shops. And whenever John and I walked on the street, people came over to us and wished us *mucha suerte* — much luck. Having their support made me feel very welcome and happy, and at the same time, I felt the burden of expectation. No one had swum across the Strait of Magellan, and it seemed that everyone in the entire city of Punta Arenas knew that this was my goal and wanted to show their overwhelming enthusiasm and support.

The pressure of expectation increased considerably during my first day training in the strait. The water temperature that day was forty-four degrees. It was so cold that I was able to get into the Atlantic Ocean only as far as my knees. For twenty minutes I stood there thinking, *How in the world am I ever going to make this swim?* Granted, in a straight line, the distance across the strait is only a mile and a half, from the tip of Chile to the island of Tierra del Fuego. But before we even started on this adventure, John and I knew there was no way I would ever swim in a straight line. The currents and tides could be as strong as ten knots, faster than a rain-fed river after a torrential downpour. This swim, we predicted, would take me at least an hour.

John and I had just traveled to the other half of the Americas; we were tired and jet-lagged, and I told myself to take that into consideration, to give myself a break. Still, that initial dip was very daunting; I just didn't know how far I could push myself.

The next day, pushing negative thoughts and feelings aside, I slid my feet in and walked into the icy water again, this time to my shoulders, and made myself stand there for twenty minutes.

On one level, my progress was incredibly slow; yet at the same time, I realized that I was doing something that had never been done before. Everything I attempted had to be performed cautiously, in small steps. I had to allow time for my body to gradually adapt.

Little by little, over the course of the first week, I managed to extend my training time in the water so that I could swim for up to an hour. My big reward came after every workout. There was a family named Fernandez who lived in a large home on the beach near my training area. Every day they would come outside and walk the beach with John, and they invited us into their home afterward to get warm and have hot chocolate with them. They let me thaw out in their hot tub and sit with them beside a fire while the two older boys played their guitars and sang Chilean folk songs for us.

One day the two sons donned their wet suits and swam out into the strait with me so they could show me shipwrecks along the shore. In a mile's area there were perhaps fifty shipwrecks, some fairly recent, others hundreds of years old. It was like swimming over liquid history, fascinating and yet eerie; we were passing over a graveyard of ships that had traveled from the far reaches of the world, from Italy, Portugal, Britain, and Spain.

After two weeks of training I was able to stay in forty-four-degree water for up to two hours. One of my most difficult training sessions was on Christmas Day. It was the first time I had ever been away from my family at Christmas, and although I enjoyed being with families in Chile, I realized how very far I was from home.

During that workout on Christmas Day the sky suddenly went black, as it had that day in New Hampshire when I was nine years old and swimming in the pool alone. This time, though, the Fernandez brothers and a small group of locals and tourists from England walked alongside me during the wild and pounding hailstorm. Once the storm subsided, they were joyful at having done something so strange and different, something all of us would remember for our entire lives.

Unfortunately, the stormy weather continued through the next day. But on December 27, the Chilean navy, which had volunteered to provide assistance for the swim, informed us that it was time to travel by bus to what is known as the First Narrows. This is the passage, at one point only a mile and a half wide, that Magellan had discovered when sailing from the Atlantic Ocean through to the Pacific Ocean.

When we reached the First Narrows, we waited for the Chilean navy ship the *Elicura* to land and drop its ramp onshore so we could walk aboard. As we watched Captain Furniss attempt to land, we held our breath. The tide was racing into the strait from the Atlantic at seven knots, moving like a flooding river. Two hundred meters offshore, the current caught the *Elicura* and spun it around as if it were a toy boat. Alarms on board sounded, as men scrambled around deck. The ship was about to run aground.

Quickly, Captain Furniss ordered his wheelman to steer offshore, but the ship wasn't responding. The captain ordered more power to the engines, and a deep rumble vibrated the air and beach. The ship still didn't move.

John pointed. "Look at the stern. See all the brown water? The propeller's in too close, and they're churning up sand. He's in trouble."

Hoping that they could ride the current to a point where it diminished and then cut across it, the captain ordered his wheelman to parallel the shore. There was only a small margin for error, and a delay between when the captain gave the order and how quickly the ship responded. Fearing he would run aground in those moments, we held our breath. The ship seemed to teeter in the current between the sea and the shore. Fortunately, the captain made the right call. As he anticipated, the current slackened, and he quickly ordered his wheelman to turn off-shore.

Watching this was terribly sobering. *If a ship can't land in that current, what's it going to be like trying to swim across it?* I wondered with a sense of dread. After that attempted landing, John and I thought the swim would have to be postponed for the day. But the captain wasn't ready to give up. He made a second attempt to pick us up, this time allowing for more time to turn the stern in to shore so they could drop the ramp. But once again the current whipped the ship around and tossed it precariously within a couple hundred meters of shore. This time Captain Furniss reacted sooner, increasing the ship's speed and pulling offshore. Then he immediately ordered the crew to lower a Zodiac inflatable rubber boat into the water. Two of his men motored in to shore to pick up John and me, as well as a number of reporters from all over Chile and the international press, who had been assigned to cover what they considered would be a historic swim.

Maneuvering the rubber inflatable was much easier than trying to land the *Elicura*, and within minutes two frogmen had picked us up and ferried us out to the ship. The ship towered at least thirty feet above us, and as we came alongside under full power, the rubber inflatable began bouncing and rebounding wildly off the port side of the ship. Waves were washing over the pontoons into the rubber inflatable, and the wind was blowing sheets of water onto us.

The only way to get on board was to climb onto a slippery pontoon, balance on it until the moment just before the boat and ship collided, then leap up to grab a ladder. It was risky. Missing the handhold would result in being squashed between the two boats or being sucked into the ship's engines.

John went ahead of me. The boats smashed together while his legs were sandwiched in between and he yelled in pain, nearly losing his grip on the ladder. Somehow he managed to hold on and pull himself up. Once on board, he leaned over and called me to follow.

It was scary standing on the pontoon with my arms extended for balance. Just a moment before I leaped, a wave caught the inflatable and it dropped out from under me. Leaning back, I tumbled into the boat, got up quickly while I had any nerve left, and leaped toward the ladder. It was narrow, slippery, and steep, and it bounced wildly in the waves. The climb was straight up. As the *Elicura* rocked and swayed, I was afraid to let go of each ladder rung so I could reach for the next. My hand missed once, and I froze there in midair, not wanting to go any farther, but knowing I had to. And the frogmen were waiting for me so they could climb on board.

"Don't look down," John warned.

Of course I did, and the sight of the boats colliding below me scared me even more. This was not what I expected at all. It wasn't supposed to be this difficult to get to a swim. If it was as hairy as this, what was the swim going to be like? *These are not helpful thoughts,* I told myself. *Focus on what you need to do now. Look at the rung, extend your arm, hold on to it, step onto the next rung, and don't let your foot slip.*

At the top, John and Captain Furniss grabbed me under each arm and hoisted me on board. My heart was racing, and I was drenched.

We followed Captain Furniss to the ship's bridge. The slight but strong-looking man welcomed us on board and had us stand by the heater, near a table covered by a nautical chart of the Strait of Magellan.

"We'll take a look at that in a moment," he

said. "First, I have to check on my men and make sure they've managed to pull the rubber inflatable on board. Here, let me introduce you to Dr. Fernandez, the ship's doctor. He's here to ensure your safety during the swim, Lynne, and this is Commander Charlie —" I never did catch the commander's last name.

Dr. Fernandez greeted me with the customary kiss on each cheek, making my face glow. Maybe it was the intensity of the swim, or being so far from home, or maybe it was simply because of Dr. Fernandez. From the moment I met him, I really liked him. Dr. Fernandez was good-hearted and caring, and he radiated enthusiasm. He was also very attractive — tall and trim, with sandy blond hair and eyes as blue as the sea. I quickly gravitated toward him.

When Captain Furniss returned, we gathered around the chart. He had been briefed on what we wanted to achieve. And he had been given orders to work with us, so from the onset we began to be a team, with John conveying our thoughts about how we wanted to coordinate the swim. I freely asked questions of the captain, Dr. Fernandez, and the commander. It was so exciting being on the ship's bridge, looking out across the whitecapped strait, feeling the ship moving beneath my feet, and knowing that we were working with one of the top navies in the world.

During the past few weeks John and I had been gathering information on the strait. We'd spoken with the Chilean coast guard, which at first had been supportive of the swim and then had decided it was too dangerous. The coast guard withdrew their support, said they would not supply any boat for the swim, and then pressured the Chilean navy to do the same.

John and I were in a meeting with the admiral of the coast guard and the admiral of the Chilean navy when this happened. There was a strongly worded discussion between the two men. Neither John nor I understood enough Spanish to comprehend what they were saying, but from their body language we could tell that they were not happy with each other.

Ultimately, through an interpreter — although he spoke some English — the admiral of the Chilean navy explained the situation. He said that the coast guard could do as they wished and that he understood the reasons for their protest, but he had given his word that he would support us for the swim. He had assured the Chilean ambassador and consul general in San Francisco that they would help us, and he would not back down on his word. Besides that, he firmly believed that we could achieve our goal with their support.

I thanked the naval admiral for his backing and asked if I could borrow the interpreter to speak with the admiral of the coast guard. It was obvious that they were a little surprised that I'd taken the initiative. I don't think they were accustomed to listening to nineteen-year-old girls, but they humored me. I didn't want the swim to create any animosity between the Chilean navy and the Chilean coast guard, so I told the admiral of the coast guard that I greatly appreciated his concern for my safety, and that it was of concern to me too. That was exactly why I had contacted him, to request his help to ensure my safety throughout the swim. He knew more about the tides and currents in the strait than I ever would; he dealt with them every day. His men boarded and piloted all the ships that traveled through the strait as a safety precaution. He also knew the mistakes people made in these waters, all the things to avoid. So we needed his help, and his knowledge. I told him I had no intention of attempting the swim if it became too dangerous.

In the end, the admiral of the coast guard

said that he was still hesitant about the swim, but he would provide whatever information and assistance he could. I asked if he could help us get in touch with a man who operated a small ferryboat in the First Narrows, who would have daily and in-depth knowledge of the tides and currents in the area. When we left the meeting that day, the admirals shook hands, and they were smiling.

As the *Elicura* sailed southward across the strait, toward Tierra del Fuego, we worked with Captain Furniss, his commander, Dr. Fernandez, and the crew to try to determine the best starting point, the swim's course, and the end point. The forecast was mixed. And neither John nor I knew it at the time, but this was Captain Furniss's first solo command. He was being prudent and cautious. He wanted the swim to be a success.

We had hopes of starting the swim that afternoon, but the wind was howling across the treeless, golden Patagonian flatlands, gaining speed with each passing hour, and increasing up to thirty knots. The Strait of Magellan was a sea of three-foot-high aquamarine waves that exploded into whitecaps and swirled and seethed around the majestic ship, the only boat operating in the strait.

It didn't seem likely that the wind would subside quickly, but Captain Furniss knew that conditions in the strait changed more rapidly than anywhere in the world. There were time constraints on us; it wasn't clear how long we could tie up the navy ship, but we knew it wouldn't be more than a few days. So Captain Furniss wanted to get the swim off as soon as it was safe. He also had other considerations at home. We didn't know it at the time, but his wife was in the hospital about to give birth. Hoping for a lull in the wind, Captain Furniss ordered his crew to cruise slowly back and forth along Tierra del Fuego's shore. It felt as if we were pacing, letting off nervous energy.

What this did, though, was to enable us to study the current alongshore by watching the movement of kelp in the water. The kelp was stretched completely out, at right angles to the shore. That meant that the current was whipping around the cove, moving at full bore, at nine knots. Tides were going to be critical in this swim, and our success would depend on the way we crafted our course.

John and I were very concerned that the current flowing into the strait from the Atlantic would be so strong that it would push me too far west, to an area where the Strait of Magellan expanded; there the distance across was at least ten miles. We were also very concerned that the current flowing from the Pacific side of the Strait of Magellan would be so strong that it would push us completely out of the First Narrows and into the Atlantic Ocean, so that we would never make it to shore.

What we decided to do was to start the swim at the tail end of the tide when the water was flowing from the Atlantic toward the Pacific, from east to west. Then the tide would go slack for a period of time. We had no idea how long this would be, but it would be when I could swim directly across and gain the most direct distance. Then the tide would turn and the current would flow in the opposite direction, from the Pacific toward the Atlantic, west to east. The change would start out gradually, then build like a freight train. Any miscalculation and we would be either too far east or too far west and would fail on the attempt.

To hedge our bets, we figured that we would make the starting point in the area of the First Narrows in the middle of Tierra del Fuego. That way, if the current carried us too far to either side, we would still be able to land onshore before being swept into the Atlantic Ocean or into the widest part of the Strait of Magellan. From that midpoint, we could aim for the center of the beach on the Chilean mainland. The beach there was seven miles long, which would give us a three-and-a-half-mile margin for error. There was another major consideration, too: the ferryboat captain had warned us that if a storm approached and the tide changed very rapidly, whirlpools would occur at the headlands, near the area where we would finish the swim. The whirlpools reached full velocity when the tide was flowing at maximum speed. They were extremely dangerous. Local people had told John and me that these whirlpools had taken down ships and small boats, killing everyone on board.

Using binoculars, Captain Furniss studied the shore, looking for a small beach where we could land. The spray off the wave tops was so thick that he had trouble seeing through the veil of saltwater mist. He directed his men to sail closer to shore, then turned the ship directly into the current and increased the ship's engines to nearly full throttle so we could hold our position and all of us could take a good look at the shore. We found a cove without many rocks or much kelp, perfect for the start of the swim. But the weather conditions were deteriorating so rapidly that Captain Furniss had to turn the ship around and head for the Chilean mainland before the storm hit.

The sea in the Strait of Magellan could become ferocious within twenty minutes. Storm fronts originating in Antarctica sweep northward across the Drake Passage, and without any real landmass to buffer them, they hit the Strait of Magellan suddenly and at full force. Fortunately, the Chilean navy had outposts and weather stations at Cape Horn, at the southernmost tip of Tierra del Fuego, and along the Antarctic Peninsula where men and equipment gathered meteorological information and transmitted it to the ship; they had alerted Captain Furniss. Without a doubt, it was an impossible day for a swim. Still, it was disappointing; we all had great expectations and underlying tensions, and we wanted to get the swim off as soon as possible. I think Captain Furniss understood this better than anyone. Perhaps it was to boost our confidence, to give us a chance to get to know Dr. Fernandez and the commander, or just to give them a break that Captain Furniss asked Dr. Fernandez and the commander to join us onshore for dinner while he stayed with the ship.

We hadn't planned to spend the night at

the First Narrows, but there was a small hotel very close by, and Captain Furniss had arranged for rooms for John and me. Over dinner, while John and the commander were engaged in conversation, Dr. Fernandez and I talked about everything from Patagonia to hypothermia. He discussed his concerns about the cold exposure; he told me to take core temperatures before and after the swim, and that he wanted me to rewarm as quickly as possible afterward. I had a wonderful time talking with him and found myself wishing the night wouldn't end, but it was nearly eleven and both men had to return to the ship. All night long the wind blew so strongly that it tore shingles off the hotel roof. Somehow I managed to block the noise and wind vibrations and fall into restless sleep.

On December 28, 1976, as I took off my sweatsuit and waited for everyone to move into position, a light wet snow began falling. John was in a skiff twenty yards off my left side, seated near the crewman who would be operating the skiff. Off to my right side, in the rubber inflatable, were the three elite frogmen wearing dry suits and an official who would time the swim. If I showed any sign of distress, they had been ordered to pull me out of the water. The *Elicura* was waiting offshore; it would stay there until we passed and then follow from behind. Captain Furniss was communicating with the two small boats via walkie-talkies.

The delicate snowflakes melted on my shoulders, which were turning bright red. I was starting to get cold. This was not good; it increased my chances of going into hypothermia. There were a few strands of bull kelp offshore that were pointing west but just beginning to relax. This was exactly what we wanted. I knew we had to start now. Impatiently I waited for something; I had no idea what. There must have been delay on the ship.

I stood on the beach, hopping on one foot and then the other, trying to generate heat to stay warm. "What's the problem, John?" I yelled through cupped hands. He was just as ready to go as I was. He borrowed the walkie-talkie from the skiff captain. The reporters were trying to convince Captain Furniss to come ashore for the start of the swim. We had already decided this was not a good idea; there just wasn't time or enough boats to jockey them in to shore and out again. We couldn't delay. The tide wasn't going to wait for us, so I decided that if I began moving into the water, everyone would follow. Shouting to John, I asked him to have the crew synchronize their watches with the official starter. Then I asked him to give me the go signal.

Quickly I slipped into the water. It was funny — after standing in the snow flurry, with tiny snowflakes melting on my cheeks, the forty-two-degree water didn't feel as cold as it had during my training sessions. Taking a breath and dipping down quickly into the sea, I began sprinting. I knew that I was going to have to race the entire three-mile distance if I was going to make it in to shore before the tide pushed us too far one way or the other. I would have to swim faster than I ever had before.

Racing across the sea with the frogmen on my right side and John and the skiff captain on the left, I felt happy that they were there with me. Taking a long breath, I turned and smiled and looked into their eyes. Startled, they looked back into mine and smiled. Everything had been so serious, but now they knew that this was about enjoying the experience and sharing it. Everything was working just as we had planned. It almost seemed too easy. The current continued carrying us to the west; and then the waves started. Three-foot waves were breaking in the direction of the current. They pushed us farther west, more rapidly than we had anticipated. Looking up, I could see that we were moving out of the First Narrows. The shoreline in front of us was dropping back, perhaps five miles away now. In waters this cold, there was no way I could stay immersed for more than two hours; it was just too dangerous. The seas continued to grow, up to four feet, and then, thankfully, the tide went slack.

From the skiff, John yelled at me to sprint, to make as much forward distance as possible before the tide changed and carried us to the east. We were racing the tide, flying over the sea surface, airborne, caught in a shower of spray, then rolling, being lifted, and spun and driven deep under the waves, popping up, surfacing, seeing the frogmen with looks of concern on their faces, laughing at them, them waving, cheering, and laughing back. Moving fast, hearing John's directions, staying near him, too. Watching him taking his gloves off, trying to wind his camera to take a picture. His hands were too cold and stiff; blowing on them, trying to warm them, he hunched over to shield the camera from the spray. Inside I laughed a little: *I can do this; I really can do this, without a wet suit or anything to warm me. It is amazing how incredible the human body is that it can do so much. That it can go beyond the everydayness of life; that it can be extraordinary and powerful, and harbor a spirit of hope and pure will.* I was so excited being out there, feeling the tide suddenly going slack. There was no more drift to the west except for the push of the waves. We were more than halfway across.

John pointed at shore and told me to aim for the beach in the distance. Lifting my head above the waves, I could see the gray-green brush and grasses. It was perhaps a mile away. Pulling harder, faster, I knew this was where I had to gain distance, where I had to get across as fast as I could before the tide changed. Catching, pulling, pushing the water, faster and faster, arm over arm, I sprinted. My lungs were burning, my arms on fire, my legs completely numb, my fingers dead. Turning, I took in a large breath of air and saw the intense blue sky, and pure white clouds rushing in. In a few more breaths, looking back, I saw big gray ones chasing them. Another storm was rapidly approaching.

I looked back again. There were bigger gray clouds, and Tierra del Fuego was sliding by to my right. The tide had changed; it was flowing from the west, toward the Atlantic, and it was building quickly, like a hose bent and suddenly released. The force was incredible — we were flying sideways to the west at three, maybe four knots. Now the waves and tidal current were in complete opposition, slamming into each other and rising up like small tsunamis. Swimming was very difficult. There was no rhythm to the sea. Turning to breathe, I drew in water; it flew up my nose and down my throat. Choking, lifting my head to get air, I looked across the sea, and it was chaos: green whitecaps darkening to a threatening gray. And the wind, sweeping across the water in forty-knot gusts, showered us with frothy spray.

John was hunched over in the bow of the skiff, using one arm to shield himself from the spray. The skiff captain was getting drenched. Both men looked miserable, and John's face registered concern. He told me that we were too far west. He was trying to get the skiff captain to make a course correction, but Captain Furniss had given him an order to hold a specific heading, and he would not disobey that order. John continued trying to convince the skiff captain to change course. He wouldn't listen.

The current was racing now, moving at up to nine knots, at full bore, like a raging river. I had never experienced swimming in anything like this. There was so much power and energy in the water surrounding me. It felt wild, wonderful, frightening, and fun. At that moment, I didn't realize we were in real danger. Sonnichsen did, though. He shouted at me, waving frantically. He told me to move close to his skiff. We were heading right for a whirlpool. It spanned fifty feet and it was spinning with dizzying speed, boiling, frothing, churning white water. I felt the whirlpool dragging us toward its center and knew that it would take us down.

John was trying to take the walkie-talkie from the skiff captain so he could talk directly to Captain Furniss. He shouted at me, but I couldn't hear him over the roar of the water and wind. He cupped his hands around his mouth and told me to sprint with everything I had for the headland at the far right. The frogmen had been ordered to stay beside me no matter what, and he thought he could reach Captain Furniss in time to catch up to us. He told me to go. The tide was racing at maybe ten knots by now, and the strength of the whirlpool was growing. Immediately, I cut to the right and swam with all my strength. Glancing back over my shoulder, I saw John and the skiff captain caught on the outer edge of the whirlpool.

The storm was strengthening, and the

tide was surging, dragging me toward the Atlantic Ocean. The frogmen in the Zodiac were cheering and clapping. We were a quarter mile from shore. When I saw one of the frogmen point toward the headland, I summoned all the power I had. A second whirlpool was forming where we intended to finish. This one was one hundred yards across, and we were headed right for it. I glanced to my left and saw John and the skiff captain motoring toward us at full speed. They were okay. But everything was happening as if on fast forward. The frogmen were shouting at me at the top of their lungs to make a sharp right and sprint for shore. We were within fifty yards of the whirlpool off the headlands. And another one was taking shape, just below it.

We turned more sharply right. Now we were less than two hundred yards from shore. But the force of a whirlpool increases in shallow waters. For the moment, I was in ten feet of water. I saw the sandy bottom rushing to my left, felt the water coiling around me, felt my breath tightening, and saw the water grow murky. The whirlpool churned up sand, filled my swimsuit with it, and chafed my skin. I slid sideways toward the whirlpool's center. The frogmen pulled within inches of my right side to protect me.

One man leaned against a pontoon, steadying himself, about to grab me and pull me from the water. They were shouting, but their voices sounded distant behind the veil of wind and waves. With everything I had left, I sprinted.

When I tried to stand, the current ripped my feet out from under me. I tried again and tumbled. I was only five yards from shore and I couldn't get in.

Sonnichsen and the skiff captain pulled ahead and landed. Two frogmen jumped into the water to help me in to shore. One attempted to grab hold of me, but I veered away. If he touched me, I would be disqualified, under channel swimming rules. I put my head down and sprinted until my stomach scraped the sand; then I crawled out on all fours. It wasn't very graceful, but it didn't matter. In one hour and three minutes we had made it across the Strait of Magellan. I was the first person in the world to make the swim.

The storm was hitting the strait hard now. This time, Captain Furniss didn't even attempt to land the *Elicura*.

The frogmen quickly helped me into their boat, and we motored out to the ship. All of us were elated, but we couldn't let our guard down yet; waves were washing into the inflatable and the skiff.

Climbing up the ship's ladder was even hairier than the first time, but I was glad I'd done it before, because this time my hands were numb and I couldn't tell if I had a good hold on the rungs. The boat was swaying more than before, and I was really scared, but kept moving up the ladder. When I reached the top Captain Furniss wrapped a towel around my shoulders, hugged me, and said congratulations. He said he was sorry, but it was too dangerous to land the ship, so we would have to ride back to Punta Arenas through the gale. Excited, I told him I thought that was great; I'd never been on a ship during a gale. Captain Furniss grinned; he was happy too — we had accomplished a lot. But he had to make sure that Sonnichsen and his men and their boat got safely on board, so he handed me over to Dr. Fernandez, who gave me a huge, warm hug.

13

Around the Cape of Good Hope

John Sonnichsen and I were driving south along the South African peninsula, toward the Cape of Good Hope, with Alex, Mario, and Doug — members of the Cape Town Police Department's elite diving team who had volunteered to help me on my attempt to become the first person to swim around the Cape.

My previous swim, across the Strait of Magellan in forty-two-degree water, had made the Bering Strait seem physically possible. I had received information from the Alaska Department of Fish and Game that water temperatures in the Bering Strait ranged from thirty-eight to forty-four degrees in July and August. The question was, How much difference would three or four degrees make? Could I endure water temperatures below forty degrees? I wasn't sure. So methodically, over the years, I had been making swims that I had hoped would be progressively colder and farther, swims between the Aleutian Islands off Alaska in the summer of 1976, between Norway and Sweden, and between Denmark and Sweden, all in pursuit of the Bering Strait goal. From one perspective or another, they were all challenging. In the case of the Aleutian Islands my swims were all firsts, and in the case of the Scandinavian swims, I set new records. Unfortunately, the water temperatures were always warmer than expected, with the exception of a swim in 1977 from Unalaska Island to Unalga Island in the Aleutian chain. There the water temperature was comparable to that in the Strait of Magellan, between forty-three and forty-four degrees. But the time it took me to complete it was long, an hour and a half. This gave me confidence that I could push further into the cold.

From a political standpoint, though, I was having great difficulty getting Soviet support. From my dorm room in 1976 I had begun a letter-writing campaign, contacting officials throughout the United States and the Soviet Union trying to obtain their support and get a visa to make the Bering Strait swim. It took months to hear back from American officials, because I actually think they didn't believe the swim was possible. Worse, I'd gotten no response at all from the Soviets. So I decided to look at another goal, one that would be exciting, challenging, and something that had never been done before. Just as significantly, I wanted to explore the world, and understand it a little better.

My folks had been supportive of my swims, putting money into my swimming ventures and the goals of my siblings, rather than into material things for themselves. But these swims were getting expensive, so I began hunting for corporate sponsorship.

From the start, I was very fortunate; a friend put me in touch with a woman named Nancy Glascock. Her family had made money in the airplane business, manufacturing airplane blowers, those little devices on the ceiling that enable passengers to increase airflow on their faces.

Glascock said she admired my ability and wanted to support a woman who had adventurous goals. She said that women just didn't get enough support as pioneers. Maybe she had discovered this for herself in business, being a company president. In any event, she agreed to underwrite the cost of the Cape of Good Hope swim.

Sonnichsen, the three policemen, and I were passing through Cape Peninsula National Park, heading toward Cape Point, at the tip of Africa. We turned a wide corner and encountered a herd of golden springbok leaping as if they had springs for legs, through dry grasses, across the beige plateau, beneath a brilliant rainbow that spanned the sky. Alex, the captain of the diving team, stomped on the brakes and told us to roll up our windows and lock our doors.

A troop of seven baboons broke from the bush, darted across the dirt road, and clambered onto the Range Rover's roof. They tried to yank the doors open. Alex told us that baboon break-ins were quite common along the Cape Peninsula. The adult males were tremendously strong and would rip door handles off vehicles or smash windows to get to whatever they wanted. They were notorious for stealing beach towels and sandals and helping themselves to your barbecue. When Alex said they once stole Mario's swim fins, the three men broke into laughter.

It was obvious that these three men were a close team. The elite diving team had been established to search for and recover human bodies and evidence. These bodies were victims who had drowned in the sea, lakes, and rivers around Cape Town, by accident or by foul play. The most difficult places to find people were in the black pools that dotted the rolling veldt. It could be dangerous and frightening work. There was no visibility in the black ponds, so after two members of the team roped themselves together, a third member would stand onshore and slowly lower them into the blackness. Sometimes the divers got tangled or pinned under tree stumps, or were sucked into thick muck, or lost their sense of direction, and were unable to figure out which way was up. Panic was not an option. If a diver moved the wrong way, he could inadvertently cut his own oxygen line. Despite the danger, he'd have to maintain his presence of mind and calmly wait for his team members to free him. This calmness under pressure was exactly what I needed for my attempted swim around the Cape of Good Hope. But they also had additional qualifications.

For fun, Alex, Doug, and Mario went spearfishing around Cape Point. The fish populations in that area were very high, due to an incredible amount of upwelling, which created an abundance of plankton, which the fish fed on. With many fish came seal herds, as well as large predatory sharks, including great whites. The great whites were eighteen to twenty-five feet long, and they could swallow a seal whole.

The white fishermen at Haut Bay, a suburb of Cape Town, told Sonnichsen and me that these great whites were common around the Cape. The fishermen even had names for them; one they called Big Ben, another the Torpedo. At first I thought they were telling us fish stories, but at Kalk Bay, another harbor near Cape Town, we found three black fishermen off-loading their morning's catch. The oldest man in the group asked if he could help us. We were out of place, but neither Sonnichsen nor I knew that in South Africa at that time there were separate harbors, ones for blacks and ones for whites.

The old fisherman walked cautiously over to us. His eyes were clouded with cataracts; his hands were dry and crisscrossed by cuts. When we asked him if he could give us some information about currents around the Cape, he said he would try and he smiled. But when he discovered what I wanted to do there, his smile disappeared.

In addition to the great whites there were other aggressive sharks, such as tigers and bronze whalers. The tigers were always in the area, while the bronze whalers were migratory and only swim to Cape Point in the summer. These sharks are so aggressive that one had recently jumped into a local fisherman's boat to get at him.

He gave us another tidbit of information: usually sharks bump their victims before they bite them, to make sure they're food.

The old fisherman asked me if I was sure I wanted to swim around the Cape. I nodded, but in truth, I had some real doubts; I'd never swum with so many sharks before. We had a solid plan, I told him. Alex's diving team would be in the water with me, watching for sharks. Another diver would be towed behind a ski boat, hanging on to a rope with one hand and carrying a shark gun in the other. If the diver sighted a shark and it looked threatening, I'd get out of the water; if there wasn't time for me to clear the water, he'd have to shoot it.

Shaking his head, the fisherman asked me if I was frightened. I nodded. He looked directly into my eyes, as if to make sure it was okay and as if to say, Don't worry. First he closed his eyes and nodded slowly, then opened his eyes, put his hand on my shoulder, and chanted something in Zulu. When he finished, a younger man said that his grandfather had just given me a Zulu blessing. He had asked the Great Spirit to keep the sharks away so I would return safely to shore.

Despite his kindness and blessing, for the next week, prior to the swim, I had shark dreams. One night I dreamed that Big Ben swallowed me whole. I rode on a stream of water over his tongue, past his enormous uvula, and down into his stomach. But my presence irritated his stomach, and he coughed me out. Another night I dreamed that a *Jaws*-sized shark came up from under the water, bumped me, and tried to bite me, but my team managed to grab me and drag me out of the water in the nick of time.

Alex and I had discussed using a shark cage, but the cage would be impossible to tow through high surf. And during the swim, if we suddenly got a set of waves, they could push the cage down, taking me with it. Besides that, the drag created by the cage would create a current that would enable me to swim up to 30 percent faster; I would be towed by the cage. To me this was cheating. So we decided to have two boats for the swim, one positioned on either side of me. The larger, thirty-five-foot ski boat would be on my left side, closest to shore, as we rounded the Cape; on my right would be a rubber inflatable, a Zodiac. Alex and Sonnichsen would be in the Zodiac, and

Mario and Doug and a few other spearfishing friends on the ski boat. They would take turns standing guard, and because of the intensity of the swim, they would change places every twenty minutes. The man being pulled along would hold the tow rope with one hand and a spear gun in the other. We had discussed using bang sticks, but the crew said they were too dangerous; they could explode by accident, injuring or killing the diver and swimmer. The spear guns sounded like a better idea. Two local swimmers, Hugh and Dennis, offered to ride along in the ski boat to serve as shark spotters.

Once the elite diving team, Sonnichsen, and I reached Cape Point, we picked our way through flowering protea bushes and shrubs to the cliffs overlooking the ocean. To the left was the powder blue Indian Ocean and to the right, the deep-cobalt blue Atlantic. Directly below us was a seething white line of foam jutting directly out from the point for at least half a mile. This was where the Indian and Atlantic Oceans collided.

From our vantage point a thousand feet above the beach, we could see the waves breaking. We couldn't tell how large they were, but the granite cliffs beneath our feet trembled as the waves impacted the beach. We could hear the concussions of waves as they broke on the shore and their echoes as the sound carried around the cove. It was ominous.

Sonnichsen and I had discussed the pros and cons of the start and finish and had finally decided to start on the Atlantic side, in an area called McClears Beach. Our route would take us around Cape Point and back into Buffels Beach, on the Indian Ocean side. The swim would cover a minimum of ten miles, all depending upon the currents.

Alex and John headed back to the harbor to get the Zodiac and meet up with the ski-boat crew. When they reached the point by boat, they would wait for us about a mile offshore. Alex was concerned about the Cape rollers. These were waves that got up to thirty feet high in the summer and one hundred feet high in winter. Caused by storms and calving icebergs in Antarctica, these rogue waves would suddenly rise up from out of nowhere and sink ships that were sailing near the Cape. Alex thought that if they stayed at least a mile offshore they would avoid any problems.

Doug led the way down a narrow rock trail; I followed with Mario and a group of journalists. Doug was carrying a long steel rod. It was the spear gun, but it measured less than an inch in diameter. I wondered how that was ever going to stop a shark.

The path narrowed, grew steeper, and became overgrown with thorny scrub. Doug warned me to be careful where I placed my hands. I thought he was concerned that I would get a handful of thorns. Unfortunately, that wasn't the problem. There were large venomous snakes in the Cape area — Cape cobras, coral snakes, ring-necked spitting cobras, and puff adders. The Cape cobra grew up to five feet long. It could spit venom eight feet away, blinding its prey, then move faster than lightning to bite it. All of these snakes liked to coil up and rest in the bushes.

As we approached a rocky area, Mario wanted me to watch my footing. He had seen puff adders sunning themselves in the area just last week. The puff adders were locally known as large lazy snakes that wouldn't slither away or give you any warning they were underfoot. If you stepped on one, it would just turn and inject its deadly venom into your leg.

I was scared to death of snakes. We managed to make it safely to the base of the cliffs, and I was relieved — until Doug told me that we might encounter one more snake in the water, the yellow-bellied sea snake, known as the cobra of the sea. These sea snakes don't attack. They do bite if disturbed, but their mouths are very small. There was a good possibility that we would see them in the sea slicks, long narrow lines on the ocean's surface where the currents converge, where debris accumulates, and where the water is calmer.

When we reached the powdery white beach, the waves towered above our heads. They were at least fifteen to twenty feet high, taller than any wave I'd ever seen. And they were breaking on the beach with so much force, I couldn't hear anything else. I'd had no experience with huge surf, but I knew that if I made a mistake, I would be clobbered.

Doug and Mario squeezed into their wet suits while I took off my sweats and handed them to a journalist. He planned to go around the Cape by car and meet us at the finish. It seemed like it was taking an awfully long time for Doug and Mario to get ready. Mario shouted in my ear that he was also a little worried about the surf.

Doug asked me to give the journalist any rings or earrings or bracelets before I got into the water. There were snook in the sea, barracuda-like fish with sharp teeth. They could be aggressive, and it was better not to wear anything that would attract them.

Doug and I walked down a slope to the edge of the beach, Mario lagging behind a little. The waves were crashing with so much force I could feel the shock vibrating through my entire body. Wave foam was flying over our heads and into our faces. Following closely behind Doug, I looked back and saw Mario licking his mask to keep it from fogging, then pulling it over his head.

Almost as soon as I entered the water, the bottom dropped out from under me. I was in foam five feet high, up to my neck. It was like entering the largest bubble bath in the world, only this tub was filled with fifty-eight-degree water. Waves were surging toward us, gaining height by the second. A rip caught Doug and me and dragged us rapidly toward a wave that must have been twenty feet high, its crest beginning to curl. I fought the water. Trying to remain near shore until the wave broke, I leaned back, then sprinted across the froth. It was so strange: I was pulling fast and hard, but the water was so full of bubbles there was nothing to push against, no resistance, nothing to grab so I could propel myself beyond the waves. Another wave towered toward me. It broke above my head. I dove deep, pulling fast through the foam, working hard to get down low, really low, before the wave collapsed on me.

The wave was tumbling, rolling forward, pulling me up, as if I were drawn by some invisible string, then bending me backward. I didn't want to go backward over the falls. Pulling as hard as I could, I tried to go deeper. My lungs were burning. I wanted to come up for air, but I couldn't. Another wave was breaking, one after the other in successive concussions. They were too large to swim through.

At last there was a gap in the set. Fighting up through the foam, I gasped for air and looked around. Doug was to my right; he told me to sprint out farther before the next set hit. I couldn't see Mario, and neither could Doug. A minute passed, maybe two; we tried to see over the backs of the waves, but they were too high. We discussed the possibility of going back in to shore to find him. Doug said it was too dangerous.

Finally, maybe a couple of minutes later, the waves subsided and we saw the journalists pulling Mario out of the surf. He was standing up, but his mask was down around his neck, and his flippers were off. He waved for us to go on without him.

Together, Doug and I kicked offshore. With a spear gun in one hand, Doug was unable to swim and he was unable to see what was below us. I wondered if he felt as much of a target as I did.

There was no sign of the Zodiac, so we decided to keep going. The water was lapis blue, clear, and felt thick with current. Warm sun shone on our backs, and puffy white clouds cast dark shadows on the water. Still there was no sign of the Zodiac, so we turned parallel to the coast and headed south, toward Cape Point.

The current twisted and turned around us, and we moved through pockets of shocking cold and warm. Finally, in the distance we saw Alex and Sonnichsen in the Zodiac and the ski boat just behind them.

Tired from kicking so far, Doug climbed into the ski boat while another diver jumped into the water, grabbed a rope tied to the boat, and held on. We started moving together; then something large bumped me on my right side. Sharks always bump their victims before they bite them, the old fisherman told me, and so I thought it was a shark and nearly jumped out of my skin. But it was the Zodiac. The wind was flowing across the Zodiac's bow, making it difficult to keep the boat moving in a straight line.

We rounded Cape Point and watched the lighthouse on the cliffs at the very tip slide to our left. We were now a mile from shore, and I watched the breaking waves outline the golden African continent with a line of white.

Quickly we reached the line of foam where the Atlantic and Indian Oceans converged. Here the water boiled with current. We changed course three or four times to find our way through the current, and it took us nearly an hour to round the point. Soon, though, we were six miles from Buffels Bay. But the wind was beginning to increase. It was gusting up to thirty-five knots, a short, rapid, hard-to-find-a-place-to-breathe chop. I was ticked off at the wind. It wasn't supposed to be blowing, and it wasn't supposed to be blowing from this direction.

Clouds passed across the sun and turned off the sunlight like a light switch. It was now impossible to see anything below. The divers changed position again. And then something rammed me. I jumped and looked over. It was the Zodiac again. In the wind and chop, Alex was fighting to maintain control and I was fighting to control my emotions.

As we moved into the Indian Ocean, the

water warmed up to seventy-two degrees, and it was clear and turquoise blue. Long strands of kelp that looked like mermaids' hair gently rolled in and out with the small waves. Brightly colored fish swam beneath us, and for the first time I began to relax, stretch my strokes out, and enjoy the swim.

Doug's voice snapped me back to reality. "Lynne, see the debris over there? That's where the yellow-bellied sea snakes congregate. You've got to move offshore."

It didn't take me more than a moment to react. I quickly swam back into the current flow, where waves slapped me in the face, but I didn't care; we were just four hundred yards from shore and I could see two wild ostriches and a crowd of cheering South Africans. It was all downhill now.

Turning to my left to breathe and to see how Doug was doing, I suddenly stopped. "Where's Doug?" I shouted, looking down into the water. He wasn't hanging on to the rope. *Oh my God, where's Doug?* I wondered. I didn't see a shark.

The crew hadn't heard me, so I shouted again, above the wind: "Where's Doug?"

Alex pulled the Zodiac close to me, then looked down. "Go on. Go on! Sprint for shore!" he shouted.

I wasn't just going to leave Doug. I looked

down again. I couldn't see him. What happened to him? Was he okay? Alex and John were shouting at me to go, insisting that they had the situation under control.

I started sprinting. I was scared for Doug, and for myself. My fear increased with each moment; without any shark spotters, I was really afraid of being attacked. Glancing back over my shoulder I could see both crews leaning over the sides of their boats and staring into the water.

It was the fastest four hundred yards I ever swam. The cheering crowd pressed in around me, and someone threw a towel around my shoulders. I excused myself; I had to see what had happened to Doug.

Alex and Sonnichsen jumped off the Zodiac and hugged me. They were blocking my view. "What happened to Doug?" I asked.

"He's over there." Alex pointed. "I'll let him tell you the story."

Doug was standing in ankle-deep water straightening his spear. He said, "A twelve-foot bronze whaler shark came up out of the kelp for you. He had his mouth all the way open and I knew he was going to attack, so I went down and shot him. I hit his dorsal fin, and the shark bit the spear, bent it in half, and pulled it out of his side. Then he swam off. The blood from his wound attracted others. That's why the crew had you sprint in to shore."

"Are you okay?" I asked.

"Sure. It's quite a good thing that the wind was blowing from the northeast, though. It only blows from that direction one percent of the year. If it had been blowing the normal way, the water would have been turbid, and I wouldn't have seen the shark," Doug said, and smiled, rightly proud of himself.

Yes, we had been lucky, I thought, and remembered the old Zulu fisherman who had given me his blessing.

I returned to UCSB to complete my junior year of college. That winter I received a letter from Sandy Blewett, the swimmer I had met a few years before in England, the one who had helped me on the Cook Strait swim. Sandy was planning to attempt a crossing of the English Channel. The year before I had coached her to swim the Catalina Channel. She had been successful and now, with more confidence and training, she asked me if I would coach her for the English Channel.

That summer, my brother, Dave, and I had been training off the California coast with David Yudovin. We had met Yudovin in 1976, when he wanted to swim across the Catalina Channel. He had asked Dave to coach him, and he was successful on the Catalina swim. We had all become good friends, and in following summers Yudovin and I trained together in the ocean off Seal Beach.

Yudovin and I had planned to swim across the Santa Barbara Channel together from Anacapa Island to Ventura, California; the distance was ten miles in a straight line. We had wanted to make the swim during the fall of 1977, but the weather never cooperated. After that our schedules hadn't meshed, and I'd finally lost interest. Yudovin had decided to continue waiting and had gotten John Sonnichsen to agree to accompany him in the boat, and I decided to help Sandy Blewett, to return the favor she had done for me. I was very excited about working with her again.

We met in Dover, England, in May 1979, and I watched Sandy swim; she looked really good. After her workout, we walked along the pebbles of Dover Harbour and talked. The air off the North Sea was fresh and sweet, and the sky was brilliant blue. Warm late-afternoon sun cascaded over the white cliffs, giving them a halo of gold. I thought of Fahmy and was glad to be back in Dover again.

As we walked along the harbor, we saw six swimmers moving between the pier and the Hovercraft port. The coach standing on the beach looked familiar. He looked like Monir. Five years had passed since I'd seen him in Egypt. I had met other men, but none of them had ever impressed me the way he had. We had written off and on, but gradually we had stopped writing. Our lives, it seemed, had gone on. But I often thought of him and wondered how he was doing.

This man seemed taller from the back, more muscular. Slowing my pace, I studied him. He must have felt my presence, because he started to turn; I held my breath. It was him, really him.

"Somehow I just knew you would be here this year," he said, and smiled. His voice was deeper, his face more mature, but the brightness in his eyes was still there.

I wanted to throw my arms around him and give him a big hug, but I couldn't; it wouldn't have been proper with the other swimmers there. In Egypt, people didn't simply hug one another. So I extended my hand, and he took it; my eyes never left his. We both smiled. It was so good to see him.

He had to finish giving the team their

workout. I waited, while Sandy said she wanted to go back and take a shower and get warm.

It was simply good to stand beside him and watch him coach. I could tell that his team loved and respected him just as much as I'd loved my past coaches. It was a wonderful thing to see.

When the workout was over and the team went back to the hotel, Monir and I stayed on the beach to talk.

He had traveled to England the year before to try to break my record but had missed it by twenty minutes.

He had thought I would return when my time was broken, to try to recapture the record. But I told him that I had helped coach the woman who had beaten my time, and that swimming the English Channel no longer had a great appeal for me; I had other things I wanted to do, things that had never been done before. But I was really sorry that he had not broken my record. It was very difficult to have that goal and not fulfill it. In the summer of 1975, Dave had attempted the English Channel. He was successful on the swim, but he didn't break the record and he was very disappointed. I thought that was sad; it seemed so much out of perspective to train so hard, to have such a high goal, and then to discount it all because you didn't break the record. There was still a great challenge in just completing the swim. Channel swimming was so different from pool swimming. So much could change in the space of eight hours. Monir laughed hard at that; he remembered that this was what I'd said to him just before we'd swum in the Nile race.

So much had happened in our lives, but it was simply wonderful to be there with him. Time had changed things, and he had changed too; but the core of him was the same, and I knew I was attracted to him more than ever before. I don't know what signaled it, but he suddenly reached out to hug me, and we kissed. From the look on his face, he felt the same way I did. I'd never experienced anything like this before. We held hands and talked about what we had been doing, and then we had to leave to take care of our swimmers.

When I saw Monir the next morning, my feelings for him were so strong that I decided I had to avoid him or see him only when someone else was around. My responsibility, I told myself, was to be there for Sandy; she was my priority. After we finished coaching I met him again on the beach. I had never been drawn to someone that strongly. It surprised me. We kissed again, almost as if to confirm our feelings, and it happened again, that electrical charge.

A few days later Sandy started her swim from England to France. The weather was good, and she was well prepared. But seven miles from the French coast she became disoriented; shivering, she disqualified herself by touching the boat. That evening, we discussed what had happened and we decided that she had simply psyched herself out. She had stopped in the exact same place the year before, just within sight of the French coast. I suggested that she take some time to collect her thoughts, rest up, wait until the following year, and then make another attempt. I promised I would be back to help her.

For the next couple of weeks I explored France and Switzerland. After I swam across Lake Geneva, I called Sandy to find out how she was doing.

She didn't sound very good. Less than a week after her attempt she had tried again. She had gotten within seven miles of the French shore and had passed out. Having been through a similar situation before in the Nile River, I tried to help her evaluate her swim. She decided to stay in England

and train and attempt the Channel again the following year.

Then I called home to check on David Yudovin, who had attempted to swim from Anacapa Island to the mainland. He had gotten within four hundred yards from shore and then gone into complete cardiac arrest. Fortunately, the coast guard had been nearby, and an emergency crew had raced him to an ambulance and then to the hospital. It had taken doctors more than an hour to get his heart beating again. He had pneumonia, cracked ribs, and was in the hospital in Ventura. I had to get home.

I stopped off in Dover on the way back from Europe and said good-bye to Monir. I had hoped to see him for a few days before I left England, but it was probably a good thing that I didn't get romantically involved. With Yudovin in the hospital, I knew I had to get home and see him. When I reached London, Dr. William Keatinge met me and had me stay at his and his wife's home. A physician and a physiologist at the University of London, Dr. Keatinge was also a friend of Dr. McCafferty's at UCSB. He and I had met at UCSB, and I had started corresponding with him to find out more about the human body's responses to cold.

Most of the evening we talked about his

research, my swims, and Yudovin's condition. In the morning, Dr. Keatinge took me to Heathrow Airport. Unfortunately, the airline I was taking home was overbooked by hundreds of people, so for four days I had to sleep in an alley with two hundred other people outside the Pan Am terminal. All in all, it was a good experience. It gave me a small sense of what it would be like to have to live on the streets, and it also showed me how situations like that can bring out the best in people. Everyone shared what they had, and told stories about their families and their homeland.

By the time I arrived in California, Yudovin was out of the hospital and was home recovering. It would take him six months to be healthy enough to get back in the water again. Years later he would make that swim from Anacapa Island, a double triumph this time.

14

Around the World
in Eighty Days

By 1985 I had been working on the Bering
Strait project for nine years. Every day I
wrote at least one letter to someone in either
the United States or the Soviet Union,
seeking permission to make the swim. To pay
the bills, I worked as a reference librarian,
wrote magazine articles, taught swimming
lessons, and worked with a group of physical
therapists. The librarian job was so helpful;
during breaks each day I could look up information on the Soviet Union, or talk with the
other librarians to find out if they had any
new suggestions for establishing contact with
the Soviets.

For years, I didn't get any answer from
them, so I tried to make contact through
congressional and Senate offices. I didn't
make much headway there either. And I still

had the challenge of paying for all of it. My folks helped by letting me live at home so I could save money; at the same time, I was writing letters to Fortune 500 companies, seeking sponsorship. The problem was that no one believed the Soviets would allow the swim to occur. My family and friends questioned my tenacity. They could not understand why the Bering Strait project had taken on such importance for me. Part of my conviction came from the realization that if I gave up, I would wonder all my life if I might have been able to make a positive difference in the world. If I gave up, I would throw away all that I had done to reach that point. In many ways, the effort to obtain permission and support for this swim reflected life and the essence of long-distance swimming: as long as you hang in there and keep going, you have a chance at succeeding. Once you give up, you're done.

To generate interest and push my physical limits, I decided to attempt a series of swims that would take me around the world in eighty days. The idea was to swim across ten of the coldest and most difficult waterways in the world. With the amount of press I had had through the years, I hoped to secure corporate sponsorship for the around-the-world journey, but I got only limited support. It was partly because I didn't allow enough time and partly, my father said, because I was a woman. Whatever the reason, I didn't get enough support for the swim around the world. So I finally asked myself, How can anyone believe in me unless I believe in myself? I cleared out my bank account and paid the expenses for Jeffrey Cardenas, a photographer from the *Miami Herald*, to accompany me and document the journey. From the onset of the trip we knew it was going to be a challenge. My funds were very limited, so I would have to find corporate sponsorship en route. That would be challenging; in addition, I would have to find boat support, coordinate each of the ten swims, inform the local press so they could document the swim, and do a major swim every four to eight days depending on our travel schedule, the time it took to coordinate a swim and find sponsorship.

We began the journey. In Washington, D.C., I swam ten miles, up the Potomac River to the Jefferson Memorial. From there, Jeffrey and I traveled to Iceland, where I planned to swim across Lake Myvatn, the third-largest lake in Iceland and one of the coldest in the country.

By the time we reached Iceland, I knew I was going to have to get corporate sponsorship. At a hotel in Reykjavík I met an American man who said there were five large corporations in Iceland, one of them being Coca-Cola. It was a consumer-based corporation with American ties, so I pulled out the phone book, found the number, took a deep breath, and asked to speak to the president of the company, a man named Petur Bjornsson. He wasn't in, but his vice president of sales was. Would I be willing to speak to him?

At the end of our conversation, the vice president said he would talk to Mr. Bjornsson and get back to me. That afternoon he called back and asked if I would meet with Mr. Bjornsson at ten o'clock in the morning, at his office.

The next morning I put on my red sweatsuit with the white stripes up the sleeve and down the leg and looked in the mirror. I looked just like a Coke can, which was what I wanted.

Mr. Bjornsson met me in the lobby; he was a very tall gentleman wearing a sport jacket and a great smile. He shook my hand enthusiastically and led me down a corridor, past pictures of him along with Jack Nicklaus on a golf course, and then he directed me to a large leather chair in his office. There were paintings on the walls and bronze sculptures on the end tables. One painting was of a white dove flapping her wings, trying to fly out of a human rib cage.

Mr. Bjornsson saw me staring at it and said that he liked to support local artists, and all the work in the room had been done by Icelandic artists. The one of the dove, the artist had said, was a symbol of herself — of her inner emotions and passions and her trying to break out of life's cage to soar. It was an amazing piece, and I thought, *If he understands this, then he will understand what I'm trying to do.*

Quickly I gave him an overview of my background and told him that I wanted to swim across Lake Myvatn because I understood that the lake had never been swum, but also because the lake was very cold and it might help me on my quest for the Bering Strait. I had also promised to supply the physiologists at UCSB and Dr. Keatinge at the University of London with data from the cold swims. And I told him that I would be willing to stencil a Coca-Cola logo on my swim cap, and tell the local media about his support.

As I related all of this to Mr. Bjornsson, I was both very excited and nervous. It had been so difficult to get corporate sponsorship, because at the time few people understood what I was trying to do. But Mr. Bjornsson completely got it. He leaned forward in his chair and said, "You know, people contact me from all over the world all the time for sponsorship. They write to me about a hot-air balloon expedition or something. But they are just talking about going out there and doing it. You are actually doing it. I greatly admire that. Yes, of course, I'd love to sponsor you. How much support do you need?"

We needed to cover the air transportation to Lake Myvatn, escort boats, accommodations, food, and communications for five days. He was very agreeable, explaining that swimming was the national sport in Iceland and would instantly gain media attention and help market his products. But more than that, he said, the people who live in the area near Lake Myvatn are like Texans; they think their region is the biggest and the best part of Iceland. He knew the local people would support the swim, open their homes, and share some of their traditions with us. He asked if I would mind meeting with the press that day and also meeting with some local young swimmers to inspire them. I was happy to do both.

The next morning Mr. Bjornsson and I met on the shores of the North Atlantic. He had come to walk with me and watch me train. He had no idea how wonderful it was to have him there; it made me feel very much at home again, having an adult walking beside me on the shore. After the hour workout in the forty-five-degree water, Mr. Bjornsson told me that when he'd heard that I was in town, the day before, he had cut his business trip short to meet with me. He was so enthusiastic. After seeing me train, he said, he was confident I would be able to swim across Lake Myvatn.

Jeffrey Cardenas and I flew to north-eastern Iceland, and for the next three days I trained in the lake. Each day an elderly woman, whose name I couldn't pro-nounce — she finally told me just to call her Sigga — invited me into her home to take a hot bath in her tub. After swimming in the forty-five-degree water, nothing felt as good. The first day she invited me upstairs into her kitchen, lit long blue candles, poured hot chocolate for me, and offered me homemade cookies. I was touched and grateful for her kindness. It didn't matter that we couldn't speak to each other; we simply looked at each other and enjoyed each other's company.

The next day, after my workout, as we stood by the window overlooking the village, she pointed out the natural hot springs off to our right. She waved to passing neighbors and made sure I saw the herd of tiny white Icelandic horses that were smaller than ponies. Without speaking, she revealed to me so much of Iceland's natural and wild beauty.

She seemed to be waiting for something, and then her daughter arrived to interpret for us. She said her mother thought I was brave to swim across Lake Myvatn. Sigga asked, "Have you been bitten by the mee flies — microscopic mosquito larva?"

"Oh, I thought I had a bad case of hives," I said. My body was completely covered with pink spots that itched like poison ivy. "Is there anything I can do to stop the itching?"

Sigga shook her head. Her husband wore gloves when he fished on the lake, but she didn't know of anything that I could use to stop the itching or prevent more bites.

I told her that it was okay; it would just be part of my story about swimming Lake Myvatn. She smiled; she liked the idea that one day I would tell a story about her home, a place she had never left. I was astonished. Hadn't she been curious? Didn't she want to see the world, understand life, have adventures? She smiled at me and said her world contained everything she needed. She had her family, the magnificent beauty of Lake Myvatn, and friends everywhere in the village. She didn't need to travel.

The following morning, on August 14, 1985, we met on the shores of Geiteyjarstönd, on the eastern side of Myvatn. Sovar Kristjansson, Finnur Baldursson, Ellert Hauksson, and Bjorguin Arnalosson, all tall, strong Nordic men from the Icelandic Lifesaving Association, prepared the rubber inflatable boats. They were excited about the swim. No one ever swam in the lake, let alone crossed it. They were volunteer lifeguards; their primary job was to rescue fishermen and tourists who fell into the lake. They each had a pioneer spirit; there was a feeling around the Lake Myvatn area that anything was possible.

Nearly the entire village of Myvatn came to see us off. All thirty or so villagers, including the family we had met the night before as well as Sigga and her daughter, lined the black volcanic beach in their parkas and hats and mittens, smiling and bidding us farewell. There was also an entourage of journalists and television people. It was an exciting day for the local people, and it was for me too.

At 9:14 a.m., I began walking into Lake

Myvatn. The water was as glassy as ice and felt just about as cold. In the background I heard people clapping as I started swimming, and I smiled. It was such an honor to be swimming in this Icelandic lake and to have the support and encouragement of the local people. Even though we hadn't spent much time together, I believed they were with me, and I felt a special connection with them. I think they understood that these swims were far more than just athletic adventures for me; they were a way of bridging cultural distances. They had made me feel very welcome there, and very special. It was thrilling to be making this swim with them with me in spirit.

The water was the same temperature as that in the Strait of Magellan, between forty-two and forty-four degrees, but for some unexplained reason, freshwater always feels colder than salt water. The distance I would be swimming across Lake Myvatn would be seven miles in a straight line, more than double the distance of the Strait of Magellan. The cold water coupled with distance would make the swim challenging and also, perhaps, build my confidence for the Bering Strait.

Positioned on my left side were Sovar and his lifeguard crew in one Zodiac; on the right were Jeffrey Cardenas, Arni Saeberg, and a couple of reporters. We were aiming for the volcanic point of Vindbelgur; it would take perhaps an hour and a half to reach that point, the deepest part of the lake. If I was not going into hypothermia, at that point I would extend the swim to include the widest portion of the lake, near Vagnbrekka.

By forty-five minutes into the swim, my arms were completely numb. The lifeguard crew watched me closely, and smiled. It was a spectacular morning, and we moved quickly across the glassy water, past two tiny lush green islands. Here the water, incredibly, changed from cold forty-three-degree water to hot ninety-degree water, as I cut across icy streams of water fed by mountain brooks and geothermal rivers from deep below the lake. It was like swimming across the face of a guitar, each string or stream a different temperature, and I never knew what to expect until my body played it.

When we hit the cold strings of water I swam faster, breathing every three to five strokes, trying to create more heat. When we crossed the hot strings, I stretched out. The contrast between hot and cold water, though, made it very difficult to adjust to the cold and it made the cold water seem even colder.

Realizing the dangers of this, Sovar and his crew didn't take their eyes off me, and I felt very confident in them and very happy they were with me. In less than half an hour we were within reach of the Vindbelgur volcano, and we decided to go for the second point. This would make the swim one-third longer, but I wanted to stretch my limits, and the crew was right with me.

Once we passed the Vindbelgur volcano, I stopped for two or three seconds for a drink of Hi-C, and for the next half hour I sprinted. Sovar guided me past a white house at Vagnbrekka, then around the Stekkjarnes peninsula. A crowd had gathered: children, grown-ups, farmers with Icelandic horses, families we had met in the past three days. All were standing and cheering. The black volcanic shore was less than two hundred yards away. When I saw the bottom, I stood up. Someone pulled an incredibly warm and beautiful Icelandic sweater over my head, an old man offered me a bottle of whiskey, and the mayor came to invite Jeffrey and me for lunch. I had completed the crossing in just under two hours, and we were thrilled.

But I was extremely cold.

Someone gave us a ride to the local swimming pool, where I jumped into the water to get warm. That was a huge mistake. The water in the pool was eighty degrees, and my skin temperature was in the low thirties.

The contrast made my skin feel like it was on fire. Worse, the cold blood from my extremities rushed into my core, and I was suddenly very cold from the inside out. It took me twice as long to rewarm as it had after the Strait of Magellan swim. But from mistakes we learn something, and I knew I would not do that again.

That night we celebrated with the people in Myvatn with a wonderful dinner at one of the villagers' houses.

The next morning we flew back to Reykjavík and met with Petur Bjornsson. He was elated, and he said that what I was doing had reached the hearts of the common people. He said I was now a hero to the Icelandic people, that they would talk of the swim in years to come. I told him that I would always remember them, that no one ever achieves great things alone.

Jeffrey and I continued our journey. With the support of a crew in Gibraltar, I became the first woman to swim across the Strait of Gibraltar, from Morocco to Gibraltar; then, with an Italian support team, I swam across the Strait of Messina. From there Jeffrey and I traveled to Greece, and I swam around

Delos Island, then across the Bosporus in Turkey, across Lake Kumming in China, and the five lakes of Mount Fuji in Japan. Each of these presented us with unique challenges and wonderful cultural experiences. But the one swim that would be the most dramatic of all in the around-the-world swim, and the most significant in terms of providing a key to the Bering Strait, was Glacier Bay.

The swim across Lake Myvatn stretched me, forced me to plod on through the cold. More important, I'd learned I could endure forty-three-degree water for nearly two hours. Now the question was, Could I endure intensely colder water for a shorter time? Glacier Bay, Alaska, would give me the answer to this question.

15

Glacier Bay

It took a lot for me to wrap my mind around it, to even begin to believe I could do it. Seeing those pure white and powder-blue icebergs bobbing on Glacier Bay's waters was enough to make me realize this was going to stretch me further than I'd ever been stretched before. It took a tremendous effort for me to even think that the swim could be possible.

On October 4, 1985, the night before the attempted swim, a sudden cold snap hit Alaska. If Glacier Bay had been filled only with salt water, this wouldn't have created a problem. But the bay contains sweet fresh-water from cascading rivers and streams and melting glaciers. The night before the swim, air temperatures in Gustavus, where Jeffrey and I were staying in a family-run lodge, and in the bay dropped well below freezing. The cold night sky was lit up with auroras. Whirling and wavering bands of light, rose, lapis blue, and neon green, particles of light stretched across the midnight blue sky. They rose, drifted, spread, and disappeared, and then out of nowhere, another shower of light swirled in the sky. The solar winds were blowing, linking and unlinking their magnetic field with the earth's. Speeding electrons were bursting through the earth's atmosphere, colliding with atoms of gas. The atoms were absorbing energy and creating showers of colored light. The auroras were a sort of meeting of the universe with the earth, and I took it as a good sign for the swim.

In Gustavus, a tiny town near Glacier Bay, at five a.m. Fritz Koshman, Dena Matkin, Debbie Woodruff, Jeffrey Cardenas, and I met at an ice-encased dock. We slipped and slid along the dock, until Fritz Koshman, the pilot, took our hands one by one and helped us carefully board the thirty-foot-long wooden skiff. Fritz was a stocky, broad-shouldered man with a bushy but well-kept beard and long brown hair. In addition to being a fisherman, he was known as a very good artist. He looked at me, and there was some hesitancy in his blue eyes.

"Is everything okay?" I asked.

"It got awfully cold last night," he said. "I'm not sure if we're going to be able to do this. Guess we'll just have to see how far we can get." But he didn't say any more. He started the motor, and we began our journey through Icy Strait.

As we entered Glacier Bay, roughly an hour later, Fritz was leaning out of the cabin, his eyes locked on the glassy, gray-blue water. "If the water was choppier, then at least I could see the ice. Or if the sun would stay in front of the clouds, it would glisten. But now the water's dark and I can't see anything at all."

"I don't understand — what kind of ice are you looking for?" I said.

"Pan ice. It's ice on the top inches of the water, about a quarter of an inch to half an inch thick. And it's round, shaped like a pan. See, there's some."

I could barely see the ten-foot-wide section floating on the water.

"I'm not sure how far we're going to be able to go. Pan ice can slice through the wooden hull of my boat. It could sink us in a matter of minutes. I don't like this at all," Koshman said.

As if we were moving through a minefield, we zigzagged northward through Glacier

Bay, past tall dark pines, small rocky islands, and fishing camps that had been closed for the season. We motored deep into the Alaskan wilderness. The sputter of the boat's tiny motor was the only engine voice in the bay. We were alone, and beside the mountain walls we were very small.

As Koshman turned his head to steer the boat, we plowed into a transparent sheet of pan ice. It sounded like something snapped, and then there was a heavy thud. The boat shuddered, and so did we.

"I don't know how much farther we're going to be able to go. I'm going to have to go slower. And I need all of you to look for the ice." Koshman sighed deeply.

"This is really dangerous for a boat," Debbie Woodruff said, staring into the water.

Dangerous for a boat — what would it do to a swimmer?

Woodruff knew how dangerous the bay could be; she'd spent years fishing for crab there. She was a large, strong, capable woman with long, wavy brown hair, a small round face, and brown eyes. As an added bonus, she was also a certified emergency medical technician. In case something went really wrong during the swim, she had spoken with her fishermen colleagues. Be-

cause of the high mountain walls surrounding Glacier Bay, it would not be
possible to directly radio an emergency
team for help. So she had contacted her fishermen friends who were fishing south of us
out of the bay, where there wasn't a problem
with ice. If we had an emergency, she would
radio them, and they would pass that information to the rescue team.

Fritz Koshman stifled a curse as a piece of
ice cracked and shattered. "I don't like this
at all," he said.

I turned to Woodruff. "If it's that dangerous, do you think I should ask him to
turn around?" I was filled with mixed
thoughts and emotions. No matter how you
looked at it, this swim was dangerous. Ad-
mittedly, that's what made it very exciting.
But there was a point where it would be too
dangerous, a point beyond any reason, and I
didn't want to reach that point before I
climbed into the water. I didn't want to endanger the lives of the crew or hurt myself;
no swim, however important to the end
goal, was worth that.

"Fritz knows what he's doing. If he
doesn't think it's safe, he'll turn back,"
Woodruff said confidently.

The boat moved as if in slow motion into
Glacier Bay.

"There's ice off the bow — ten yards! Steer right, more right!" Debbie yelled.

Koshman turned the wheel, leaning and pulling with his entire large body, and he managed to steer the thirty-foot boat out of harm's way. He kept adjusting the course, making sudden abrupt turns. This took an enormous amount of concentration, skill, and nerve — especially when he came upon a section of pan ice and had to choose whether to steer around the larger pieces, knowing that he was going to snap through smaller pieces and possibly damage his boat.

We motored deeper into the bay, where there was more freshwater runoff from streams, rivers, and brooks, and the pan ice became even more abundant. Navigation was a nightmare. We heard ice snapping and crunching beneath the bow, then more crackling as the boat moved over it. The sound penetrated the boat's floorboards and traveled through our bodies.

Fritz ran to the bow and looked over the side. The wood hadn't been cut — at least, not yet. He hurried back to the steering house. He wiped sweat off his brow and sucked in air nervously. "I'm not sure we can go much farther," he said. "I don't want to damage my boat, or sink us." He looked ahead, as if trying to decide the best starting point for the swim.

No one saw it coming, although we all had been completely focused on the water. We hit an iceberg. It was what Debbie Woodruff described as a baby berg, just two feet wide, and most of it was below the water's surface, except for a patch of ice that was only a foot wide. When we hit the iceberg, the impact sounded like a giant boulder had slammed into the boat. Fortunately, the berg just bounced off us without making a hole, but this first encounter heightened our anticipation. We watched the water, hoping we wouldn't miss another submerged berg. Our anticipation continued to increase when we sighted two larger bergs, two to three feet high and wide. When we passed within a couple yards of them, it felt as if we were standing naked in front of an open Sub-Zero freezer.

How could I even believe this swim was possible? What was I thinking? *Maybe it's time to reconsider. Maybe the smart thing to do is to gather up all my marbles and just go home.* Sometimes I wasn't sure why I did these things. I stifled a shiver. This was more than I had expected.

Strong currents began coming at us from a multitude of directions now, flowing at up to a knot, pushing pan ice and bergs into us. It was like getting hit by comets flying at us from outer space, smashing into us from every direction.

Suddenly, the boat lurched to one side when a piece of ice connected with the propeller. Koschman checked the line; it seemed to be okay. He told us he couldn't make the boat go any slower, to reduce the impact of the icebergs. If we hit one hard and it punched a hole in the side of the boat, we would sink quickly. Survival time in this water for an untrained person was less than ten minutes.

Shaking his head, Koshman turned to me and said reluctantly, "Maybe we should turn back now. But if we do that, we won't be able to come back tomorrow. The ice will be worse. You won't have a chance to try this swim until next year. And I know you really want to do it now."

"I really do. It's important for my long-range plan. But if you feel that we are putting your boat and the crew in real jeopardy, then I think we have to turn back," I said, unable to conceal my disappointment.

"We have only a couple miles to go. The thing is," Kochman said, "I want to get the swim off as soon as possible. It's late afternoon, the sun's going to set soon, and when that happens, the air temperature here will plunge. More pan ice is going to form, rapidly. And that will make our trip home very difficult. But I'm more concerned about getting locked in the ice. The air temperature could drop more rapidly than I've anticipated, and if that happens, we could get stranded."

"You mean like Shackleton's expedition? You mean we could be trapped in the ice?"

"Yes, it happens easily here. We could be stranded for a day or two, or more. The ice can also freeze around the boat, compress the two sides, and crush the hull. So if we're going to do this, you're going to have to hurry. We've got to get in and out of here fast."

"I will go as fast as I can," I promised.

There were bears in this area. Dena Matkin had told me all about them. She worked with the Forest Service as a biologist, spending her time studying bears and humpback whales. She said that older adult bears who were no longer strong enough to fight younger bears for territory with an abundance of food were pushed north into the Muir Inlet, near the Riggs Glacier, where we were headed. Here, because of the glaciers and glacial rock, food was scarce. The bears in this area were always very hungry, and it was dangerous to camp there. Against the warnings of park rangers, one tourist had decided to go camping in Glacier Bay and wandered off on his own. After a couple of days the rangers began searching for him; all they found were his feet in his boots. No, we would not be camping.

The air temperature dropped a few more degrees. It was probably in the mid-thirties, and I blew my breath into my jacket to trap the warm air and keep me warm. I couldn't afford to get cold before I started swimming. If I started warm, I had less of a chance of going into hypothermia, or at least more time to work with before my temperature dropped too low. This was scary stuff. *How am I going to do this? How am I going to be okay? How am I not going to get cut by that pan ice?*

Matkin provided a solution. She was an expert with small boats. While studying humpbacks, she spent a lot of time rowing out among them, and she had developed skills that enabled her not to disturb them. She said we would not encounter any humpbacks because the water was too cold; they had already swum to Hawaii. On my swim, she would row a small dory in front of me, and would act like a mini ice breaker while Koshman, Woodruff, and Cardenas monitored us and the ice from the boat.

Woodruff pulled her long wavy brown hair back into a ponytail to get it out of the way, then began radioing her fishing friends down the bay to inform them of our status. The captains were relaying this information to Matkin's friends at the Forest Service, and they were updating an airplane pilot who was on standby in case of an emergency. The airplane would be able to provide support as long as the weather held, and as long as there was light.

Muir Inlet narrowed to a mile. Here we were surrounded by an awesome towering amphitheater of majestic serrated white glacial peaks and steep shale midsections and bases. In the distance, half a mile at most, was the Riggs Glacier, a breathtaking mountain of white, blue, and green ice compressed for millions of years, a sort of massive frozen history of time. Its enormous beauty and power seemed to say, "Look at me; I am Alaska, the heart and essence of it, wild, pristine, and enduring."

Fritz suddenly turned and started to land the boat on a crumbly black shale beach about a mile from the Riggs Glacier.

"Can't we get closer to it?" I asked. I wanted to see it more closely, from many sides.

Koshman shook his head. "It's not safe. The glacier can calve without warning, and those huge blocks of ice weigh thousands of pounds. They tumble into the bay at thirty or forty miles an hour, and when they hit the water they create waves up to twenty feet high. A large berg can capsize a boat or take it under. I've seen it happen before. We'd better get moving," he said.

While Matkin rowed the tiny boat into position and Koshman picked his way through the icebergs to the beach, I pulled off my parka, sweats, shoes, and socks, and looked to the opposite shore for reference points. In a straight line the distance across was one mile, but with the ice, current, and icebergs, we wouldn't be going straight. I knew this would be the longest mile I'd ever swum.

Small shale pebbles from the mountain ridge above our heads began sprinkling the beach with rocks. They were dropping every minute or so, and starting to increase in size. Once Koshman landed the boat, he said, I'd better hurry; we could be in for a rockslide, and he wanted us offshore before that happened.

Quickly I climbed up on the boat's railing. As I started to come down over it, the part of my Lycra swimsuit where the strap joins the chest got caught on a hook inside the railing.

The strap was stretched out like a rubber band, and I was at an angle where I couldn't pull myself back into the boat and I couldn't reach over the railing and free myself; I was suspended in midair, bouncing up and down and laughing really hard.

I tugged on the strap, yanked it. It was strong material, but finally I ripped a hole in it and tore myself free.

On the ground, I tied the suit together, but the knot wouldn't hold. It kept slipping out. "Okay, forget it. I'll just swim like this. I'll just keep my right arm in front of my chest until I get into the water," I said.

"You can't swim like that, with your top torn off," Matkin said.

It didn't matter to me. I just wanted to start. God, I just wanted to start. But she was right; I couldn't swim without a top. I needed some protection from the ice, or I could really get cut.

Rummaging through my swim bag, Woodruff pulled out two spare Tyr swimsuits and tossed me the blue one. Crouching in front of the bow for some privacy, I pulled off my torn suit and changed into the spare.

More rocks were sliding down the ridge; it was becoming increasingly unstable. Rocks the size of oranges were bouncing off the bow. Koshman reversed the boat's engines and started pulling offshore. Matkin turned the rowboat around and told me she would stay right beside me.

The avalanche happened at the best time. It pushed me offshore quickly. I had to move fast without thinking. Quickly I tugged my yellow cap onto my head, stuffed my long hair into it, pulled my goggles over my head, licked them so they wouldn't fog, licked them again just to make sure, adjusted the straps on my swimsuit, took a deep breath, and slid my feet into the Muir Inlet of Glacier Bay. Immediately the frigid water dulled my feet and then my hands. My arms turned bright red and ached with a deep pain. I had asked the crew not to tell me what the temperature was.

At first, I swam freestyle with my head up; an inefficient way of swimming, but it allowed me to conserve body heat a little longer. More than that, I was afraid of the pan ice. I was afraid that I would slice my face with it. As I chopped it with my hands I felt it crack, and I felt the sharpness of the edges. It was like swimming through shards of glass. I didn't want to get cut. I was scared.

The crew was shouting at me. Icebergs were being pushed toward me by the current from the left and directly head-on. There were five or six icebergs, in different shapes and sizes, from six feet wide to one foot wide, and up to three feet high. They were flowing from the left, down the bay, and swimming near them was like running a gauntlet, but this gauntlet was moving toward us, and it was hard to judge the speed of the current. Could I get past them before they reached me, or did I have to slow down and let them slide by?

Dena Matkin was rowing ten yards ahead of me, her petite body working hard. Moving through the ice fields was difficult work. She had to get us through the ice patches and around the ice blocks without getting the rowboat caught up on the ice. At the same time, she was keeping an eye on me, making sure I wouldn't ram into the back of the boat. Dena used her oars like a sledgehammer, slamming them down against the pan ice with all her might, repeating the action rapidly until the pan ice cracked.

Her boat became a mini ice breaker. She parted the ice and I followed her through the break, feeling the sharp ice sticking into my chest and forearms.

"Watch out for that berg!" Dena shouted a warning. "Head right. No — more. More.

It's wider than you think."

Turning hard right, I followed Dena around a large iceberg six feet high and eight feet wide. We were within a foot of the iceberg, and as I swam, I stared at it. This was the first time I had ever been so close to an iceberg, and it was magnificent, a piece off the Riggs Glacier. At the bottom, the iceberg was bright glacial blue. In the middle, it was deeper blue and marbled with snow. The top of the iceberg had been sculpted by wind and rain into a thin, wavering, and silvery edge.

I swam as fast as my arms would turn over, trying to beat the cold and create heat. With my head up, I was able to see the bay ahead and to my right and left sides. The sun emerged from behind a cloud, and I looked across the Tiffany blue water, where a dozen icebergs shimmered like diamonds, bobbing slightly as they slowly slid downstream toward us.

"Look out, pan ice!" Matkin shouted. She broke a wedge through it with her bow so I could follow. It was a wide piece, and the unbroken part shifted around in front of me. I thought, *Maybe I should wait and let it flow past me; then I won't have to swim through it. That won't work. It's too cold.* Dena was yelling for me to swim around it, but that would take too much time. I had to swim through it. Using my right arm I made my hand flat, as if I were going to do karate. Then I chopped it down onto the ice. It hurt; my hand only bounced back up, reverberating like a bell. I did it again, harder this time, and felt the ice start to give. I hit it again in the same spot, and my forearm went through the ice and down into the water. I used my left arm next, and slammed it down. It worked. The ice cracked a bit more. I checked my arm. No blood. I hit the pan ice again, and it snapped and cracked open. *Hmm, this is actually kind of fun.* I carefully swam between the sharp pieces. I felt them jab into my arms, but I now knew that they weren't cutting me, and somehow that made me feel more confident.

Another piece of pan ice bobbed in Dena's path. She rowed onto it and smacked it with her oars. It wouldn't break. Turning my arms over quickly, I swam in place. She tried again. It still didn't break. She tried hitting the ice with one oar at different angles, but it still didn't work. Dena was struggling now. Gripping the gunwales, she stood up and jumped down in the boat, trying to use her weight to crack the ice, but she was such a featherweight, she couldn't do it. She held the gunwales, coiled her knees up to her body, and bounced up and down in the boat. I couldn't help myself; I started laughing. It was contagious — soon Debbie and Fritz were laughing so hard they were bent over.

Dena wouldn't give up. She rocked the boat back and forth, and then pushed herself high into the air. When she hit the floorboards, the pan ice heaved, groaned, and cracked. Dena grinned triumphantly, then laughed, her brown eyes radiating sheer delight, and she motioned for me to follow quickly.

This time, it felt as if I were swimming through ice soup. Tiny blades of ice ricocheted off my body. With a quick sigh, I made it through that section. But a large berg was now directly beside us. There was no way I could swim over it, so I decided to stop for a moment and let it slide pass. That was a mistake. The icy cold water quickly seemed to pull the warmth from the marrow of my bones.

We were about halfway across the Muir Inlet now, and I was starting to think about the finish. When we landed and I climbed out of the water, the cooled blood from my extremities would be pumped back into my heart. If the blood was too cold, it could cause my heart to beat irregularly. Getting cold now could have more serious consequences later. In the afterdrop phase, I could go into severe hypothermia and pass out, or my heart could stop. So far I felt I was okay. Actually, my confidence was growing. It was really strange; I could feel heat from my abdomen as if it were a radiator, and I could feel it moving up through my body. I dipped my chin into the water, then my lips and face. Instantly my face went numb, but I didn't get a headache. I tried again, longer this time. The water tasted sweet, just a little salty. Glacier Bay was different from any waterway I'd ever swum. My lips were numb.

Jeffrey Cardenas looked at me from the boat; I could tell he was becoming increasingly concerned. We had traveled around the world together, and we had become good friends. Jeffrey had been the person who had suggested this area; he said it would be an incredible spot for a swim. Jeffrey knew that my original plan had been to keep my head up during the entire swim. Knowing that a person loses up to 80 percent of their body heat through their head, I'd thought I would be able to keep my body temperature up by keeping my head up. But during the crossing I changed my mind.

"Are you okay?" Cardenas shouted. His

teeth were chattering. He was from Florida, and he didn't like the cold.

"I'm fine. Just experimenting," I said between quick breaths. My neck and shoulders were sore from holding my head up for so long. But I also wanted to see what I was capable of doing. I needed to know for the Bering Strait. The farther I could push myself now, the more I would know.

Kicking my feet to increase my tempo and to get my numb arms to turn over faster, I put my head down for a couple of minutes and sprinted. My face ached. But I could do it. I lifted my head and looked around. Dena was waving at me again, telling me to swim around another iceberg.

When I cleared it, I put my head down again. My face was already numb, so it didn't feel as cold this time. I counted my strokes up to one thousand. This time my face was in for maybe three minutes.

Jeffrey Cardenas shouted, "I thought you were going to swim all the way with your head up." He was worried. I think he thought I was losing it, or on the verge of hypothermia.

It took so much additional energy to talk. "Don't worry. I'm okay. I just need to see what I can do," I said.

He looked at me through his Nikon's long

lens. "Your face is bright red and swollen. So are your shoulders. Your lips aren't purple, and I don't see any discoloration in your shoulders."

"Thanks, Jeffrey." He was telling me I wasn't hypothermic. That was very good news.

I continued sprinting. We were three-quarters of the way across the inlet, and to our left, the Riggs Glacier was calling. Wind-driven plumes of snow were rising above the glacier's face. Massive chunks of ice were exploding into pieces as they tumbled into the inlet with such force that the waves reached us in a matter of minutes. They were a couple feet high, making the icebergs twist, turn, and bob around us. Swimming around them became trickier. We had to give them more space — they were becoming tipsy and they could roll over on Matkin and submerge her or me. We watched more intently, reacted more rapidly. The intensity of this swim was like nothing I had ever experienced. It was unbelievable. There was so much to be aware of, and yet, throughout it all, I had to stay absolutely focused on how my body was responding. The icebergs I passed seemed to be exhaling breaths of icy air. Despite the cold, I was enjoying the swim. It was absolutely beautiful, seeing the icebergs dancing in the water currents, watching them as they changed colors — blue, green, white, silver, and gold — and brightened with light and deepened with shadow.

The Muir Inlet was like a natural amphitheater as the wind in the bay increased to five knots. The sounds of the moving ice, creaking and moaning, grew louder, and with the movement of the water and wind, the earth and trees, the high notes became sweeter and longer sustained. We were listening to a symphony of Alaska sounds. This was something I had never heard before, something I had never imagined, something beautifully new.

Koshman checked the thermometer and noted that the air temperature had dropped to thirty-three degrees. The sun's warmth was completely extinguished by thick gray clouds. If the temperature dropped any further, we would have real problems with pan ice and getting back home.

My feet, arms, and legs felt like stumps, and for the first time I noticed sharp, cold pain shooting into my armpits. Matkin and I approached another iceberg and she motioned for me to go left. But I didn't follow her. She had taken a course against the current that added twenty yards. It would take too much effort. Instead, I swam right toward the iceberg, thinking that the current would move it out of my way before I reached it. Poor physics. The iceberg and I were moving downstream at the same speed. Caught on an underwater ledge, I had to drag my chest, stomach, and legs off the iceberg, and it felt like I was sliding naked down a snowbank covered with rough ice crystals and nodules.

Matkin broke through another ice panel and pulled ahead. By the time I reached the panel, it had twisted completely around in the current. There wasn't time for me to swim around it; I was too cold, too tired. It was thicker than the pan ice from before, and I knew I had to break it with my arms. I was scared. I lifted my arm and slammed it down against the ice. It didn't break. I tried again. It hurt a lot. I was glad my arm was already numb. I took three quick strokes and used the weight of my body to break through it, the ice splintering around me.

"Swim closer to me," Matkin urged, pulling her red cap down tightly on her head.

This time I listened to her and stayed right behind her stern.

Debbie and Jeffrey were leaning over the boat's railing, shouting ice warnings for us and for Fritz. We continued twisting and turning, abruptly shifting from one direction to the other, until we were four hundred yards from the landing point. I began sprinting with my head down, with all the strength I had remaining. I didn't see the iceberg on my left and I smacked my left hand into it. The impact and pain rang through my arm and body, and I shouted a curse into the water. Oh, it hurt. I scraped the torn skin off, and my arm was bleeding.

I couldn't afford to stop and examine the wound, but looking down through the water, I tried to determine how bad it was without interrupting my stroke. I couldn't see anything. The water was filled with glacial silt, and it was milky white and opaque. *It's okay. It doesn't matter,* I told myself. *We're almost three hundred yards from shore.* I looked down the beach. *Maybe I can swim to that next beach. It's another half a mile. That would increase my distance by half, and it would help me see if the Bering Strait is really possible. Maybe I can push farther.* "How are you feeling?" Jeffrey called from the boat. I couldn't feel my arms or legs or my face; they were numb. And my eyes ached.

Maybe I can go farther. That's not a good idea. Because if you do, and you're okay, you'll want to go farther again. What's wrong with that? You can't feel your body. You're ice-cold. Can you imagine what's going to happen when you stop swimming? I don't want to think about that. Right, and it's going to be worse if you keep going. Remember, you have to think of the afterdrop. You're going to get colder if you continue. The cold will penetrate deeper when you're tired. You had better stop now. I know. But I really want to try it. The crew's watching me. Sure they are, and they're making sure you're coherent, but your brain could have cooled down without them or you knowing it. And you know that's bad news. You may be losing your sense of judgment without knowing it. And that means you could push yourself too far. Remember what happened to David Yudovin on his Anacapa attempt? He thought he was fine. He had no idea he was dying. His brain had cooled down and he lost all sense of reality. I think I'm okay. Sure, but if you cut right and head for that other beach, you'll be riding the current, and you'll be in this iceberg-filled water for at least twenty more minutes. You've been going flat out for more than half an hour. And this cold is sapping your energy. Do you really think you can continue? Do you think you can make that shore? No. I'm too cold. Okay, then you'd better get out. But where am I going to get a chance to swim in water as cold as this before the Bering Strait? I don't know. But you'd better be satisfied with what you've done today. You'll find another time to test yourself. Honestly, you've reached your limit. Be happy. You've made it. You're fifty yards from shore.

It looked like it would be an easy landing, but the current along the shore suddenly increased, and there was a cluster of icebergs and huge boulders clogging the entrance to the shore. We tried, but the ice pack was so tight we couldn't get through them. Fritz shouted at Dena, directing her to paddle to the right, to a smaller cove. I was hitting icebergs with each arm stroke; it was like swimming through an ice maze. Suddenly I felt waves of cold rippling through my body. Something had broken. Some defense mechanism that had kept me warm had been breached. Tremors were surging through my body, radiating out across my back and shoulders. *You've got to sprint now. Now, with all you have. Don't let up for anything. I can't. I can't find a place for my arms to move. Then push off that berg with your feet, cut left, no, right — that way you won't have to swim against the current. Go around the berg. But Dena's on my left; we'll get separated. It's okay. It doesn't matter now. You're only ten yards from shore. Keep going. Fast. Okay, careful. There are rocks below your feet. And rocks between the bergs. At least there's no surf.*

Put your feet down carefully. You're not going to be able to feel them at all. They are dead numb. So watch them when you put them down. Don't step on anything that can hurt them. You're fine. Oh my God, we're almost there.

Turning back for one last second, I looked at all of the Muir Inlet. I wanted to hold that image in my head forever. When things got difficult in life, I would pull it up and remember how amazing it was to be there, to push the limits with the crew, and remember how inspiring the entire experience was.

When my body cleared the water, I could hear the crew cheering. *Remember, you're going to have a big blood-pressure shift when you go from lying down to standing up. It's going to make you feel dizzy. Whoa, wow, the world feels very unsteady. Whoa, I think I'm going to fall on my face. Stick your arms out, just get your balance. Ah, there's Dena. Oh, she's putting a blanket over your shoulders. She's holding your shoulder, helping you balance. Smile. Your hand, it's bleeding — just a superficial cut, and water always makes it look worse. You're okay, right? Your entire body's numb and you're shaking so hard your head's bouncing, but you're okay, right? Yes. Okay, then, get back into the boat. Look, Fritz is pulling onshore. Debbie has the hot-*

water bottles to put under your arms, the back of your neck, and your groin area to start rewarming.

You can crawl into the sleeping bag now with the hot-water bottles and a blanket. Won't that feel great?

Oh, yes, I'm so cold. It will feel wonderful. I'm breathing so fast and hard. My body is shivering hard; my muscles are instinctively working to make heat. Okay, stop thinking and just get into that bag and get warm. The air temperature now has to be below freezing. Ah, they have the heat on belowdecks. Wow, how wonderful it feels to be immersed in swirls of heat. Fritz must have put the heater on full force. I can feel my body thawing. It's going to feel like pins and needles all over, but it won't be that way for long, and then you'll be warm and you can rest. Hot chocolate. That would taste so good, once I can feel my lips and tongue. Dena and Debbie are all smiles. They did so well. What an incredible team. Jeffrey must be on deck with Fritz. I can feel the boat turning; he's probably helping Fritz spot ice. Hope that we can get out of here okay.

"Dena, did anyone get my time for the swim?"

"Yes, you were in the water for twenty-eight minutes. You've changed a lot of minds about people's ability to handle the cold," she said, her voice high with excitement.

I felt so fortunate that I had been able to find a group of people who thought of what could be instead of being stuck on what was. That's where progress came from, imagining the possibilities. Alaskans were like that, though. Maybe because of the openness of their environment or maybe because of the danger of it, they had to find new ways to work together to survive. They lived a lot on the outer edge, so I think that's what made it easier for them to understand what I wanted to do and then to embrace it.

After the swim, Dena told me that I had swum in thirty-eight-degree water. It took me at least two hours of shivering to get my body temperature back to normal. We took it immediately after I got out of the water, and it was the same as when I'd started the swim. I'm sure it dropped once the swim was over, but I wasn't interested in trying to get a temperature by that point; all I wanted to do was to get warm.

When we reached Gustavus, we celebrated with a great Alaskan salmon dinner — you are what you eat. All of us were happy and satisfied. A day later, Jeffrey Cardenas and I flew to San Francisco so I could finish my around-the-world swim with a crossing of the Golden Gate. It was a fun, current-filled swim. It was challenging, and it was so beautiful to swim through San Francisco Bay.

When I got home to southern California I knew that the Bering Strait might be possible. I knew that I could swim one mile in thirty-eight-degree water. Could I swim five times as far in water that cold? Could I swim if the water temperature was colder? I wasn't sure, but I was sure that the only way I would ever know was if I tried.

16

Facing the Bomb

Pulling my hood over my head, zipping my raincoat, and stepping out of the taxi, I ran across Green Street through a series of puddles and gutter spray, to the black wrought-iron fence rimming the perimeter of the Soviet consulate in San Francisco. It was the spring of 1986, and for ten years I had been working, nearly every day, on trying to obtain permission from the Soviets to swim across the Bering Strait.

I had written to Brezhnev, Chernenko, Andropov, and Gorbachev, as well as ambassadors and other diplomats. No one in the Soviet Union, at the Soviet embassy in Washington, or at our embassy in Moscow had responded to my inquiries. At the time, there was only one man at the State Department who believed that I had any chance of getting permission. But then a friend put me in touch with Armand Hammer.

During our meeting, Dr. Hammer agreed to contact Alexander Terehkin, the cultural attaché at the Soviet consulate in San Francisco. After six phone calls, I finally reached him, and we set a time to meet.

When I heard the gate at the Soviet consulate, and then the heavy metal door, clang shut and lock behind me like a prison door, I began to perspire and shake. Deep down, I was scared to death of the Soviets. When I was a child, we'd be drilled by our teachers to duck under our desks and cover our heads. This, we were told, would protect us from nuclear missiles. Even then, I knew we weren't being told the truth, that my teacher was lying. It was a lie she wanted to believe, one she wanted everyone to believe, but I didn't. My father was a radiologist, and he used to let me accompany him to the office, where he put on a heavy lead jacket to take X rays. X rays and radiation were dangerous; they could kill people.

I knew my parents were just as afraid of the Soviets as everyone else was. During the Cuban Missile Crisis, my parents had the radio or television on throughout the day and night. They tried not to show their fear, but people were talking about the end of the earth, how if the Soviet Union dropped a bomb on us, all of us would die. Everything, all the animals and plants, would die too. I didn't want that to happen to me or my family or friends or my dog, Beth. Why did Khrushchev want to drop a bomb on us? Why was Castro letting him put nuclear missiles in Cuba? Watching Walter Cronkite on television and listening to him, and seeing President Kennedy's face blank of emotion, his voice filled with controlled tension, as if he were really angry or frightened or both, made me really scared. At night, when I heard the engine sounds of an airplane flying above, I wondered if it would be my last night on earth, and I would hug my dog, Beth, praying that it was just another airplane. Why did they want to hurt us? Why couldn't we be friends with them?

Standing in a narrow, stark-white waiting room inside the Soviet consulate, I felt like I was alone. I was now in Soviet territory and I was nervous about being there.

Somehow I got my feet to start moving again. Stepping carefully across the wooden floor in my high heels, afraid I would slip and fall, I walked over to a bulletproof window and smiled at a Soviet man in uniform sitting behind the glass. I asked if I could please meet with Mr. Terehkin. Unsmiling, the Soviet guard picked up the phone and dialed an extension. I really wanted to turn around and leave. In the Soviet consulate, I knew I was standing on Soviet soil, and it was just frightening. None of these thoughts were helpful at all. But more than anything, I wanted to believe that the Soviet Union wasn't the evil empire. Soviet citizens were people like us. Why did they have to be enemies? Why did we have to fear them?

For at least five minutes the man behind the bulletproof glass memorized my passport, noting every stamp and visa. He wrote the information into a ledger. Then he picked up the passport again and compared it with my face. Staring directly at me, it seemed as if he were memorizing every feature. Finally he asked for my handbag. He poured everything out on his desk and went through it item by item. I offered him one of the wintergreen Life Savers, but he declined, shaking his head as if to say, Don't bother me.

Nothing could have prepared me for the moment when I met a real live Soviet official. My impression of Alexander Terehkin was: *This man looks like a thin Santa Claus.* He had beautiful white hair, bright blue eyes, a rosy complexion, and a wonderful smile. When he extended his hand and enthusiastically shook mine, my fear was almost completely converted to excitement. Mr. Terehkin led me into a small, musty room with heavy red drapes, opulent dark wooden furniture, and a plush Oriental carpet, and offered me a chair. The room was dim, the drapes were drawn so no one could see into or out of the room, and high in the right-hand corner of the room, near the ceiling, was a tiny, almost imperceptible red light. It was blinking. Beneath the light was a video camera, and it was focused on us.

Instead of being afraid or paranoid, I decided, this was my chance to take full advantage of the situation, to be bold and explain concisely to Mr. Terehkin, and whoever would see the video, what I wanted to do and why I wanted to do it. Mostly, this was my chance to let the Soviets know that my motives were straightforward and genuine.

Mr. Terehkin offered me a chair directly below the camera, and then sat down behind a large, imposing desk. For a moment he excused himself; he put on his reading glasses and glanced at a letter from Dr. Hammer. He asked me if I had been in touch with Mr. Potemkin, the cultural attaché at the Soviet embassy in Washington. I explained that I'd tried to reach him by letter and by phone at least five times. In fact, I told him I had begun writing to Soviet officials in 1976, beginning with Brezhnev, then Chernenko, Andropov, and finally Gorbachev. When there was no response, I wrote to Anatoliy Fedorovich Dobrynin, the Soviet ambassador to the United States. At the same time I wrote letters to President Reagan, Secretary of State George Shultz, Assistant Secretary of State Rozanne Ridgway, U.S. Ambassador to the Soviet Union Arthur Hartman, and the Soviet desk at the State Department. When there was no response, I wrote to Senators Frank Murkowski and Ted Stevens from Alaska, and Steve Cowper, the governor of Alaska. When I couldn't get through to them, I contacted Congressman Dan Lungren, the pianist Vladimir Horowitz, the astronauts involved in the joint Soviet-U.S. space mission, and other people who were known for having some contact with the Soviet Union.

I did get a call from Congressman Lungren's office saying that they would like to help, but I hadn't heard back from them yet. And Vladimir Horowitz had called me from New York City and told me that I was on the right track. He couldn't suggest anything further I could do. But his call had given me confidence that it was a good idea to pursue the Bering Strait crossing.

As I spoke, Mr. Terehkin's interest increased; he smiled and nodded, and I could tell he was impressed with the time I'd spent and the number of contacts I had made. He asked me a number of questions about where and when I wanted to swim, and now my heart was pounding in my chest from sheer excitement. For so many years I had tried to get someone who could do something to listen, to understand, and Mr. Terehkin was perched upright in his chair, listening to every word.

He asked me about my background and what I had done to prepare, and he looked astonished when he found out I had swum the English Channel. Oh, but that was just the start of it all. The more questions he asked, the more excited I became. He was really interested. I spoke faster and faster, and sometimes had to slow myself down to make sure he understood. Then I got to the most important point, the part I hoped he would understand more than anything else.

"This swim is meant to be a gesture of goodwill between the United States and the Soviet Union, to open the border between the two countries," I said.

Mr. Terehkin jumped as if he had been struck by a lightning bolt. He drew in a deep breath, rocked back in his chair, and grinned like a Cheshire cat. He loved the idea; I could just tell. I was so scared he would say no, but I had to ask; that was why I was here, that was the whole point of going through all of this for so many years. So I asked, "Do you think your government will give me permission to make this swim?"

Slowly he sat up and leaned forward in his chair. He removed his glasses, rubbed his eyes, set his glasses on the desk, and let out a deep, long breath. "It's a very complicated situation. Where you intend to land, it is a very sensitive area," he said. But I could tell he was contemplating the idea.

"I know it is. But we can work with your government and we can find an area on Big Diomede that is less sensitive," I said, trying to show that I was willing to work with him any way I could.

Mr. Terehkin nodded, but he was looking far away, into some open space.

I waited until I couldn't hold back any longer, and then I nearly whispered, because I was afraid he might say no and I didn't want to hear that. "Do you think it's possible?"

He brought his eyes back and looked at

me. A smile came to his lips, and he nodded slowly.

"Yes, yes, I do. It's a very good idea. I will forward this information on to Moscow today," he said emphatically.

We stood up to shake hands and I gave him a bear hug instead — I couldn't help myself. "Thank you. Thank you!" I said.

He held on to me and we laughed together. He was grinning. The idea was growing on him. "This is a very good idea. I will call you as soon as I hear from Moscow. But if you don't hear back from me this week, please call me. Here's my card. And please call me Alexander." He handed me his card with a big smile.

It was amazing. I felt like I was starting a friendship with a man from the Soviet Union. And I didn't want to lose contact with him. He was really the only person who now believed in this. "Alexander, if I have difficulty reaching you, is there a second number I can call?"

"I've given you my direct line. You will have no problem," he said. Then he opened the door, collected my passport and bag, and handed them to me. "It was a great pleasure meeting you. I will call you as soon as I hear anything. But don't forget, you can call me too."

We shook hands again. I was so excited, I don't even remember how I got out of the consulate. All I heard was the door shutting behind me with a metallic thud. I stood on the street corner, a little dazed. And then I looked up and let the cold rain splatter on my hot face. I smiled; I loved rainstorms. So much happened during rainstorms. Pulling up my hood, zipping my rain jacket, I jogged down the stairs and opened the second gate. It clicked behind me.

I had no idea what to do next. There was no way I could get into a cab; I had too much energy. Instead, I decided to walk around; eventually I would find somewhere to have lunch. I walked up and down the hills, winding my way through the city, with no idea of where I was or where I was going, just wandering, feeling the wind gusting around me and the rain splattering across my face. It was so good. Somewhere near the Embarcadero, I spotted a large puddle. It was a little crazy, but I couldn't help myself. No one was looking; I kicked off my shoes and danced in the puddle. How can you contain happiness like that?

With three hours to fill before my flight home, I decided to have lunch at a small family-owned café. I sat in a far corner so I could watch people coming and going and ordered quiche with some fruit. While I waited I went over the details of the conversation in my mind, making sure that I hadn't misinterpreted anything. And I noticed a man sitting at the opposite corner of the room carrying a newspaper. He ordered coffee, and he glanced up at me a couple of times and smiled. He didn't really seem to be reading the paper.

After lunch, I randomly toured the city, getting on and off city buses until I reached the Transamerican Pyramid building. With an hour remaining before my flight, I wandered through downtown, window-shopping. In one store was a pair of Ferragamo shoes, and I strained to see the price tag. Someone bumped into me so hard my hood flew off, and I nearly landed on the ground. Someone caught me by an arm. Something dropped. A man — tall, athletic-looking, with short, light brown hair and hazel eyes, wearing a navy blue rain jacket and a beige rain hat — was the one holding my arm.

"Oh, sorry. Did you twist your ankle?" he asked, studying my face.

"No, I'm okay," I said.

"Good. I must have slipped on some mud — so clumsy of me. You're really all right? Have a nice day," he said, releasing my arm and collecting his umbrella.

It didn't occur to me then that this was anything but an accidental meeting — not until later that day, at the airport. Before my flight home, I went into the rest room and noticed a heavyset, kind-looking blond woman following closely behind me. As I headed for the gates, I suddenly realized I had left my book on the sink and returned to retrieve it. When I entered the rest room, the blonde was just leaving. A look of shock crossed her face, and she turned quickly and walked the other way.

On December 22, 1986, a man who identified himself as Dave Beiter called me. He said he was with the FBI and asked if he could come to my home that afternoon to talk with me. He said because of security concerns, he could not discuss on the phone why he wanted to meet with me.

Before he entered the house, Beiter, a compact man with very short salt-and-pepper hair, showed me his identification card. He followed me inside and sat down in a chair beside me, and for the next twenty minutes we talked about everything from dogs to scuba diving. All the while I kept thinking, *What's this all about?* Finally I just asked.

He cleared his throat, shifted forward in the chair, then leaned back in a practiced relaxed and open position and said, "We understand that you visited the Soviet consulate. Could you tell me the purpose of this visit?"

This surprised me. It had been more than six months since I'd been to San Francisco. So I explained the Bering Strait project to him. He listened, although it seemed as if he already knew about it. He began asking a series of questions: Whom did you meet with? How did you contact Mr. Terehkin? What did you discuss? He asked if I had any friends, family, or other contacts in the Soviet Union. Then he asked a question that perplexed me. He wanted to know if I had visited the Soviet Union or if I had any Soviet friends. No, I told him. And then I asked him if I could ask him some questions. He seemed surprised, but he nodded and smiled.

"How did you know that I visited the consulate?" I asked.

"I'm sorry. I'd like to tell you, but I can't. It could jeopardize our way of getting our information," he said.

Then I remembered what had happened to me after visiting Mr. Terehkin at the Soviet consulate: the man from the café, the other athletic man who bumped into me, and the woman at the airport. Suddenly I wondered if these events were somehow connected.

"Why are you asking me these questions?"

"We want to make sure that you aren't being pressured by the Soviet authorities to do something you wouldn't ordinarily do," he said.

"What do you mean?" I asked.

"You've heard of the KGB, haven't you?"

"Yes. I've read a lot of spy thrillers," I said.

Beiter grinned. Then his voice deepened and his expression became serious. "There have been certain circumstances in the Soviet Union where people were forced into situations that were beyond their control. They don't realize it at first — they're only trying to help a friend or family member — but suddenly they find themselves in way over their heads."

"Cloak-and-dagger stuff," I said.

He nodded his head slowly, making sure I understood. "We just don't want you to find yourself in that situation."

"You know, I have to be in contact with the Soviets if I'm going to make this swim. Are you saying that the FBI doesn't want me to do this?"

"No, not at all," he said. "This interview isn't meant to discourage you. We want to

366

encourage exchange between our people and theirs. Personally, I think that this change in the Soviet government with Gorbachev and his policy of *glasnost* is good. I think it would be a much safer world if the Cold War ended." He paused. "If the Soviets contact you again, will you call me?"

For a moment, I hesitated. I didn't want him to think that I wouldn't cooperate with the FBI. I was an American citizen, after all, but I didn't intend to be a part of any spy game. What I was doing was based on trust. That was at the core of my project: trying to encourage trust between the Americans and Soviets. How could people trust you if you were collecting information on them? What was the real reason for Beiter's visit? Was he there to warn me, or did the FBI have other intentions?

He took a card from his wallet, handed it to me, and said, "When you call the main number, it will take a few minutes. I'm in and out of the office so much, the operator has to page me, but I'll get back to you quickly."

I nodded, but I decided that there was no way I was going to report to anyone about anyone. That's what they did behind the Iron Curtain, or maybe behind the "Ice Curtain" between Alaska and Siberia.

"You know, you don't have to feel like you're alone in this. If you have any questions, call me. We can just talk." He patted me on my shoulder and left.

After the interview, my phone began clicking and echoing every time I had a conversation with anyone. Friends joked that it was probably the FBI or KGB. A new friend at the State Department said it was probably both.

17

The A-Team

At the beginning of 1987, I realized that I could spend my entire life working on the Bering Strait swim, trying to get Soviet permission and sponsorship, and training for it physically and preparing mentally, so I decided to set a deadline. Based upon weather conditions, I decided to attempt the swim in August 1987. By April, there was nothing to indicate that the Soviet support would come through.

But on the home front, I was getting replies to my phone calls and letters. Ed Salazar, who worked at the State Department on what was known as the Soviet desk, was the first U.S. diplomat to take me seriously. He called me from Washington and said he was thrilled about my project and wanted to support it in any way he could.

Salazar asked for a summary of the people I had contacted and asked if I was following up with the contacts. My most recent contact had been with Ted Turner, who'd had the idea of creating the Goodwill Games in Moscow, a new forum for athletic competition between the United States and the Soviet Union. I had asked Turner if he had any contacts who could help me obtain Soviet permission. His assistant had called me and suggested that I get in touch with Bob Walsh in Seattle. Walsh was organizing the Goodwill Games.

I called Walsh's office and spoke with Peter Kassander, who had a Ph.D. in Soviet affairs and had worked at the State Department. He was now a consultant helping Walsh deal with the Soviet officials who were working with Walsh and his team to organize the Goodwill Games. Peter promised to relay the message. That same afternoon I received a call from Walsh saying that he would be having meetings with the Soviet Sports Committee in Moscow and would approach them with my proposal. He sounded excited about the idea, knowing somehow that sports could be a bridge between people. Walsh promised to get back to me.

It turned out that Ed Salazar and Peter

Kassander were best friends; at one point, Kassander had worked with Salazar at the State Department. When Salazar told me about this friendship, I felt that finally things were starting to move into place. Salazar agreed, which made me even more excited. Then I told him I'd also written to President Reagan and his wife, Nancy, as well as Secretary of State George Shultz. Salazar asked if I'd gotten responses. President Reagan's office hadn't responded; Nancy had said she couldn't get involved in the politics of what I was doing but had wished me luck. Secretary of State Shultz said he had passed the proposal on to Assistant Secretary of State Rozanne Ridgway. I had spoken with her. She said she would meet with the Soviets on my behalf about the project. Salazar explained that Roz Ridgway was his boss and that he would brief her about our conversation and serve as my point man. If I had any questions at all or needed any suggestions, he would do his best to help me.

We immediately began working together. I told Salazar that I had been in touch with the Soviet consulate in San Francisco and that I had met with Alexander Terehkin. Salazar suggested that I write to him as well as Mr. Potemkin, the cultural attaché at the

Soviet embassy, with updates on my progress and news about my contacts with Bob Walsh and the Goodwill Games.

What we were working toward at that point was simply a response from the Soviets. Would they permit the swim to happen? We waited. On a daily basis I began talking with Salazar, Kassander, Evans, and Bob Walsh's assistant, Gene Fisher, discussing what to do next. I also kept writing more letters and making more phone calls. Eventually, they began talking to one another, and they came back with suggestions for me. This team knew how the world worked and how the Soviets worked, and they gave me insights into how our government and the Soviet government worked. With their help, I started getting calls back from the Soviets.

Then a call came from Congressman Dan Lungren's office. Lungren said that his office had sent letters to the Soviet embassy as well, and they would let me know when they heard anything. Meanwhile, Bob Walsh met with Mr. Gramov of the Soviet Sports Committee in Moscow. Gramov was thrilled with the idea, and he put his best man, Alexander Kozlovsky, in charge of the project. Kozlovsky began contacting the Soviet Foreign Ministry, the KGB, military officials, the governor of Siberia, various diplomats, and people within the Soviet Sports Committee. His job was to secure Soviet permission; if he managed to get it, he would be in charge of organizing the swim from the Soviet side.

Kozlovsky was given carte blanche by Mr. Gramov to do and to spend whatever he needed to on this project. At that point, I didn't know all of this, only that Mr. Kozlovsky was our guy on the inside trying to get Soviet support.

One of the largest considerations on the Bering Strait swim was the cold and how it would affect me. I had been writing to Dr. William Keatinge at the University of London, William McCafferty's friend who was the world's foremost expert on hypothermia. Dr. Keatinge wrote to me and said that yes, he would like to come on the swim and provide medical backup. He could also use the swim as an opportunity to take my core temperature readings during the crossing, information that would be very useful in his research on hypothermia.

I also received a call from Dr. Jan Nyboer. Nyboer was a physician and long-distance runner in Anchorage, who read about me in a local newspaper. He was calling to say he would like to offer his help, to join the swim crew as a medical support person. He also offered to open his home, so that my crew and I would have a place to stay if we needed one when we stopped over on our trip from Anchorage to Nome. And he offered to bring his father along. His father was a world-renowned cardiologist from the Detroit area who had done research on physiological responses to the cold and was very interested in the way blood flow was altered. I thought it was a good idea; my only worry was that his father was eighty years old, and I wasn't sure how well he would do in the difficult conditions. Dr. Nyboer said that his father would be fine. Dr. Nyboer was so energized over the swim that he made me even more excited.

One of my largest concerns was what kind of boat we would use for the swim. When my brother Dave had flown to Wales in 1976, he'd reported that the only boat support on Little Diomede were umiaks, walrus-skin boats. While the distance from Little Diomede to Big Diomede in a straight line was only 2.7 miles, I knew that we would go farther, which meant that we would need some kind of backup for these boats if something went wrong. I wrote to the U.S. Navy; to the coast guard; and to Elizabeth Dole, who was in charge of the Department of

Transportation — I hoped that through her we could get coast guard backing. A letter came from an admiral in the U.S. Navy saying that they would look into it, but he didn't think we should count on their support. Nyboer offered to follow up with a call to Washington to the admiral, and also to make contact with local officials. The admiral suggested contacting the coast guard. So as a follow-up to that, I asked Bruce Evans in Senator Murkowski's office if he would send a letter of support to them as well.

Then a call came from the office of Steve Cowper, the governor of Alaska. Governor Cowper offered to send a letter of endorsement for the project to Soviet officials in Siberia, as well as to the Soviet embassy in Washington, D.C., and to the coast guard. Now there were people in Washington, Seattle, Moscow, Alaska, and Siberia working toward the same objective. One of my largest concerns, though, was how I was going to pay for this.

For years I had continued trying to secure sponsorship from large U.S. corporations, but I had not gotten anywhere. It was very discouraging. Didn't they understand what it would mean to open a market with something like 286 million Soviets? And maybe through this swim, not only American projects could pass through Soviet borders, but also American ideas and ideals. Maybe this could be a way to further bridge the distance between the two countries.

I didn't know the right people in high places in corporate America. Because of support I'd received from Coca-Cola on my around-the-world swim in Iceland and, later, in Japan, I decided to go to Coca-Cola headquarters and try to make contact on my own. I flew to Atlanta not knowing how I was ever going to meet with Mr. Goizueta, the CEO of Coke, but I had to try. I had tried calling but I had gotten nowhere, so I hoped that appearing in Atlanta in person would help me meet with him.

When I got to the entrance to the Coca-Cola building, I had no idea how I was going to get inside. I didn't have an appointment and I didn't know anyone there, but I did have letters of reference from Iceland and Japan, as well as newspaper clippings.

As I paused outside the building, a young man said, "Oh, you must have forgotten your employee pass. Here, let me help you." He slid his card into the electronic lock.

There must have been at least ten women sitting side by side in a receptionist bay at the entrance to the international division.

One kind woman in her thirties with chestnut brown hair looked up and gave me a big smile. "May I help you?"

The way she looked at me, I knew she meant that she did want to help. So I explained to her why I needed to see the head of Coca-Cola. She was very impressed and picked up the phone to call his secretary. The secretary wouldn't let me see him. The receptionist kept working on her, but she could not gain entrée. I was visibly disappointed. I couldn't help it; it seemed like it would work. The receptionist got an inspiration and called the vice president of the international division. He met with me, and he liked the idea, so he brought in his assistant, who had been a swimmer for the Spanish National Team. But this man was totally opposed to it. He had certain money earmarked for his own project, and he didn't want any of it going anywhere else. So they wished me well, and I flew off to meet with two editors at *National Geographic*, William Graves and Tom Smith. I had written to them off and on since 1976. By 1987, they'd said they were very interested in the swim. They had flown me to Washington to meet with them over lunch. I was ecstatic and hopeful that they would embrace the project; ever since I was seven years old I had been looking at the pictures in and reading *National Geographic*. What a privilege it was to meet the top editors at the magazine. I hoped that I could write a story for them.

Intentionally, I got to the National Geographic building early so that I could wander through Explorers Hall, see the photographs on display, and find out where they housed the map section. There, a mapmaker invited me in to see their map collection. I loved maps. Naturally, I asked if I could take a look at some of the Bering Strait region, hoping that I could study a chart or just be able to see what the coastline of each island looked like. There were a few good maps of the region, but no nautical charts. I would have to wait until later for that.

Mr. Graves met me in his spacious office. He was a tall man with dark, curly hair who moved like a hummingbird, in quick bursts, then hovered over his desk. We met Mr. Smith in the lobby. He was smaller in stature, soft-spoken, with a fair complexion. When we stepped outside, he complained of the cold. He had forgotten his jacket, so I offered him mine. He thought that was kind of odd, but he was cold and I wasn't.

During lunch we talked about kiwifruit

propagation. Mr. Smith had a male and female vine, as did I. His were producing fruit. Mine weren't, even though I was using a paintbrush to hand-pollinate them. He had some suggestions and I think that is how we connected — but not strongly enough.

Over crab cakes we discussed the swim. Mr. Smith and Mr. Graves thought the idea was very exciting, but then I told them I did not have Soviet permission yet, though it was already early May. They didn't say so, but I knew that they didn't think I would get it in time. They said they'd enjoyed meeting me, asked me to stay in touch, and added that if it came together I should make sure to take some good pictures. How was I ever going to take pictures when I was in the water swimming? Plus, I had no idea how I was going to be able to purchase a new Nikon on my budget or learn how to use it in three months' time. I flew home feeling frustrated, but then thought that at least I'd had a chance to meet them, and although they didn't completely support my project, they'd shown an interest. And if they did, there would be others, and maybe from that I could gain the support the project needed.

In the meantime I continued working a variety of jobs to earn money both to pay my bills and also to save money for this project, and I continued writing letters to corporations and smaller companies seeking corporate sponsorship. The problem was that no one believed that the Soviets would allow me to make the swim. No one thought that it could happen, so no one was able to support it. How do you get people to think a new way? People were still afraid of the Soviets. How do you make people less afraid? Is it through trying to understand them, trying to see them differently? That's what I thought, and that's why I was trying to do this swim. What else did I need to do to try to get people to understand?

But the Alaskans seemed to understand what I was doing. I got a call from David Karp, who worked at the Visitors and Travelers Bureau in Nome, and he immediately offered to help once I arrived in Nome. He said that I could use his office for incoming phone calls from the people on the team coordinating the project and from the media. Karp said he would try to help us. Aware that I had written to Alaska Airlines requesting their sponsorship, he told me that there was someone there he thought would really get behind the project. Also, in summertime, the only way to travel out to Little Diomede was by helicopter. He would make some calls to Evergreen Helicopter for me.

My own efforts were easier now because all of a sudden there was momentum. Each day I heard something from a team member, or discussed another idea with someone, or sent a draft and had someone read it and send it back with comments.

Gradually the path became clear too. Dr. Nyboer said that he had a patient in Nome named Dennis Campion who was a member of the Rotary Club; he had a teenage son and a home where I could stay while I trained in Nome in preparation for the swim. Dr. Nyboer thought it would be a good idea for me to stay with Dennis because he thought I would need a quiet place away from the fray. So I called Dennis, felt very comfortable with him, and, grateful for his offer, I accepted it. Then Dave Karp called and said he had a friend who had a rental house with four bedrooms where the team could stay.

In the middle of June I decided to leave for Alaska. I had some sponsorship from local companies and individuals. Some of the kids whom I had taught to swim handed me their week's allowance and wished me good luck on my swim. Their parents wrote out checks too. I was so touched. Alaska Airlines came through with one airline ticket, which I used for Dr. Keatinge; an outdoor clothing company gave us some sleeping bags; Quaker Oats gave me a check for five thousand dollars; and Johanna Zinter, a friend from Los Alamitos, had T-shirts made and sold them to raise money for the swim. The local high school swim team did a swim-a-thon and raised $230. Friends sent checks, and so did some people I had never met before but who believed in what I was trying to do. It was wonderful and very humbling. I knew I would think of all of them often, especially whenever I hit a major stumbling block.

All of this was helpful, but it wasn't nearly enough pay for the project. Once again I asked myself, How can anyone believe in me unless I believe in myself? So I emptied out my bank account. That, along with the contributions, paid for the crew's transportation, the rental house, food, phone calls, a helicopter (if we could get a group rate), and the support boats (if they were reasonably priced). Unfortunately, I didn't have enough to pay for my plane ticket. I couldn't take out a loan from the bank, so I took one out from my folks. All of this was hard; it took everything I had, emotionally, physically, and financially.

Dr. Keatinge called and confirmed that he would provide the medical support along with Dr. Nyboer; and Dr. Nyboer said he would bring his father out for the swim. Out of the blue I got a call from a man from New York named Joe Copeland. He had read about the swim in April in an article in the *New York Times*. He said we had a friend in common. Joe had a background in fundraising for major events, and he offered to help in return for having his expenses covered.

And I had another volunteer, Maria Sullivan. We had met through the Special Olympics. She had volunteered as an organizer for the Special Olympics, and I'd gone to the games as a guest athlete, to meet with the athletes who were participating.

Maria had read an article in *People* magazine about me while she was in a hospital bed in Los Angeles. She said what caught her attention was what I said about cold and pain — that I didn't focus on the pain of the cold; I focused on getting through it to the other side. She said she was using this idea with her own pain. She had fallen four stories from a building and had broken her back. She'd had rods implanted in her back, and she was just starting to sit up again. She asked if she could help me. She knew I needed support, and it would divert her mind from her pain. I thought about it, and eventually she started making phone calls for us. She had her mother lighting candles at a local Catholic church and saying prayers for us. Then Maria offered to come to Alaska at her own expense to help out. It was a tough call for me because I was worried about her health. Finally I realized that she needed a chance as much as I did. I said I would love her help, but she had to watch herself. I didn't want her to have any problems in Nome. In fact, as a precaution, I asked her to speak with one of the physicians at the hospital in Nome to make sure they could take care of her if the rods presented her with a problem. And I told her that if permission came through from the Soviets, I wanted her to remain on Little Diomede. I was afraid she would have a problem in the umiaks, and more than that, we would need someone to stay in touch with us as well as with the outside world. Maria would take some of her first steps in Nome. And she would become an incredibly valuable member of the support team.

When I arrived in Anchorage in mid-June, Jeff Berliner, a reporter from UPI, met me at Dr. Nyboer's office to interview me. After an hour, he put down his paper and pencil, scratched his head, and said, "So you mean to say you don't have Soviet permission, you don't have escort boats, you don't know how cold the water is, and you don't have sponsorship, but you think you can do it?" My reply was confident. "Yes, I think I can," I said, and a sudden surge of excitement filled the room. It was electric. Berliner shifted forward in his chair and said, "Gorbachev has been talking about *glasnost,* a new openness between the United States and Soviet Union. Do you think he is aware of you and this project?"

"I sure hope he is — I've written to him at least four times," I said.

"If Gorbachev approves of this swim, this action could signal a new relationship between the United States and the Soviet Union," Berliner said. Contemplating the depth of his statement, he shook his head and hurried off to file his story.

As he rounded the corner, I was overwhelmed by his questions. In all my planning I hadn't looked at all of the challenges piled one on top of another, as he had presented them to me. Instead, I had kept everything horizontal, dealing with each challenge one at a time. When he'd asked me if I thought I could do it, I'd had to say yes, because otherwise there would be no point whatsoever in going through all that I had so far. But I still wasn't sure how it was going to happen. I just continued believing that it could.

In Nome, Dennis Campion, Dr. Nyboer's friend, met me at the airport, drove me along the main dirt road to his home, and showed me to the guest room. He immediately made me feel welcome. A large Irishman with dark eyes, dark hair, and a rumbling laugh, Campion was an amazing person. He had traveled the world as a dredger, using special equipment to remove silt from harbors, canals, and, in this case, the gold mines around Nome. Campion had a nautical chart of the Bering Strait, and the day that I arrived at his home, he spread it out on the kitchen table. He was so excited about the swim, and he provided me with some valuable information. As a dredger he was well versed in reading nautical charts, especially in looking at changes in the ocean floor. He pointed out a deep trench immediately off Big Diomede. He said that there was a strong current immediately offshore and it was cutting away at the ocean floor. In summer the prevailing current flow was from south to north; in winter it flowed from north to south, bringing with it pack ice. Campion suggested that I start at the very southern tip of Little Diomede and compensate for the strong current flowing north. In calm water the current between Big and Little Diomede Islands ranged from half a knot to one knot. That meant that I would have to crab against the current, go sideways into it, always angling to the left. I had to do this: Big Diomede was only four miles long, and if I missed the island, I would end up in the Chukchi Sea. There would be no way to turn back and fight the current. The current was too strong, but more than that, the water was even colder there than in the Bering Strait.

That same afternoon I received a phone call from David Karp, from the Nome Visitors and Travelers Bureau. He had contacted Evergreen Helicopters, and they said that they might be able to help with transportation for the swim if we were willing to fly out with the mail. Otherwise we would have to charter the helicopter, and that would be a minimum of five thousand dollars per flight. Flying out with the mail sounded like a great option, since I couldn't afford chartering the helicopter.

A day after I arrived in Nome, I met with David Karp at the visitors bureau and set his office up as the place to take calls from reporters and from my brain-trust team. After I finished making the calls, a man named Larry Maine introduced himself. He knew

David Karp and said that he was a fisherman from Petersburg, Alaska, who'd come to Nome to dredge and sift the beach sand for gold. He camped on the beach and dressed in worn-out clothes. There was a lot of time and weather etched in his face, but he seemed very kind, and that day he offered to walk on the beach with me as I swam. He did it every day, even when it was raining, or there were fierce winds, or even sandstorms. I remember asking him why he had volunteered and he said that sometimes you just need to have someone with you, to know that he cares. Although I never told him, I think he knew how much it meant to have him walk beside me. There were days when I didn't want to swim, especially during the sandstorms, but I knew Larry would be waiting for me. He not only inspired me, he also represented all those people who had sent me their prayers and best wishes.

Person by person, the support was growing. Then Claire Richardson, a reporter from KNOM radio station, began doing daily updates about the planned swim. Soon KICY and other radio stations in Alaska started picking up the story, then radio stations in southern California. The *Los Angeles Times* ran a series of stories. Then the *Orange County Register* joined in, then the *Seattle Times* and the *Anchorage Daily News*. Then CNN did a story, and all the network television stations began calling. The media was intrigued with the idea. But they all knew that nothing counted unless we managed to get the Soviets to open the border. And then I'd have to make the swim.

The phone was ringing as David Karp and I entered the Nome visitors center. It was Gene Fisher, Bob Walsh's assistant. Walsh was in Moscow organizing the Goodwill Games and was meeting with Soviet officials. Fisher sounded excited. He had heard from the Soviets. They had sent a telex requesting the names of our crew members, their dates and places of birth, and their passport numbers. The Soviets also wanted to know if there was anything in particular we would need at the end of the swim. I requested blankets, a hot-water bottle, hot drinks, and a babushka. I later learned that *babushka* in Russian means grandmother, not, as it has come to mean in English, a brightly colored shawl or scarf. The "babushka," I thought, would identify us as landing in the Soviet Union and it would symbolize the brightness and warmth of our meeting.

I asked Gene if this meant that we had Soviet permission. He said it didn't, but we were making progress.

Whatever it meant, to me it felt like a warm breeze was stirring around us after a very long, cold, hard winter — a promise that the ice would thaw and spring would arrive. But we were less than three weeks away from the target date.

My hand was shaking as I dialed Bruce Evans at Senator Murkowski's office. He had just spoken with the Soviet embassy in Washington, D.C., and they hadn't heard anything from Moscow, but he promised to keep the pressure on. He would convey the news to Senator Murkowski and he would ask the senator to put a call in to the Soviet ambassador in Washington with the hope that Ambassador Dobrynin's inquiry would prod Moscow to provide further information and even commitment. Meanwhile, Ed Salazar would check with the State Department and send another prompt to our embassy in Moscow with a request that they touch base with the Soviet Foreign Ministry.

18

Mind-Blowing

Joe Novella, an ABC television producer, called and said that ABC wanted to take a gamble. They wanted to cover the story with or without Soviet approval. They planned to run a preswim story as well as one during the swim, and immediately afterward they wanted to fly me to New York City for an interview. If President Gorbachev didn't know about the project by now, we could send him the news story with the hope that it would help persuade him to grant me a visa.

From an elevation of a thousand feet, the Alaskan tundra rolled out before us in a tapestry of red mosses, white lichen, jade shrubs, and emerald grasses. Woven throughout the land's contours were brightly colored wildflowers, silvery blueberry bushes, and countless clear rippling brooks and streams. In the warm, intense arctic light the land sparkled and vibrated with energy and life.

Joe Novella and Randy Tolbin, his cameraman; our pilot; and I flew north by northwest, skirting the North American continent, bound for Wales, Alaska, the jumping-off point for Little Diomede Island. Crosswinds shook, turned, twisted, and jarred the plane. Looking at the pilot, I wondered how he kept us in the air. He saw me and turned slightly in his seat, grinned, and said, "Don't worry, it will smooth out after we pass the mountains. You know, I think what you're attempting is great, and I am very happy I'm the one getting you to your starting point."

As we rounded the foothills of the York Mountains, our small Cessna cast a tiny, bouncing shadow on the wide golden hills. There was great contrast — we were dwarfed by the magnitude of the environment, yet there was something so expansive about Alaska, something that infused the soul, that made you believe you could reach enormous dreams. It might be because the land in Alaska is so open, untouched, wilder than wild, and bigger than any imagination can hold; or it might be that the colossal size of the mountains, like the Brooks Range in the northern part of the state, matches the way Alaskans think. They carry with them a pioneering attitude, a belief that impossible things are possible.

From Anchorage to Nome, and now to Wales, whenever Alaskans heard about our plans, they did what many others hadn't — they immediately embraced and supported the idea of swimming the Bering Strait, and that was truly inspiring. They made me feel the way our pilot did that day, like we were finally on the right path at the right time.

As we rounded some foothills, suddenly off to the left were sparkling, deep, lapis-blue waters. There it was! After eleven years of dreaming, working, and believing, I was seeing it for the very first time in real life, the Bering Sea. I stared at it, trying to match up what I had envisioned in my mind's eye with the reality of what I was seeing. It was almost too much to comprehend. Yes, there it was — the Bering Sea. It was right below us, so blue, so vast, so wild, so beautiful and awesome. And somewhere in the middle of all that blue were Little Diomede and Big Diomede. We were getting closer, and my spirits were soaring high over the sea.

Studying the water more closely, I tried to tell how high the waves were. But I had no way to gauge distance or height from the air, so I asked the pilot. Rapidly breaking waves, four to five feet high, covered the Bering Sea to the horizon. This was typical weather, and that was sobering information. With only one week remaining before my proposed departure for the swim, we still hoped that we would hear from the navy or coast guard and that they would support the swim. There was a good chance that the water would be much rougher in the middle of the Bering Strait. We had to have a safety net.

To our right, on the very edge of the Bering Sea, in a flat section of land between the foothills, was the village of Wales. Thirty small, dark wooden homes were clustered together around an unusual community center: a three-story-high building painted snow-white and shaped like an igloo.

The pilot fought strong crosswinds and landed us on the runway. As we stepped out of the plane, he said another pilot would meet us for the return flight, then radioed Eric Pentilla, our helicopter pilot to Little Diomede. The weather was very unstable in a village to the north of us, so he would have to wait to see if it would be possible for him to take off. In the meantime, we were invited to stay at the community center.

A local villager driving a beat-up old van

gave us a lift into town. We drove along a narrow dirt road past small, storm-worn homes, most with plastic tarps for windows and doors. I imagined how cold and how difficult it must be to live there all year long. None of the homes had fireplaces, and there were no trees; I wondered if they had electricity or any way to heat their homes. In their backyards were clotheslines covered with the black drying carcasses of walruses and seabirds, and some backyards had satellite dishes. The village looked so small and fragile against the great expanse of land and sea.

At the community center, a young Inuit woman with a long black ponytail greeted us and invited us up to the third floor. As we climbed upstairs, we saw a group of teenagers playing pool and talking. The young woman led us to an office and offered us hot coffee. She explained that about 150 people lived in Wales. The men in the village were primarily walrus hunters. They and their families ate the meat, and they carved the tusks and sold them to tourists in Nome and Anchorage, or used the scrimshaw as money in trade. She was very interested in what we were doing and said that we were welcome to stay the night if the weather did not improve.

For three hours we waited, pacing the edge of the Bering Strait in an icy cold wind. Finally, we heard from Eric Pentilla. He would wait another hour. If the weather conditions improved, he would pick us up, but if they didn't, he would have to fly to another village to deliver mail and supplies. That would mean that we would be delayed in Wales for a day, maybe more. Everything in Alaska seemed to depend upon the whim of the weather.

Another hour passed and we began making plans to spend the night. Then we heard the throb of helicopter engines. The van driver explained we had to hurry. This was only a break in the weather, and we had to get out of town immediately. Clambering into his van again, we were taken to a flat piece of land at the edge of the village, where Pentilla was waiting. Quickly we loaded the helicopter and climbed in. Pentilla, who looks like Harrison Ford but taller, handed us headphones and told us — so quickly that I wanted him to repeat it — what to do if he had to ditch the helicopter in the Bering Sea. He said there were life jackets under our seats, flares, and an emergency kit. But the sense of his message was: I'm telling you this because I have to. In reality, your survival time in these waters is five to ten minutes maximum, and there are no rescue boats between Wales and Little Diomede, so you don't need to worry. If the helicopter crashes, you will die.

Pentilla opened the throttle, checked his watch, and said that if we made it to Little Diomede, we wouldn't have much time there; it was late, and he had been flying all day. He flicked a series of switches; spoke into the radio, telling someone somewhere about our destination; did a quick visual inspection; got a weather update; and opened the throttle further. The engine sound heightened, the helicopter trembled, and we lifted off.

This was my first helicopter ride, and sitting there inside the glass dome, I felt like I was riding inside an enormous bubble. Sunlight poured into the cockpit, warming it to at least eighty degrees. Everything inside the bubble sparkled. Once through the cloud layer, we floated across the intense blue sky with a puffy white carpet rolling out before us as far as the eye could see.

Finally, after eleven years of dreaming about Little and Big Diomede, I would see the islands, and I couldn't wait to get out there. But the cockpit was so warm and the air was calm, and I was enjoying every second of the experience.

At the edge of the horizon, there was a great hole in the cloud carpet. Circling the hole and tipping the helicopter forward, Pentilla looked straight down. Then he pulled back up, deciding where to descend. When he started down it suddenly felt as if we were free-falling into a giant vortex. It was as if a great whirlpool in the air were sucking us down, shaking and twisting us like we were in a coffee grinder. The helicopter itself seemed to be screaming and hollering as the blades tried to hold on to unstable air. Pentilla clenched the joystick and tried to control it. "It's a little bumpier than I expected," he said, his voice shaking from the helicopter's vibrations.

The wind was plummeting into us so hard that I wondered if it would project our bodies through the glass bubble. Just ahead of us, to our right, emerging from the clouds and mist, was Little Diomede, a cone-shaped volcanic island, rocky and green and seeming to bound up and down on a viscous sea.

"I'm going to try to descend to two hundred feet," Pentilla shouted.

The wind gusts were shifting us from side to side. It was as if we were riding at the tip of a nervous dog's wagging tail. Pentilla fought to hold the helicopter in a straight line, but he couldn't control the aircraft in the windstorm. He couldn't descend farther. Suddenly a gust caught the helicopter and tossed us down to within fifty feet of the sea. Fear registered on Pentilla's face.

The waves right below the helicopter's runners were large. I couldn't tell how high they were, but they were creating choppy air, and the helicopter wasn't responding to Pentilla's commands. Holding on tight, we watched Pentilla and felt the waves pulling us down. Suddenly, to our left, the wind lifted a cloud bank like a huge curtain, and there was Big Diomede — the Soviet Union, less than three miles away. I was too focused on what we were doing at that moment to be excited. Only the image registered — *Oh, there's the island.* The clearer thought was, *Are we going to make it down alive?*

Pentilla shouted to us over the radio, "We're going to try to land on that barge."

The barge was a rusting old ship that had sunk during a storm. The upper section of the ship had been cut off and transformed into a landing ramp. From our position, the barge was the size of a postage stamp. But the island itself was composed of black rocks and boulders; there was no alternative place to land.

"Eric, will you be landing?" a man's voice

asked over the radio. "The wind's from the southwest at forty to forty-five knots." It seemed like the man strongly questioned Pentilla's actions. But so far, all Pentilla had done was show us that he was an incredible pilot.

"Yes, that's an affirmative," he said.

The wind was bouncing us and shaking us radically. Pentilla dropped the nose slightly, and just as we reached the barge, eight feet above the landing area, a huge gust tossed us to the left, way off target. Quickly Pentilla added throttle; the helicopter teetered between flying and falling. Somehow we surged upward.

Pentilla made a second attempt, but the wind tossed us nearly sideways, into the island.

"I'll try one more time. If we don't get down this time, we'll have to turn back. We don't have enough fuel to make another attempt," Pentilla said.

Our necks were snapping from side to side, and I wished I had gotten more out of Pentilla's safety demonstration.

We circled around and descended again. To our right, we could see tiny, brightly painted houses on stilts built into the hillside of the extinct volcano. Below us were two men bent over against the wind, signaling Pentilla with flashlights. He dropped to ten feet above the barge and hovered, waiting for a moment to center the helicopter. Slammed sideways by a wind gust, we dangled over the water.

For a split second I hoped that Pentilla would abort the attempt; but he waited, felt the wind, held out for a pause, maneuvered the helicopter into position, crabbed sideways, and set us down.

We cheered and then sat there, unable to speak, while two villagers latched the helicopter's runners to the dredge so it wouldn't be blown into the sea. Then Pentilla let out a deep breath and grinned. We slapped him on the shoulder. He grinned again and admitted that the landing had been more difficult than he'd anticipated.

When I stepped out of the warm bubble, a blast of cold arctic air nearly blew me off the barge and into the water. Waves were crashing close by, over a small breakwater. One of the villagers, a young woman, grabbed my hand and guided me to a place where I could climb down onto the rocks and land.

Once there, I turned around and looked at the Bering Sea. I was horrified. It was rougher than any ocean I had ever seen. Rougher than the Strait of Magellan, rougher than the Cape of Good Hope, rougher than anything I had ever dreamed in my worst nightmares. I couldn't register what I was seeing. *It can't be like this,* I thought. *How is this ever going to work?* There was no way a walrus-skin boat or even a navy ship could navigate these waters without sinking. Staring across at Big Diomede, I thought, *That island is only 2.7 miles from us, but it might as well be a million.* At that moment I felt farther from the crossing than I had in eleven years.

Novella, Tolbin, and Pentilla joined me on the beach. The air was frigid, it felt like it was going to snow, and the wind was blowing so fiercely we had to shout into each other's ears. Tolbin pulled a cap over his red hair. His blue eyes were tearing up from the cold. He asked me if I was going to train along a ten-yard-long strip of beach.

It wasn't safe to train even three feet from shore. The current was so strong that it would whisk me out to sea. "It's too rough," I said.

Tolbin and Novella nodded like they understood, and I was surprised. They needed film footage, but they weren't going to pressure me.

Following Pentilla, we climbed a steep embankment to the community center, where Pat Omiak, the mayor of Little Diomede, was waiting for us. He was wearing a green-and-white baseball cap that read, "Patrick was a saint but I ain't." He led us down a rocky path to a wooden rack where seven umiaks were stored hull-side up. They were thirty feet long, made of walrus skin stretched over a wooden frame and stitched together with walrus gut, and had outboard motors. Omiak pointed out that the stitches were close together so the boats wouldn't leak. And the hides were replaced every three to five years, because they had a tendency to rot and tear.

The boats seemed flimsy, but he quoted me a price of five thousand dollars. That was beyond anything I could afford. I asked him to consider five hundred dollars, still more than anything I had paid for a boat that would travel only ten or fifteen miles. Omiak said he would consider it, but he had to talk to the boys about it. "The boys" were a group of men who were the walrus hunters, and they were the ones who fed the village. Omiak said he would let me know.

While Novella and Tolbin filmed, I walked back to the edge of the sea. Two young boys joined me. The older boy, maybe twelve years old, told me that no one on the island knew how to swim, not even the walrus hunters. "The water's too cold. If they fall in, they die," he said.

A teenage girl in a red parka with long brown hair and large brown eyes came over and joined in our conversation. When the boys wandered off, she stayed beside me. "We are very close neighbors with the Soviets," she said. "I hope someday we can be friends with them. That has been my dream for many years."

It was as if she was the voice of the child within me from so many years ago. It was as if she had come to me to remind me of why I was there. I had to remind myself that so many things had seemed impossible so many times, all along this odyssey. I had to alter my thinking. If I didn't try, everything would be lost. Oh sure, I'd learned many lessons along the way, but my reason for all of this would remain unfulfilled. I couldn't stand that.

"Is the weather always like this?" I asked.

"No, it changes every day, sometimes every twenty minutes," she said.

"So the weather conditions get better?"

"Yes, sometimes the water is even flat. That won't happen today. But it's not always like this," she said reassuringly.

"Thank you for telling me that — I feel much better now," I said.

"Are you really going to swim over there?" she asked.

"I'm going to try," I said.

"No one here thinks you can do it. But I do," she said.

Our takeoff from Little Diomede was white-knuckle frightening, but once we cleared the cloud pack, the trip to Wales was bumpy but uneventful. Novella and Tolbin returned to Nome in the airplane chartered by ABC television, and I flew back with Pentilla. He was tired, and I appreciated all that he had done for us.

A few minutes after we lifted off from Wales, we heard someone speaking Russian over the radio. Pentilla explained that it was Russian air-traffic control. The Soviets had a lookout station on top of Big Diomede, where radar and other military devices enabled them to monitor the Alaskan coast. Our frequency was picking up Russian pilots conversing. Pentilla said that even though there was nothing to mark the border between Little and Big Diomede, everyone knew where it was. If an American helicopter ventured into Soviet airspace intentionally or inadvertently, it would be shot down. Once when he'd been caught in a fog bank, he had strayed across and had a close call with a Soviet helicopter. The only reason he wasn't shot down was that the Soviets were as lost as he was.

Were the Soviets monitoring our conversation? I asked Pentilla. Without a doubt, he said, nodding his head. Smiling, he said the KGB was also listening to us. So I got an idea. I decided to talk to them about the swim, to tell them everything I could about the upcoming ABC television coverage, my crew, and my contacts in Moscow with the Soviet Sports Committee. Pentilla helped by interviewing me over the radio, providing the Soviets on Big Diomede and, hopefully, in Moscow with my background information. I told them we were now just waiting for final approval from Gorbachev.

At the end of the conversation, Eric Pentilla said that he definitely would help us. He wanted to be our air pilot for the swim. Up until that point, Pentilla admitted, he, like the people on Little Diomede, didn't believe that I was really going to attempt the swim. Now he understood why the swim was so important, how determined my crew was, and how much it was taking to make it happen. He said he would speak with the administration at Evergreen Helicopters and make sure we could fly out with the mail. After seeing Pentilla fly the helicopter, I knew he was a very skilled pilot, and with his help I could afford to rent the helicopter.

All night long, I rolled around in bed, trying to figure out what to do next. When morning came, the wind was blowing so hard that Nome resembled a ghost town out of the Wild West. Swirling dirt clouds blew along Front Street, blasting the ice-heaved homes, tourist shops, and businesses that lined Nome's main street. The boardwalk that ran along Front Street was buried under an inch of sand. I didn't want to get up and work out that day. Just wanted to roll over and pull the blanket over my head. I was in a bad mood, really glum, but I knew that Larry Maine, the man who had volunteered to walk with me, would be waiting for me in his beach tent. So I put on my swimsuit and sweats and walked across town, leaning sideways into the wind, holding one hand over my face. The weather was so foul no one was outside. Its bleakness matched my mood.

It was July 29, 1987. More than a week had passed since we replied to the Soviets' telex, providing them with information on the crew and myself. The Soviets knew that we intended to make the crossing in less than two weeks. Something had gone wrong; I was sure of it. But no one on our side of the border knew what it was. Much later, we would be informed that the KGB had denied our request to land on Big Diomede, and they had convinced high-ranking Soviet officials to withdraw their support.

Salazar at the State Department, Evans in Senator Murkowski's office, and Kassander, as the consultant for the Goodwill Games, my brain trust in Washington, D.C., knew something was wrong. They had been in touch with the Soviet embassy, and with Gene Fisher, Bob Walsh's assistant in Seattle, and there had been no word at all. We kept talking, kept working on it, kept trying to figure out what to do. And I kept wondering, Why won't they talk to us?

The media was calling from all over the world. They sensed a big story. Journalists kept asking, Do you think the Soviets will support the swim?

I didn't want to go into the water that morning. Didn't want to train. When I reached the beach the wind was ripping across the sand, lifting it and spraying it along the beach and into my face. *This is crazy,* I told myself; *I'm working out in a Sahara sandstorm. What's the point?* But I kept putting one sand-stung foot in front of the other. Larry Maine would be waiting for me. He'd promised that he would be there. He had said he would. Every day since he'd volunteered to walk with me, no matter how bad the weather, Larry had been there.

Outside his tent on the beach, I hollered his name. He didn't answer, and I hoped he'd be out. It would be better to just go back to Dennis's home and sleep. It would be better to just hide from the world for a while. Then Larry unzipped the green tent flap, stuck one old shoe out, and then another, and unfolded himself outside the tent. He stuck his head out, grinned, and shouted over the roaring wind and surf, "Good morning, Lynne. Ah, look up there!" He pointed.

The wind was tearing the gray clouds apart, and an enormous pinwheel of light was spotlighting the sea.

"If you hurry, you can swim in that trail of light," Larry exclaimed. "The sunshine will warm your back."

I felt that day that Larry was truly a godsend. Bent completely in half against the wind, fighting to move forward and hold his balance, Larry walked on an incline, keeping pace beside me as I swam. Every ten steps or so, he would turn, wipe the wind, spray, and salt from his face, cup his hands around his eyes, and search the sea for me.

The water was turbid brown and churning with heavy sediment and glacier silt as fine as baby powder. It was a tough workout. At times, the sand sprayed across the water and stung my face. And that made me think of how hard it was for Larry out there, just walking along beside me. It was a lot easier for me then, knowing both that he was with me and that my job was much easier than his was.

At the end of a two-hour training session, Larry wrapped a towel over my shoulders and said in my ear, "That was a brutal workout. You did a fine job."

"I almost didn't make it, Larry. Thanks so much for walking with me."

He smiled. "I used to run track. And for many years I was a track coach in Oregon. I found that sometimes it helps just to have someone with you. Sometimes just going through the motions helps you get where you need to go. See you tomorrow morning," he said.

"Don't leave yet, please, Larry. Part of my support crew arrived last night. They've been setting up some research equipment on the beach. See? Over there."

Maria Sullivan, my friend who had injured her back, Dr. Nyboer Jr., and Dr. Nyboer Sr. were setting up a table with Dr.

Nyboer Sr.'s medical equipment: an impedance machine, an experimental device that was supposed to measure changes in blood flow within the body. There was also an infrared device to measure heat-flow changes. They expected to see enormous changes in blood flow and heat flow due to my immersion in cold water.

For more than an hour the doctors tried to get some measurements, and I lay on the table freezing. They tinkered with the equipment, but they kept getting false readings. Maria Sullivan finally figured out what was causing the problem: gold dust.

Sullivan had noticed that when I'd climbed out of the water, my face, arms, and legs had sparkled. A fine layer of gold dust had adhered to my skin, and the gold had caused the electrical current within the impedance machine to short-circuit. When we brushed off the dust with a towel, the machine finally worked, and the doctors were able to successfully run the experiments.

Dr. Nyboer Sr. immediately confirmed that my response to the cold was perfect. I was able to shut down blood flow to my extremities and maintain that closure, which enabled my body to keep the blood around my core warm.

Three hours after my workout, I finally returned to Dennis Campion's home. He informed me that word had come from the U.S. Navy: they could not provide support for the swim. They didn't have any vessels in the area, and they didn't feel it was their job anyway. They suggested that we contact the coast guard, who had a new state-of-the-art cutter anchored directly off Nome.

Getting on the phone, I called Bruce Evans and asked if he would have Senator Murkowski call the director of the coast guard in Washington and request the coast guard's support. The location of their vessel seemed perfect, and I thought, *Maybe this is the way it's supposed to work.*

On August 3, 1987, one by one the support team assembled in the rental house in Nome. As each person arrived, the excitement intensified. Dr. Keatinge, Dr. Nyboer Jr., and Dr. Nyboer Sr. commandeered a bedroom and eagerly transformed it into a medical testing unit.

Stretched out on one bed were an experimental charcoal-heated sleeping bag, a blood-pressure cuff, and a doctor's bag filled with pills, syringes, adrenaline, and a stethoscope. On another cot was a forty-foot-long spaghetti-thin wire — the rectal probe that at the end of the swim would be plugged into a telemetry device to measure my core temperature. On a kitchen table was a portable defibrillator, the infrared heat-flow measuring device, and the impedance machine.

Maria Sullivan assisted them as they tested and repacked their equipment. Maria had trouble walking, but she didn't care. She was having the time of her life. And I needed her there so badly. It was exciting, but also crazy. The doctors wanted to run experiments on me each day after training. And there were phone calls coming in from all over the world, from reporters, well-wishers, even Mom and Dad, whose voices sounded stressed.

In the living room, the journalists — Rich Roberts from the *Los Angeles Times*, Jim McHugh and Jack Kelley from *People* magazine, the ABC television crew, Claire Richardson from KNOM, a reporter from the AP, and one from UPI — set up a makeshift media center and began filing stories.

Then there were the people from Nome. They had been listening to interviews daily about the plans for the swim, and the *Nome Nugget* and *Anchorage Daily News* were doing daily stories. It felt like a wave of interest was building around us and, with it, support. A businessman who owned a mining company called Inspiration Gold heard over the radio that I was trying to find life jackets for the crew in our umiaks. He brought over a dozen jackets that we could borrow for the swim. A shop owner, knowing that we had limited funds, sent over crates of apples and oranges. The local hospital let us borrow whatever medical equipment we required for the swim and said they would be on standby if we needed them. The town priest invited me to dinner to get me away from the crowd, and he said he would be praying for me. The town minister did the same. And then Libby Riddles, the first woman to win the Iditarod, the dogsled race across Alaska, came over to the house to wish me the best of luck and said that she hoped that we could succeed at opening the border. Neighbors, saloon owners, the whole town of Nome, it seemed, came by to offer support or wish us luck or just to let us know they cared. It was absolutely amazing.

Then CNN, NBC, and NHK, from Japan, arrived to do stories. CKO from Canada, the BBC from Britain, and ABC radio called for live radio interviews. Reuters, the *Long Beach Press Telegram*, the *New York Times*, the *Philadelphia Inquirer*, the *Manchester Union Leader*, the *Boston Globe*, the *Orange County Register*, the *Chi-*

cago Tribune, and so many others were calling for interviews. All of the journalists were asking the same question: Will the Soviets open the border for you and allow you to swim? Trying to sound positive, I told them I thought they would, but I had no idea if they would do it.

Suddenly it occurred to me that I had overlooked a very important detail. Our request for permission to land had been for the physicians and journalists, but I hadn't supplied the names of the pilots for the swim, nor did I know if the coast guard would support us. Obviously we wouldn't be able to pass into Soviet waters without our pilots and boats. This oversight was a major mistake and could have blown the whole project.

I immediately called Bruce Evans at Senator Murkowski's office, Gene Fisher, and Ed Salazar. Evans said that the Soviet ambassador had put his other projects on hold, giving this one priority; it appeared that the ambassador had joined our team. He was in contact daily with Moscow, trying to find out the status of the project from the Foreign Ministry.

That evening, my crew gathered with me at the bar in the Gold Nugget Hotel in Nome to watch the preswim story produced by Joe Novella and Randy Tolbin. The piece was moving. They conveyed the awesome beauty and sheer vastness of the Alaskan frontier. They also ran an interview with me explaining the reason for the swim. And then they did something brilliant. They used a film clip of Gorbachev stepping off a plane, and the commentator ended the piece by saying, "The question is, Will General Secretary Gorbachev give Lynne permission to make her swim?"

Now the swim was directly linked with Gorbachev, and we asked friends to immediately express-mail a copy of the ABC tape to the Soviet ambassador and to General Secretary Gorbachev at the Kremlin. We hoped he would see the video and do something to help. We didn't know then that communications had broken down between the different groups inside the Soviet Union or that something else was happening behind the scenes.

19

Debate

After the airing of the television story, Dr. Nyboer Jr., Dr. Nyboer Sr., Maria Sullivan, Dr. Keatinge, Rich Roberts, Claire Richardson, Jim McHugh, Jack Kelley, and I met at an Italian restaurant in Nome to do some serious carbohydrate loading.

We got our menus and ordered; while we waited for the food to arrive, Jim McHugh voiced the question that was on everyone's minds: "If the Soviets don't give you permission to swim to Big Diomede, will you go across anyway?"

This was the question I had been contemplating for the past three days.

"You know, it would make a fabulous story," McHugh said, bouncing a little in his chair, his brown eyes lit up and his dark brown eyebrows pulled up into question

417

marks. He was very excited. He was a passionate, highly reactive guy, a photographer I had met before when *People* magazine had done a preswim story.

Jack Kelley, his friend and the writer for the story, was a strong contrast. He was contemplative, gentle, and very balanced.

Both were great guys. It had taken a lot for them to convince their editors that this swim could happen, and I was happy they were with us.

Jack Kelley pushed his glasses back and ran his hand through his wavy salt-and-pepper hair. He sat back in his chair and objected to McHugh's suggestion. "I don't think it's a good idea. If you cross into Soviet territory, they could lock us up in prison indefinitely."

"Oh, come on, Jack, do you really think they'd put Lynne in prison?" McHugh argued.

"They certainly could," Jack said.

Rich Roberts, a reporter for the *Los Angeles Times* whom I had known since I was fourteen, when he'd started doing stories about my swims, entered the conversation. Rich was a strong, compact man in his midforties, an avid sailor who had grown up in the newspaper business. He knew the way the world worked. And he agreed with

Kelley. He said, "What you meant, Jack, was that they'd put all of us in prison. But Jim's right — the story would go worldwide." Rich smiled, a twinkle in his brown eyes. He was willing to risk it.

"Just think, I could get some great first shots from inside a real Soviet gulag," Jim McHugh mused.

"That is, if you can get the film out," Jack Kelley said, and then laughed.

"We could smuggle it out in Lynne's bathing suit," Rich Roberts suggested.

As Kelley twirled some spaghetti around his fork, he said, "You know, it would be very dramatic, especially if they sent gunboats to meet us. I doubt they'd put us in prison. It would look bad for Gorbachev and his new policy of openness."

"He's right. Lynne, you've trained a long time for this," Dr. Nyboer Jr. said. "You've put a lot of effort into it, and you should go for it." He knew what it was all about. As a marathon runner, he understood the commitment it took to reach this point as well as anyone could.

Suddenly Dr. William Keatinge sat straight up in his chair and said, "Look, Lynne, I think we're all getting a bit carried away here. I've been trying not to make any comment, but I really believe I ought to let you know that I don't think you should swim into Soviet territory without clearance. It would discredit what you're doing, what we're doing. And it could provoke a serious incident."

This was my concern too. The last thing I wanted to do was to create a problem between the two countries.

Dr. Keatinge was politically astute; his father had been a member of Parliament, and Dr. Keatinge had maintained strong ties to the British government. He was right. If we went forward without clearance, the fallout could be really bad.

Dr. Nyboer Jr. was deep in thought, chewing on a piece of pepperoni pizza. "As much as I hate to admit it, I think Bill's right. We'd look like that crazy guy who tried to walk across last winter. He was put in a Siberian prison for three or four days. Then the Soviets figured out he was mentally unstable and returned him to the U.S."

"I don't want to be connected with anything like that," Keatinge said emphatically.

"It would be a great story, though," Jack Kelley said to me.

I sat there listening to both sides of the argument, and I was very torn. Part of me wanted to go out there no matter what happened. This was everything I had worked for. Anything short of it would be very disappointing. The other part said I should just swim halfway. I could then at least make the point that we had tried.

The debate continued for more than an hour, and I kept hoping that the discussion would help me decide what to do. But then it occurred to me that the debate was starting to split the team. The doctors had decided that they would only go halfway, and the journalists indicated they would go all the way. This left me with more questions. If the doctors only went halfway, where was my safety net? Would it be too risky to go on without them?

Jim McHugh pressed the question: "So what do you think you're going to do?"

Finally I arrived at the solution. "I will swim as far as they'll let me," I said.

"Does that mean that you'll cross the border without permission?" Kelley asked.

"I'll decide that when I have to," I said, and thought, *I guess I'm only going halfway. Well, at least that's something. Not at all what I wanted, but at least it will give us a start.*

The next morning, on Tuesday, August 4, we packed to leave for Wales but no flights were departing. The winds were so strong that all flights had been canceled. But we got good news from Eric Pentilla: the weather between Wales and Little Diomede had been terrible too, and he had been grounded. If we reached Wales the next day, we could fly out with the mail.

All day long we waited, as calls came in from all over the world. Interviews, training — it was crazy and intense, and I felt very fortunate that I could escape to Dennis Campion's home and have some coffee with him and talk about his world travels.

On Wednesday morning, August 5, the airport was fogged in. We waited all morning, and at 1:00 p.m. we decided to leave the airport for some lunch. In the middle of the meal, David Karp came running into the restaurant at full speed and said, "Grab your bags — the flight's leaving in an hour. You'll arrive in Wales just in time to connect with Eric. He'll fly you to Little Diomede." David was as excited as we were.

As soon as we took off, I knew that the flight to Wales was going to be rougher than the first. Jim McHugh, who hated to fly, made me laugh very hard. "The editors tell me to ride the wild dragon, fight the hungry tiger, capture the running elephant, and I do all that, but they know I hate to fly in little tiny airplanes. Oh, my mother is lighting candles and praying for me. Oh, this is terrible," he said, and held his head with one hand.

I took his other hand. "Don't worry, it won't take us long to get there," I said.

"How long does it take?"

"Maybe an hour, and we've already been in the air at least fifteen minutes."

He groaned loudly. I talked to him to distract him, so he wouldn't be afraid, and so I wouldn't be either.

Finally we arrived in Wales, just as the fog closed in. Chris Shaeffer, whom I had met very briefly on my first trip to Wales, met us at the airport. Her husband had been posted there by the navy to monitor all shipping and aircraft activity in the Bering Strait. She was smiling when she saw us, assuming that we had been given the go-ahead by the Soviets to make the swim. When I told her that we still hadn't heard anything, she pulled me aside and said, "I don't know if you've heard this, and I'm not sure if I should be telling you, but for the last two days, there's been significant military traffic in the area."

In the middle of our conversation, the clerk from the community center ran over and said, "You've got an urgent call from Senator Murkowski's office. You can take it in the community center."

We ran across the village and up three

flights of stairs. Breathlessly I picked up the phone. Bruce Evans was on the line. He said he had finally gotten a response from the U.S. Coast Guard, and they would not support the project. They said that if the swim was too dangerous, they wouldn't allow me to do it. And if the swim wasn't dangerous, we didn't need them.

Very disappointed, I hung up the phone, only to get a call from David Karp. He had been talking with Pat Omiak, the mayor of Little Diomede, for us. Omiak still had not wavered in his boat-rental fee.

Worse than that, Omiak had been watching Big Diomede for the last two days through the telescope in the community center. The Soviets had moved two ships the size of football fields just a mile south of Big Diomede.

All day and evening long, the Soviets had been deploying ships to the island. They had been digging in, posting guards around the island, and off-loading men, guns, and equipment. Omiak said he hadn't seen as much activity on Big Diomede since the Cuban Missile Crisis.

Omiak didn't trust the Soviets at all. He had had relatives who once lived on Big Diomede; people from both islands used to go back and forth, visiting. But in 1976,

Omiak's relatives had been removed, forced to relocate on the Siberian mainland, so that Big Diomede could be transformed into a tightly secure military installation.

More recently, the Soviets had arrested three villagers from Little Diomede who had been out walrus hunting and inadvertently strayed into Soviet waters in the fog. They had been detained for fifty-two days in a Siberian prison.

With all the troop movement in the area, it appeared to Omiak and the elders on Little Diomede that the Soviets were about to blockade the Bering Strait. Omiak radioed the Alaskan National Guard and alerted the U.S. Air Force. The air force immediately sent pilots up to check out the situation.

When the Soviets saw the U.S. jets on their radar screens, they scrambled their own planes, and sent out fliers to see what the Americans were up to.

Bruce Evans called me from Senator Murkowski's office and confirmed all of this. Murkowski's office had been in touch with the air force and with the Soviet ambassador, and the ambassador promised to find out what was going on.

In the morning, I looked at my watch. One day away from my proposed swim date, and I couldn't fathom why we hadn't heard from the Soviets. I was just about to enjoy a bite of a bagel when Claire Richardson, the reporter from KNOM, ran into the community center, grabbed me by the arm, and said, "Lynne, come quickly, David Karp's on the phone.

"David has heard from the Soviets. Come on, hurry, run! He's on the phone at a friend's house. Hurry, he might get disconnected. He's frantic. He's been trying to reach you all night long, but he couldn't get through, so he called my friend."

We ran through the eerily quiet village and barged into the home. No one was there, so I grabbed the phone that was lying off the hook on a small end table and said hello.

It was David Karp. He started crying. He tried to talk, but he couldn't get the words out. He began to cough and choke, he was crying so hard.

Oh no! Oh no, no, no! my mind screamed, *The Soviets have said no. After all this, they have said no.*

Bracing myself against a counter, I waited for the weight of his words. My heart was about to burst into a million pieces. An eternity passed in those moments as I waited for David to stop sobbing. He had worked so hard on this project. He had coordinated the press, helped with the sponsors, given us his office — he had put so much into it.

Finally I couldn't stand it any longer. "David, what happened?" I said in a soft, soothing voice, ready to burst into tears myself.

He took a deep breath, and his voice quavered. "Gene Fisher just got a call from Bob Walsh in Moscow." There was a catch in his voice; he paused and cleared his throat.

I thought I was going to lose it.

"The Soviets said yes. They said yes. Yes! You can do it!" He was crying again.

"Are you sure? Really sure?" I was completely stunned. With the news about the troop buildup on the border the day before, everything had become so much more uncertain.

"Yes. Yes. They said yes." David was laughing now.

They said yes, I thought. *Oh my God, now I've got to go the whole way. Oh my God.*

Claire threw her arms around me, and we nearly landed on the floor.

"Oh, I almost forgot to tell you," Karp added. "I was able to get Pat Omiak to agree to rent you the two boats for five hundred dollars. I told him it would really look bad if the Soviets came through and he didn't.

You'd better get back to the community center — Gene Fisher's going to call you there."

Claire and I ran back to the community center so fast that I can't remember how we got there. We were gasping for air when we reached the third floor. When the crew saw us, they encircled us.

It was as if a lightning bolt struck everyone in the room at the same moment. The crew threw their arms into the air and exploded into jubilant cheers. It was a wonderfully strange feeling; all the pressure had suddenly been released, but there was no letdown. It was as if the pressure had been transformed into energy, and all of us were charged by it.

The doctors eagerly checked and packed their equipment. The journalists dictated stories, and the photographers snapped what seemed like hundreds of pictures. When Gene Fisher called, everyone clustered around the phone to listen in. Fisher's normal monotone voice was filled with excitement. He said, "Let me read the telex from the Soviet Sports Committee: 'Please inform where Miss Cox is at present time and what day until August 12 she intends to carry out the swim. We need exact Greenwich and Moscow time. We are ready to render assistance. Your group will be met at the international date line.' The telex is signed by Alexander Kozlovsky, director of the Soviet Sports Committee."

We'd planned to make the swim at eight o'clock tomorrow morning — or any of the following mornings, depending upon the weather. "We will signal the start of the crossing by releasing red, white, and blue balloons," I said to Fisher. "If there is a problem, is there someone we can contact on Big Diomede?"

"I don't think so. I don't think there's a telephone on Big Diomede."

"That could be a problem. That means we have to contact Moscow, and that's fourteen time zones from us, right? If we reach Moscow, how can we relay information to Big Diomede or how can they reach us?"

"Here is Kozlovsky's number in Moscow. If there is a problem and I'm not reachable, contact him," Fisher instructed.

"Gene, do you know why it took them so long to respond to our telex?"

"Kozlovsky said there was a breakdown in communication, and their security forces rejected our request."

"How did he get them to change their minds?" I asked.

"Bob Walsh told Kozlovsky that you intended to swim with or without their approval. He said you would swim as far as they would permit. And it would be very embarrassing for Gorbachev if he didn't allow the crossing, because opening the border symbolized *glasnost*. When Gorbachev saw the ABC tape he had Gramov, the head of the sports committee, put Kozlovsky in charge of the project. Kozlovsky said the visa requirements have been waived for the Inuit crew in your support boats. And he wants to know if there is anything further you will need to support the swim."

"Are those ships supposed to be our escorts? They may be a bit big for us," I said.

"They're just a staging area. They have smaller boats, and they'll meet you on the border with them. Anything else you need?"

"Yes, a sleeping bag for rewarming and a babushka," I said.

"A babushka?" Gene asked.

"It's a brightly colored Russian shawl. In many ways it symbolizes the warmth and brightness of the Russians," I said, still not knowing what the word meant in Russian.

What we didn't know at the time was that Kozlovsky and Walsh had been certain that this project would glorify *glasnost* and Soviet relations with the United States.

Kozlovsky had worked night and day, going through party channels; but somewhere along the line, key people in Gorbachev's cabinet who should have known about the swim hadn't heard anything about it.

That left an opening for the naysayers, and they had the power to move in and set up roadblocks. But Kozlovsky was used to navigating around them. At one time, he had been a world champion cyclist in the Soviet Union. He was still a national hero, and he had friends everywhere. Most people knew him simply as "Mischa," like the popular bear mascot of the Moscow Olympics. Kozlovsky promised Walsh he would do his best to see that the project would happen, though it was very late.

Kozlovsky had less than two weeks to pull it all together, and in a country where the normal first, second, and third responses to anything were *nyet,* two weeks was very little time. He called his friends in the highest echelons of the Soviet government, in the military, and at the KGB. He knew how to package the proposal. He copied the American newspaper clippings and had them translated, along with the letter of support from Senator Murkowski, and he called his friend at the Foreign Ministry. He strongly suggested that Edvard Shevardnadze, the foreign minister, contact Ambassador Dobrynin in Washington. Kozlovsky knew that Ambassador Dobrynin's endorsement would push the project along. He also gave the story to the Soviet Sports Committee's public relations department, and they passed it on to the Soviet press. Then Kozvlosky had one copy of the ABC television video hand-delivered to the foreign minister, and another handed directly to Gorbachev's assistant.

On Thursday, July 30, with less than a week to go before the proposed swim, a new answer came back from the Soviet government. Kozlovsky immediately wired it to Walsh's office in Seattle. The telex read: "Your proposal is being reconsidered, and we will advise you of our decision later."

Later? Kozlovsky fumed. How much later?

At 2:00 a.m. on August 1, a directive came from the central government for Kozlovsky to drop everything. He was put in command of the Bering Strait project. His office became the base of all operations, and he was given carte blanche. Everything was put at his disposal — ships, planes, helicopters, personnel, press, and funds, nearly a million dollars' worth.

Nothing like this had ever happened to

him before, and he was having the time of his life. It was like a chess game, and chess was Kozlovsky's passion. He set up a series of meetings with top officials from the government, commanders in the military and the security forces, and immediately began implementing the plan.

On Tuesday, August 4, one by one the welcoming party began arriving on the Siberian mainland. Most of the group had never met, but they had plenty of time to introduce themselves. There was a world-champion boxer, the governor of Siberia, journalists from across the country, a military commander, the head of the KGB for the Siberian region, and one of Gorbachev's assistants. More than fifty people had been sent to Siberia as part of the welcoming committee.

The fog that had prevented us from flying to Wales also grounded the welcoming committee on the Siberian mainland. The military commander called Kozlovsky and informed him of the Soviet team's delay.

Meanwhile, the military commander on Big Diomede built special ramps so the American team could land their umiaks safely without being worried that the walrus skins would be punctured by the rocky shore. Kozlovsky wondered if the U.S.

Coast Guard would be escorting us. He was eager to see the new coast guard boat.

On Wednesday, August 5, the fog cleared and the Soviet team was mobilized. They flew to Big Diomede, set up tents, and moved in equipment and supplies. When everything was in place, they took turns staring through binoculars at the Eskimo village on Little Diomede. For hours they searched the shoreline, straining to see where the American team was.

Then a military lookout shouted from the beach. He had spotted something in the water heading toward Big Diomede. Sure that it had to be the American swimmer, they scurried from their mountainside tents, down a rocky and slippery cliff face to the beach. When the head coach for the Soviet national swim team took his turn looking through the binoculars, he started laughing out loud. It wasn't a human swimmer moving toward shore; it was a seal.

The following morning, on Thursday, August 6, the Soviet welcome party crawled from their tents wondering again where the American team was.

We stood on the other side of the strait in the early evening — six o'clock. The sea was peaceful, and we could see the very top of

Big Diomede's volcanic cone. It looked so close, I just wanted to put on my bathing suit and swim across, but we had told the Soviets we would leave here at 8:00 a.m.

Rich Roberts, Dr. Nyboer Jr., and I stood onshore and studied Big Diomede. We didn't know it then, but the Soviets were looking back across at Little Diomede through binoculars, wondering what had happened to us. They had had three more false alarms — all seal sightings — and they were beginning to wonder if we were ever going to come across. The last thing we had heard from Moscow was that at 8:00 a.m., we were supposed to release our balloons and push off from Little Diomede, then meet the Soviet boats at the border.

The Inuit families sang and danced all night long in celebration of the border opening. At 7:00 a.m., when we were supposed to shove off from shore and motor to the southern tip of Little Diomede, most of the villagers were sound asleep. Looking out of the window from a schoolhouse apartment where I had spent the night, I could clearly see Big Diomede, a snowcapped volcanic cone rising majestically out of the Bering Sea, which was as flat as a mirror, reflecting the wide blue heavens. It made me feel that there were no limits to the sky, and the world seemed to be filled with energy; everything seemed possible. I wanted to go, to start. I was so excited and nervous, so ready, I didn't want to wait another moment. But we needed to wake the villagers and I needed to tell Kozlovsky that there was a delay. I called and reached an operator, but I couldn't speak much Russian, and she couldn't speak much English. She did know my name, though, and Kozlovsky's, but that's as far as I got. So I tried to reach Gene Fisher in Bob Walsh's office. He was on his way to work.

Worse than that, a milky-gray fog bank was rapidly moving into the strait, snaking its way in front of Little Diomede. In a span of ten minutes the visibility to the north and south of us had dropped from one mile to less than half a mile, and I was becoming agitated. I hated fog. I had been lost in it during the Catalina Channel swim and scared out of my wits. If I got lost in the Bering Sea, in water this cold, I wouldn't only be lost, I'd be dead.

Fog continued streaming into the strait, filling it with clouds that were strangling the light. I knew we had to move, so I started to gather the crew together. I asked Dr. Keatinge if we could get started now. That's when I found out that the Soviets and my crew already knew about the delay. Without consulting me, someone in my crew had spoken with Gene Fisher at Walsh's office and had postponed our departure time until noon. Fisher had immediately transmitted this information to Moscow, and they'd confirmed the update. The Soviets would have their boats at the border to escort us at noon. There was no way we could wait until then; it was too dangerous. And there was no way I wanted to delay the swim for another day. Conditions could get worse, and we had only a small window of opportunity to make the crossing. On our side of the strait it was August 7, while on the Soviet side it was August 8. We had only five days to get this off, and then I didn't know what would happen.

Looking out the window, I could see wind ripples on the sea surface. I was getting nervous. Just the week before, I had seen the straits when they were rough, and I couldn't get that image out of my mind: the Bering Sea as a raging hell. If the wind increased quickly, I knew, we would have to postpone the swim. Even though the distance was only 2.7 miles in a straight line from our side to theirs, we couldn't start in marginal conditions. It was just too dangerous. There was no way I was going to wait until noon. I thought that any delay now reduced our chances of getting across.

Dr. Nyboer Jr. came down to the beach to find me. He said that Dr. Keatinge wanted to begin the preswim tests on me. I asked him if he could make it quick. I had changed the plan, I told him; we were going to start the swim at nine. But Dr. Nyboer Jr. didn't think we could get our Inuit crew together in that time.

We couldn't wait. I told him conditions were beginning to change. He said he would go tell Pat Omiak, and he asked me if I'd lie down and relax in a room in the community center so he and Dr. Keatinge could get their preswim readings.

As I lay on the table waiting for Dr. Nyboer's return, I heard Dr. Keatinge talking with a crew member. They had found an uninflated Zodiac and had decided to inflate it and tow along it on the swim. The Zodiac would provide a more stable base for them to hold their equipment and get readings. Dr. Keatinge unrolled the rubber boat, and Pat Omiak began reading directions for inserting its floorboards.

While this was happening, Dr. Nyboer Jr. returned and took my pulse. He couldn't believe how slow and calm it was: forty-four beats per minute. I was doing my best to be calm, but I was itching to go. This wait was killing me. My skin temperature was the same as the air temperature, seventy degrees, and my core temperature was all the way up to 100.7, three degrees above my normal temperature. My mind must have told my body to turn up the heater.

Dr. Keatinge handed me a large silver capsule and explained that it was the thermopill, a metal pill the size of a horse pill that contained a radio transmitter. This device would measure my internal temperature. As backup, I would insert a thin rectal probe connected to a twenty-foot-long lead that would be coiled up in the bottom of my swimsuit. To get a body-temperature reading, the doctors would have me roll over onto my back while they held a receiver attached to a long broomstick near my stomach, to get a transmission from the thermopill.

Dr. Keatinge handed me a large cup of coffee, explaining that some subjects had difficulty swallowing the thermopill. I wasn't worried about swallowing; I was more concerned about getting it out afterward. But I wasn't sure how to ask Dr. Keatinge this delicate question.

Fortunately, he volunteered the information. The pill was worth about a thousand dollars, and Dr. Keatinge wanted me to recover it once it passed through my system. He told me that a plastic bag worked nicely for the recovery phase. I hesitated before I swallowed it, wondering, Was this pill new or had it been used? Dr. Keatinge assured me that it was new. They wanted to sterilize it and reuse it for future experiments and to check the calibrations after the swim.

Everyone in the village turned out for the swim — the village elders, men, women, and children. Some were blowing up red, white, and blue balloons, while others carried the umiaks from the racks and placed them in the water.

The journalists — Rich Roberts, Jack Kelley, Jim McHugh, and Claire Richardson — climbed into one umiak with David Soolook, their pilot, while the ABC cameraman and Pat Omiak boarded the other umiak. As Dr. Nyboer Jr. and Dr. Keatinge climbed into the Zodiac, the village children released the balloons to signal the start of the swim.

The fog was so heavy it was drizzling, and the balloons sank to the water's surface and floated rapidly northward. No one on the Soviet side of the border could have seen them anyway; the fog was too thick.

Just as we were about to shove off and

head to the very southern tip of Little Diomede to start the swim, David Soolook said something in Inuit to Omiak, then jumped out of the boat and headed uphill toward the village. While we waited, the fog grew heavier and the villagers put five more boats in the water. Pat informed me that the villagers wanted to share in this celebration, so they had decided to join us.

What's going to happen next? I wondered, shaking my head. This created a real problem. None of these villagers had clearance to enter Soviet waters except our immediate crew. None of their boats had life jackets, and none of the villagers could swim. Worse, they were using some of the older boats, and the skins were stretched, tattered, and worn. I voiced my concern to Omiak and he assured me that the boats would be fine and promised that the villagers would not enter Soviet waters. They would only go halfway. None of this made me feel comfortable. And then it got worse.

When David Soolook returned, he was carrying seven rifles. The crew had decided to go seal hunting during the swim. Somehow I had to tell them that it wasn't the right time to hunt seal. I was concerned that they might miss and hit me, or attract sharks, but what worried me more than that was the Soviets' perception of the rifles. What would they think if they saw the Inuit landing with rifles?

David Soolook and his crew were not prepared to relinquish their weapons; they didn't trust the Soviets. So I explained that things were changing, that the reason for this swim was to foster trust; we had to put aside the fear and work together.

After a tense and long discussion with David Soolook and Pat Omiak, the villagers agreed to leave their rifles at home. But by now our visibility was less than two hundred yards, and it was drizzling hard. We were just about to push off when David Soolook again jumped out of the umiak and ran back up the beach. Ten minutes later he returned with a rusty old compass. When he tried to start the motor, it wouldn't start. Finally, after another ten minutes, we were moving.

On the outer edges of Big Diomede, long trailing bands of fog were forming, like warning signs. Fog was gathering into sheets, and trying to see through these bands was like looking through cotton batting. How would we see the Soviets if the fog filled the strait? Where would we meet them? What would happen if we landed in a spot where we weren't supposed to? What would they think when we reached the border ahead of schedule? Would they understand? All I knew was that I had to get in and swim soon, because I couldn't stand one more delay.

By eight-thirty, the entire village had finally assembled by the edge of the Bering Sea. They shouted good wishes to us in our two boats and to the group of villagers, along with Maria Sullivan and Dr. Nyboer Sr., who were climbing into the five additional umiaks.

20

Across
the Bering Strait

We motored south in the umiaks, along the craggy shore of Little Diomede toward the southern tip of the island, where we would begin the swim. Ethereal clouds swirled around the island, and the air was filled with the smell of seabirds and salt and charged with expectation. As we reached the southern section of the island, we moved through a heavy blue fog. Our visibility decreased to one hundred yards; we could just see the shore. It was very rocky, and we could not land the boats. We were afraid that the rocks would puncture the walrus skins.

At that same time, I was thinking of my own skin. *Take your sweats off. Let your skin cool down to the air temperature. That way it won't be such a shock when you hit the water.* I cringed. I knew it was going to be cold, really cold, but I had asked that no one tell me the water temperature until I finished. I didn't want to psych myself out before I got into the water. I told myself, *Be calm; focus on what you are going to do. Don't get distracted, don't get overwhelmed, take it all as it comes. You are ready for this; you've prepared for years. This is it, your time to shine. Go forth with all your powers. Go forth with everything in you. Make it work.*

Oh, shoot. Okay, wait a minute; wait until everyone is in position. When it's time to go, you just want to go; you don't want to stop for anything. The water's going to be too cold. You can't stop for anything. You will lose heat too fast if you do. Don't stop for a second. If the boats stray off course, just head straight. Keep going. Move forward. Sprint. Sprint the whole way across. Stop for nothing. This is it. It is time.

Take a deep breath. Okay, take another one. Steady your heart. You're shaking. You're scared, cold, excited. You'll be fine. You'll do fine. Look at the crew. They are smiling. They are excited. They are so ready too. Okay, climb onto the Zodiac's pontoon. Look, Dr. Nyboer Jr. is offering a hand. Take it. Don't let him see you shaking or he'll be worried. Okay, balance yourself. Let your feet feel the water. Oh, it is cold. Wow. It's colder than I expected. Okay, take another breath. You're ready for this now.

You're smiling. Good. Okay, you're going to have to slide in, off the pontoon. Take a deep breath first, let your body drop underwater, turn, swim toward shore as fast as you can, climb out of the water and clear it, and then shout to the crew that you're starting. The journalists will keep track of your time.

The boats have moved into position. Dr. Keatinge's telling you he's ready. The thermopill is working.

Everything is set. Okay, slide feet-first into the water. You don't want to have a heart attack. Oh my God. It's like liquid ice — The frigid water punched the air out of my lungs. I popped up, gasping. *Catch your breath; swim for shore. Put your face in the water. Sprint as fast as you can. My arms are numb. I don't care. Climb out on the rocks. Oh, shoot, I just slipped, ripped the back of my thigh on some barnacles. It stings. It's bleeding. So what — it will stop. Get focused. All right. You've got to stop smiling. But I'm so happy. After so many years, it's hard to believe I'm here. You'll believe it in a minute when you hit that water again. Come on. Let nothing stop you. Okay, they're ready. Go!*

My heart was pounding in my chest. Hitting the water with a splash, I began stroking as fast as my arms would turn over. Nothing had ever felt as good as that moment. Finally I was swimming across the Bering Strait from the United States to the Soviet Union. I swam with absolute elation. My strokes — what I could feel with numb arms — were strong and powerful, and I moved rapidly across the Bering Sea's calm surface. The sea's tranquillity was in such contrast to the way I felt, so full of energy, of excitement, of utter happiness. I had dreamed, and so many others had embraced my dream. We were doing this together. Sure, I was out there in the water, but I had so many people I carried along with me in this dream and who carried me as well. It was absolutely fantastic.

Within moments, the two escort boats were behind me, and in the fog. I had nothing to use in front of or behind me as a reference point for navigation. Little Diomede had already disappeared in a fog bank. The escort boats weren't following the plan; they were supposed to be right beside me, guiding me. I started to get worried. I didn't want to get lost. I later found out the water temperature at that point was forty-two degrees.

The boats slid farther behind, and the crew didn't appear to know where they were heading. In water that cold, every moment we strayed off course reduced our chances of making it across.

Looking back over my right shoulder, I could barely see Dr. Keatinge and Dr. Nyboer Jr. in their black wet suits. They were fidgeting with the equipment, trying to get it to work properly. I became more agitated. Precious moments were ticking by, moments we would never get back.

Lifting my head, I drew in a deep breath, continued spinning my arms, and yelled, "Bill, are we going straight or what?"

Dr. Keatinge was involved with the equipment, so I shouted again.

"Go straight ahead," he shouted, then realized that I was being consumed by the fog. He shouted to Pat Omiak and David Soolook to move their boats to either side of me.

I was still swimming as fast as my arms would turn over. It was like being on the very edge of life. Every moment I had to be acutely aware of everything, to stay attuned to my body, to make sure I wasn't going into hypothermia.

Looking down through the clear, icy, gray-blue water, I examined my hands. My fingers were together, my hands like paddles; that was good. It meant that I was maintaining fine motor control, and that my brain was warm. If my fingers started spreading apart, that would mean I was losing fine motor control and my brain was cooling down. This was dangerous. It was a sign that I was going into hypothermia, and also possibly losing my sense of judgment. I was okay. But my hands were numb. With each arm stroke, I had to wait to feel the water pushed by my hands against my thighs to know that my hands were pushing water and I was moving forward. I glanced at my shoulders; they were splotchy red and white. The blood from the exterior of my body was pooling in the core to protect my heart and vital organs. I began sprinting, faster and faster, trying to generate more heat than I was losing to the Bering Sea.

Dr. Nyboer and Dr. Keatinge were waving and shouting at me.

"Lynne, swim close to us and roll over. We need to take your temperature," Dr. Nyboer said, grabbing the receiver attached to the broom handle. Dr. Keatinge moved to the opposite side of the Zodiac to counterbalance Dr. Nyboer. I rolled over onto my back and started backstroking, turning my arms over as fast as I could. When I did the backstroke, I didn't produce as much heat as when I swam freestyle. So during this experiment, the cold water was rapidly sucking the heat from my body. It was like standing wet and naked in front of an air conditioner on high.

Dr. Nyboer was trying to hold the receiver near my stomach to get a transmission from the thermopill, but the ocean waves were bouncing him slightly up and down and sideways. A freak wave hit the Zodiac and Dr. Nyboer missed the reading, nearly plunging headfirst into the water with me.

I knew these temperature readings were necessary, to make sure that my core temperature was staying at normal levels, but I was getting annoyed. This was slowing me down and reducing my ability to create heat, and I was losing more now than I was making. I didn't want to wait for him.

"Let's try again. Roll onto your back," Dr. Nyboer shouted.

He held the receiver near my stomach while Dr. Keatinge stared at a digital readout in a black box. This procedure would take only two or three minutes, but that was way too long. It was making me cold.

"She's cooling down a bit. She's down to ninety-seven degrees. Lynne, are you doing all right?" Dr. Keatinge asked. His voice sounded edgy.

"Yes, this is great," I shouted happily, covering my real feelings. I didn't want Dr.

Keatinge or Dr. Nyboer to panic, to think that I was getting too cold. I didn't want them to pull me out of the water. I had to appear warm to them — as if this swim were easy. But I was a little worried. Before the swim, my temperature had been 100.7. That was pretty normal for me before a big swim, but it had already dropped three degrees, and I'd been in the water for only about half an hour. My cutoff point was ninety-four degrees. That was the beginning of hypothermia.

From the onset, Dr. Keatinge, Dr. Nyboer, and I had decided that I would have a three-hour limit in the water. By that time, the water would have cooled my peripheral areas down, and after the swim was completed, my core temperature would fall further. We didn't want it to drop too far.

The fog deepened so that our visibility diminished to fifty yards. The crew was covered in a fine mist, the droplets clinging to their hair like dew and saturating their parkas. Huddling forward, they stared into the consuming grayness. We crossed the border, we thought, though it was hard to tell. There was nothing in the middle of the strait to indicate exactly where the border was. Scanning ahead, we strained to see the Soviet boats, but we couldn't make out

451

anything in the gray void.

The current was pushing us north, and we were cutting across it. Our concern was still that we would be pushed into the Chukchi Sea before we reached shore. Then ghost-like fog blanketed us, constricting the light, and our visibility dropped to ten yards. It felt as if we had become detached from the world, a tiny blip of warmth on an icy, gray sea. We were moving in a void between the two islands. I felt like screaming. I was losing sight of the boats. That fear from the Catalina swim had come back to haunt me, only this time it was worse; it gripped me so hard that I was shaking in the water. I sprinted closer to the umiaks for human warmth. I needed to stay near them. I couldn't lose them.

David Soolook checked his compass and noticed that we were thirty degrees off course. He shouted something to Pat Omiak in Inuit, and suddenly both boats made sharp forty-five-degree corrections to the left.

Now the current was broaching the left side of my head. *Do they know what they're doing?* I wondered. *Don't they realize that every moment we stray off course, we diminish our chances of making it across?*

How could I expect them to know this?

They hadn't expected me to get into the water. They didn't think anyone could swim in the Bering Strait and survive.

Heavy drizzle began falling as Dr. Keatinge and Dr. Nyboer waved me over for another reading. I rolled over onto my back, impatient and grumpy. These readings were taking too long. Every time I slowed down, I got colder. Tremors were racing up my back.

Dr. Nyboer was doing his best, but he couldn't get a reading. He waved me away from the boat, then back again for another attempt. This time I ignored him. I had to start swimming faster, had to stay warm. The point wasn't to be a human subject; it was to get across. This was slowing me down.

A few minutes later, Dr. Nyboer waved me over again. He held the receiver right above my stomach while Dr. Keatinge studied the monitor. The receiver was malfunctioning. Although the doctors were working hard to fix it, cold was moving into my muscles, and they felt like wood. At that moment, I decided I would not stop again for tests. I couldn't afford it.

Suddenly we made another sharp correction to the left. *Why can't we stay on course?* I wondered. *Have we missed Big Diomede? Is that why the Soviets haven't appeared?* We had to be at least halfway by now. We had to have crossed the border. *Where are you? Can you hear us? Please find us.*

I didn't know it then, but Pat Omiak and David Soolook weren't sure where we were. They had hunted walrus only along the border, never crossed over it. So they didn't know what the currents were like on the other side. Pat Omiak asked Dr. Keatinge what heading he should take. Neither Pat Omiak nor Dr. Keatinge knew how far north we had already drifted. Rich Roberts, the journalist from the *Los Angeles Times* who was also a sailor, asked Pat Omiak what heading he was on, and then Rich helped Pat make a critical correction.

The crew searched the fog for the Soviets, knowing that we needed them to guide us to shore.

At first I thought I heard a sound through the water. It sounded like a small boat's motor, but then it disappeared. I heard it again. It grew louder, and then faded again. *Please find us,* I thought.

The sound of the motor grew louder. I could feel the water trembling around my body. I could hear the engine's soft putter. The crew heard it too. The Soviet boat was circling somewhere out there. It was them.

It had to be them! They were searching for us! The putter grew deeper; then the sound changed. They were moving away. *Oh God, no!* I thought desperately.

The crew was shouting at the top of their lungs, waving their arms in the fog. No one could see them, and their voices were muffled, and no one could hear them, either. Jim McHugh and Jack Kelley began whooping. The entire crew yelled. The motor sound grew louder again.

Turning to breathe, I saw Claire Richardson bouncing up and down in the umiak. Jack Kelley was pointing. "Look, there they are! It's them. It's the Soviets!"

It was one of the most beautiful sights of my life. The dark gray Soviet boat motored slowly out of the fog toward us. They were there. Really there. And they were going to help us.

For eleven years I had imagined this moment. I had imagined meeting Soviet sailors in the middle of the Bering Strait. But I never could have imagined the way I would feel. All the work, all the hope, all the faith, all the belief, all those people who'd believed and who hadn't, and now, the Soviets were right there.

"It's them! It's the Soviets!" I heard the crew shouting.

Claire Richardson yelled to me, "What day is it, Lynne?"

"It's tomorrow. It's tomorrow!" I shouted.

We had crossed the border and the international date line; we had reached from the present into the future. We had done it. My goggles filled with tears. Finally, we had found each other.

The Soviet launch stayed at a distance of fifty yards, and the sailors on board maintained stoic expressions. I couldn't understand why they weren't coming closer. Had we arrived too early or too late? Had there been another breakdown in communications? Were they angry at us for allowing the other umiaks to join us? Some of the villagers had come across with us, although during the swim I hadn't seen them. Someone aboard the doctors' umiak said that two of the villagers' umiaks were turned back. But that was expected, as they hadn't gotten clearance to land on Big Diomede.

With the Soviet pilots guiding us into their territory, we moved directly toward Big Diomede. One of the crewmen, a fellow with curly brown hair, wearing a green uniform and a brown leather jacket, introduced himself. He said his name was Vladimir McMillian, and he was a reporter for TASS. He spoke perfect English. I shouted to him,

"Vladimir, is there something wrong? Some reason why they don't want to be closer to us? Please, I want to see your faces."

The crews talked back and forth. I couldn't listen because I had to keep swimming to stay warm. But when I looked up again, both crews were smiling and the Soviet launch was moving in close to us, just ahead of the journalists' umiak. They hadn't wanted to be in the way. But they were smiling, and I felt like we were doing this together now.

"Your stroke rate is dropping to fifty-six," Dr. Nyboer said. "Down from seventy strokes per minute. You've dropped way off pace. You've got to pick it up."

My hands reached deep into the gray sea. I couldn't feel them at all. There was no sensation. *Put your head down. You're wasting time looking up. Focus. You haven't finished. Come on. Pick up your pace.*

Slowly the sun began melting the fog, and the top of Big Diomede Island towered above us. We were less than four hundred yards from shore. That's when it happened, exactly when Dennis Campion had said it would: the current grew stronger, and the water temperature dropped to thirty-eight degrees. My body shuddered. My teeth started to chatter, and chills were crawling continuously up my spine. The water was only six degrees warmer than an ice cube, and my body was screaming, *Get out! This water stings. Oh God, it's so cold!*

Go through the pain. Just swim through it. Don't focus on it. Don't give any energy away to it. Keep focused. Keep swimming. Seabirds nesting in the cliffs on Big Diomede were calling. We were almost there. Fifty yards. I was tiring, and I was so ready to finish. I couldn't wait to get out of the water and crawl into a warm sleeping bag. That thought made me swim faster.

Turning to breathe, I saw the crew in the Soviet launch pointing to a snowbank a half mile south of us.

Vladimir McMillian, the man with the curly brown hair, shouted excitedly to me, "The Soviet people are waiting for you over there. They could not manage to climb down these cliffs. But they would like to meet and see you at the finish."

"Lynne, you can stop now," Dr. Keatinge shouted. His voice was heavy with concern. He was afraid that my temperature would drop more. He hadn't been able to get a reading.

"You know, if you stop now, you will have succeeded," Dr. Keatinge said.

"How far is it to the snowbank?" I asked.

Vladimir asked a crewman, then told me, "Half a mile."

"Bill, it's okay if I stop now?" I asked Dr. Keatinge, trying to decide what to do.

"Yes. Yes. You can finish right there," he said, pointing to a rock.

We were fifty yards from our goal.

"She's heading in to shore," I heard Dr. Keatinge say, his voice filled with relief.

But when I turned to breathe, I saw the bright snow on the beach and I saw the little black dots that must have been the Soviet people standing there. I asked myself, *Will you be satisfied if you stop now? Everything you have done has been about extending yourself, about going beyond borders. You've had to go beyond your physical and psychological borders. Everything everyone has done for you and for themselves to this point has been about extending themselves, too, beyond their own borders, about believing when there was little to believe in. But now you can stop. You're only ten yards from shore. You can stop now and know that you have succeeded.*

God, I want to. I've got to think about how cold I'm going to be when I climb out of the water. I took a few more strokes forward. *You've got to decide now,* I told myself. *In a moment the crew will be preparing to land.*

"You can finish on that rock," Dr. Keatinge coaxed. "It's the flat one. Over there. It should be smooth."

I knew I would regret it all my life if I didn't push on. I turned left and began paralleling shore. I glanced at Dr. Keatinge. He looked surprised, then worried. He must have thought I was becoming disoriented and going into hypothermia.

"Bill, it's all the way or no way," I shouted.

He grinned, and the crew started cheering and clapping and waving their arms in the air. I rode their wave of energy, took it all in, let it carry me. They continued cheering. Oh, did I need their support.

Look into their faces. Look at their smiles. Draw from their energy, I coached myself. But it was really hard swimming. The current was flowing into us at one knot, diminishing my speed by half. We were moving in slow motion, and all I wanted to do was to get there.

Dennis Campion had said that the current might be easier closer to shore, so I angled in. The crew thought I was getting ready to stop. "No. We're not stopping. I'm just trying to find a way to break through the current," I said. It took so much energy to talk.

Dennis was right; it made all the difference. We started moving faster. And then I heard Jack Kelley shouting, "Look, you can see the people on the snowbank. They're waving!" I counted thirty black figures on the bright white snowbank.

I looked at my hands pulling through the water. They looked like the purple-gray hands of a cadaver. My shoulders were blue, the color of blueberries, and my arms, legs, and trunk were splotchy white. They felt heavy, like meat taken out of a freezer. My thighs could no longer feel water being pushed past them. My face no longer felt like a face; it felt detached from my head. I started swimming faster, faster. Looking up, I could see the colors of the Soviet people's clothes, red, blue, green, and black. And they were moving. They were running, slipping on the ice, picking their way down to the water's edge.

Dr. Nyboer and Dr. Keatinge shouted, "Sprint! Sprint in to shore!"

That sure sounded great to me.

The journalists' umiak zoomed ahead as men in military uniforms set out small wooden ramps for the umiaks to land on.

The journalists were leaping out of their boats, onto shore. Dr. Keatinge and Dr. Nyboer were leaning over the pontoon right beside me. Their smiles were very big.

Then I saw it: the sea floor rose up to meet

me. I could almost climb out. There were people, real life-sized people towering above me on the snowbank. They were cheering. And they were speaking Russian.

A man in a green uniform reached down toward me alongside Vladimir McMillian. I pulled off my goggles and stuck them in my mouth. After more than two hours in the icy water, I needed both hands to crawl out of the sea. I tried to move forward, but the incline was steep, and I slid backward. I stepped up. Three men were leaning toward me, extending their arms as far as they could go. They were smiling and shouting in Russian. I leaned forward and reached as high as I could. I felt the warmth of their hands in mine.

A Soviet man was talking to me, draping his coat over my shoulders. A woman with dark reddish-brown hair who said her name was Rita Zakharova was piling blankets over me. They were heavy. My legs were so wobbly. I had to bend my knees to stand.

Vladimir McMillian was kissing me all over my face, as if I were his long-lost relative. Someone else wrapped a green towel on top of the blankets. Dr. Keatinge and Dr. Nyboer were on either side of me, supporting me under each arm. Dr. Keatinge said in a controlled, calm voice, "We've got to get her to the tent as quickly as possible to get her warm."

Vladimir wasn't listening; he was too excited and happy. His mother was Russian and his father was American. They had met after World War II, had married, and his father had stayed in the Soviet Union. That was why he spoke English so well. He was thrilled because half of him was Russian and the other half was American and he had seen with his own eyes the two nations, like the two parts of himself, coming together that day. It was something he never thought he'd see.

Vladimir kept talking, introducing everyone on the beach to me. It was very hard to concentrate. I was so cold, and I just wanted to curl up into a ball somewhere and get warm. It didn't help that I was standing on the ice in bare feet, or that the air temperature was in the low forties. Vladimir introduced me to the Soviet press, but I couldn't concentrate on what he was saying. More than once he had to repeat himself. But his comrades were only too happy to wait. "That man is from Radio Moscow. This woman is from *Pravda*." He said their names, and I couldn't catch them at all.

In the background, Dr. Keatinge was insisting that we head for a tent pitched on a steep hill on the rocky island. But Vladimir was holding my arm, and he wasn't about to let go. I didn't want him to; I wanted to meet everyone there, to see their faces, to see real live Russians, people I had been afraid of all my life.

It was so strange; they were all smiling, all excited, all thrilled to be there.

Vladimir introduced me to a man from *Vremya*, on Russian television. It's called *Time*, like our *Sixty Minutes*. Vladimir himself was the reporter from TASS, he repeated, and then explained that the Soviets on the beach had been specially selected to be on this beach and to greet the Americans. They had been transported from all over the Soviet Union to meet us on Big Diomede. He introduced the Soviet national swim coach, a world-champion boxer, the governor of Siberia, the commander of a military garrison, a KGB officer, and three Siberian Inuit women doctors.

An Inuit woman wearing a bright red parka told me that she was a pediatrician in Magadan and kissed me on both cheeks. At the same time, I kissed her the same way. She was small and pretty, with black hair and delicate Asian eyes, and her lips felt so warm. Smiling, she handed me a bouquet of wildflowers that she had gathered from her village on the Siberian mainland. The flowers were the same ones I had seen on the Alaskan mainland — magenta fireweed, turquoise forget-me-nots, lavender wild asters, and goldenrod. And she said that at one time the two countries had been joined by a land bridge that connected Siberia and Alaska. When the sea rose in the Bering Strait, the continents were separated. She said that she was very happy that I had swum between Big Diomede and Little Diomede because she understood that it was the human way of reconnecting the continents. She was fighting to hold tears back as she said that she had family who lived on both sides of the Bering Sea, on Little Diomede and on Big Diomede, but they had been separated by political differences that none of their families believed in. She told me that after today she thought they might see each other again; maybe this was a beginning. She smiled, and her eyes filled with tears. Mine did, too, and I just had to hug her again and say, "*Da*. Yes, someday this will happen, I just know it."

Vladimir pulled me away by the elbow and said that the Soviet press wanted to conduct a news conference. Would I be willing to talk with them? Sure, I said, but I knew my body temperature was dropping. I was shivering hard, and Dr. Keatinge kept urging me to go to the tent, but I wanted to talk to them, to answer their questions. I wanted to find out who they were. I didn't realize what I was getting myself into.

The Soviet press's questions were direct, complex, and very difficult to answer. They phrased their questions in three or four parts, making sure they could get as many answered as possible. The problem was that each question was translated by Vladimir immediately one after the other, and I was so cold. I was trying as hard as I could to respond, but by the third or fourth question, the reporter would have to repeat him- or herself before I could understand. One reporter from Russian television asked me, "Do you think your swim will contribute to a reduction in nuclear missiles in the United States and the Soviet Union and further the INF treaty? Do the American people really view the Soviet Union as the evil empire? Why did you make the swim? What do you feel now?"

My speech was slurred, and my numb lips weren't helping me speak. I tried to quickly sort out my thoughts and feelings. How could I possibly speak for the American people?

But this was what they were asking me to do.

Vladimir translated what I said into Russian. "The reason I swam across the Bering Strait was to reach into the future, to cross the international date line, and to symbolically bridge the distance between the United States and the Soviet Union. It was to generate goodwill and peace between our two countries, our two peoples. I would not have swum here if I believed that this was the evil empire. I can't say if this swim will contribute to the reduction of nuclear weapons, but I sure hope it does. We need to become friends. That is why I did this; that is why *we* did this," I said, pointing to my team.

The media fell silent and did something I had never seen before from the press: they nodded in agreement.

Dr. Keatinge and Dr. Nyboer were getting agitated. They could see that I was starting to stagger.

"We've got to move her now. She's really cooling down," Dr. Keatinge said.

But the reporter with Radio Moscow asked in English, "Who were the corporate sponsors?"

Suddenly I was embarrassed. I saw all that the Soviets had done — they had moved ships, helicopters, people, everything to this island. Later I would find out they had spent nearly a million dollars. What could I tell them? That no large U.S. corporation had really supported us? That none of them had believed the Soviets would open their border? I didn't want to embarrass the United States.

Thinking for a moment, I said, "Our sponsors were the American people. They were individuals from all over the United States. They were the ones who supported us. And we had some support from companies like Rocky Boots, Alaska Airlines, and Monotherm." My teeth were chattering so hard I couldn't talk anymore.

The Soviet press didn't understand. They looked perplexed. Didn't corporate America, the free-enterprise system, support you? Didn't you get paid millions of dollars for doing this?

I tried to explain that it was the American system that gave me the freedom to make this swim, but that I hadn't done it for money. I didn't tell them that I was now in debt trying to pay for it. Instead, I tried to explain that becoming friends with them was the most important thing.

"Look, Vladimir," Dr. Keatinge said sternly, "her temperature is dropping. It could affect her heart. We've got to move her immediately. Can you walk, Lynne?"

I couldn't flex or grip with my feet. I had no idea how I was going to walk barefoot across the rocks and ice sheet. But two Siberian women emerged from the crowd and presented me with a pair of sealskin slippers with brightly colored red and blue beads on the top of the slippers, and fur surrounding the rest of them. Vladimir explained that the Inuit people who lived on the Siberian mainland, in the Chukhoka's Luorovetlian region, had made the slippers. They'd chewed the sealskin with their teeth to soften it, then hand-stitched the skin together. With the help of the two women, I slipped them on. They fit perfectly. How had they ever known my size?

Stumbling and sliding across the rocks toward the tent, I walked with my arms outstretched for balance. The distance to the tent was only two hundred yards, but it felt like half a mile. When we finally arrived at the tent, there was a cot with a heavy sleeping bag, extra blankets, and hot coffee. Standing at the tent entrance, holding a blanket for me, was a woman with dark reddish-brown hair.

Everything we had requested by telex was in the tent except for the "babushka," the colorful shawl. My body was shaking like a blender turned up on high. My hands were lifeless clubs. I pulled the coiled wire out of the bottom of my swimsuit and extended it to Dr. Nyboer so he could plug it into the monitor to measure my core temperature. Vladimir entered the tent and explained that the woman with the reddish hair was a Russian doctor. She had been sent specially to take care of me. And she was beside herself. She could see how cold I was, and she was worried. Using hand gestures, she told me to take off my wet swimsuit before I climbed into the sleeping bag. It was one thing to be naked in front of her, but another to do so in front of the two men on my team. I pretended not to understand and tried to climb into the sleeping bag. She wouldn't let me get away with it. Finally she got it, and waved Dr. Nyboer and Dr. Keatinge out.

Quickly the Russian doctor placed hot packs at key sites: under the back of my neck, in my armpits, and in my groin area. She felt my cheeks with her hot hands. I just wanted her to keep her hands on my face. They felt so good, and I couldn't imagine how my face felt to her. She leaned on top of the sleeping bag, giving me the warmth of her body. It was so strange; I felt like her daughter, the way she was fussing over me. My breathing was very rapid as I shivered, laboring to generate heat.

Dr. Nyboer stepped back into the tent. "What was my time for the swim?" I asked. My teeth were chattering.

"Two hours and six minutes," Dr. Nyboer said and he checked the monitor. "Her temperature is down to ninety-four, but I can see it's beginning to climb back up."

Dr. Keatinge was right there beside him and suddenly I felt like their patient. It was a weird change; I'd been the team leader for so long. Dr. Keatinge reached down, took one of my arms between his hands, and slid his hands down to my hand. The warmth of his hands felt so good, I didn't want him to let go. "Her skin is still very cold. It's probably about forty degrees."

They set the cardiac defibrillator on the table. When the Russian doctor saw it, she bolted out of her chair and shook her head vigorously. She clearly thought they were going to use it, and she quickly moved between them and me. She gave them a look that said, You'd better not touch her.

Dr. Keatinge tried to explain that it was there just as a precaution. He asked Dr. Nyboer to check my heart.

Dr. Nyboer opened his black bag, threw the top of the sleeping bag back so my entire chest was exposed to the thirty-degree air, and put the icy stethoscope on my chest, which was suddenly covered with goose bumps.

"Sounds strong and even. You doing okay?" Dr. Nyboer asked.

I nodded and covered my head with the sleeping bag so I could breathe into it and trap body heat. This troubled the Russian doctor — she wanted to see my face. She wanted to be able to rub her hand on it so she could tell if I was rewarming. She pulled the sleeping bag back down.

A minute later, Dr. Nyboer returned, threw the bag back again, and placed the stethoscope on my chest. My body was fighting like mad in a refrigerator-like tent to get warm, and every time I'd start to create a warm airspace around me, someone would open the bag. I knew they needed to make sure my heart wasn't going into fibrillation, but I couldn't stand it.

In the background, I could hear voices and people singing, both in Russian and in a different language. It sounded like they were celebrating — it was a Siberian beach party. I wanted to be out there with them, but I just couldn't manage it yet.

Fortunately, my old friend Rich Roberts came into the tent and said that the Soviets had set up two buffet tables on the rocky beach. They were covered with starched white tablecloths, and waiters wearing white smocks were serving hot tea in china cups, dried fish, bread, and chocolate-covered coconut candy. On the cliffs above the tables two army officers were watching everyone with binoculars and taking pictures. There was also a soldier posted to guard my sweat suit, which I had dropped outside the tent.

About an hour later, when I finally felt warm, I looked up at the Russian doctor and said, "Hi, my name is Lynne. What's yours?"

"My name is Rita. Rita Zakharova." Quickly she opened her wallet and started showing me family pictures.

"Your children?" I asked, pointing at the pictures.

"*Nyet,* no." She shook her head and said something in Russian that I didn't understand, then: "Not children. I babushka."

"You're a babushka?" I asked — a colorful shawl?

"Yes." She nodded quickly. "Grandchildren." She pointed to the pictures.

Rita Zakharova was the babushka I'd requested — a grandmother. To me, she was the warmth and color of Russia.

She opened a bag, reached in, and excitedly handed me a gift — a beautiful hand-painted lacquer bowl decorated with bright orange, red, and gold flowers. *Oh, what can I give her?* I thought. I picked up my cap and goggles and handed them to her. Rita motioned that she couldn't accept them. When I insisted, she took them as if they were precious gifts. If only I could tell her what a precious gift she had given me, sharing her warmth with me. Somehow I think she understood without my having to speak any words. Both of us were almost in tears. She felt my cheeks again and nodded. They were finally warm, and I could feel my lips. Rita smiled, hugged me, and gave me permission to leave the tent and see what was happening outside.

21

Success

I heard the Inuits singing more clearly. There were people standing around the table and waiters serving them great cups of tea from a huge stainless steel samovar, and there were people standing side by side, Americans and Soviets, just talking. The Soviets had welcomed us with heartfelt gladness, as if we were long-lost friends.

Claire Richardson said that Pat Omiak had tried to communicate with Zoya and Margaret, the two Siberian Inuit women who had given me the sealskin slippers, but they spoke a different Inuit dialect, called Siberian Yupik. Pat knew, though, that the elders on Little Diomede used to hunt and trade with the Siberian Inuit and could speak Siberian Yupik. He knew that the elders on Little Diomede were at the community center waiting to hear from us, so Omiak called them on the two-way radio. Zoya and Margaret got on the radio and spoke to the elders while the entire village of Little Diomede, including Maria Sullivan and Dr. Nyboer Sr., listened in on the conversation.

Zoya and Margaret asked about the walrus hunting and whaling around Little Diomede. Margaret said it wasn't good for the Inuit in the village of Magadan, on the Sea of Okhotsk. Most of the whales were gone. She also asked about John Kiminock, who had sailed from Siberia to Nome in the 1930s and never returned. The elders knew John. He was now eighty-six years old and lived in Nome. Then the elders asked about John's family, whom he hadn't heard from for more than fifty years. Margaret said two of John's sisters had died, but three were still alive. They continued talking to each other, learning what had happened to their relatives during the past forty-eight years. On Pat Omiak's radio, caught up in emotion, we heard someone singing; then the whole village of Little Diomede joined in. They were singing Siberian Yupik songs that they had memorized from old records. Zoya and Margaret joined in; these were songs they had learned as children. As they sang back and forth to each other, some of the villagers started performing traditional Inuit dances. The gap created by all the years of separation had been bridged.

We continued to celebrate. One man gave me an Olympic Games pin, another man gave me a dove pin with the word *mir* — "peace" — etched on its wing, and the woman from the KGB gave me a pin with the U.S. and Soviet flags crossed together. When it was time to leave, the sun was shining brightly and the sky was blue and clear.

When we reached Little Diomede late that afternoon, all the villagers came out to greet us. We were fogged in that evening and couldn't leave until the next day. Eric Pentilla met us in the morning and helicoptered us off the island to Nome. Our departure to Nome was late, but Pentilla radioed ahead, and Alaska Airlines held the plane for us. When we boarded, twenty minutes late, everyone on the plane burst into applause. The captain had given them the background on the swim. Later, after takeoff, he came out to meet us. It was strange too; once we were in the air, people started asking me for autographs. I was happy to oblige, until the pilot asked the passengers to return to their seats, because there was too much weight on one side of the plane.

The celebration continued that night in Anchorage, and in the morning, as promised, I flew with Maria Sullivan to New York City to appear on ABC's *Good Morning America*. The other members of the crew had to return home, but Maria had offered to stay on and help with anything that came up. I was glad she was with me. Once we reached New York, the media barrage was unbelievable. Journalists were calling the hotel night and day from all around the world. Finally Maria asked the hotel manager to hold all calls.

Going from Nome to New York City was a real shocker. It was August, and in Alaska it had felt like winter. In New York it was eighty-five degrees and humid. All I had left to wear were my sweats, and they smelled like dead walrus from the ride back to Little Diomede in the umiak. But it was wonderful having a hot shower and clean sheets, and ordering room service, sharing chocolate and cheesecake with Maria.

I was so worried that I was going to have to wear the walrus-smelling sweats on the television program. There was no money left in my account for clothes, or anything. Fortunately, Maria had spoken with Joe Novella, the ABC producer, and in the morning he handed me his company credit card and said, "Buy whatever you need."

Good Morning America had me scheduled for an interview between Boy George and Colin Powell. When I entered the green-room, Colin Powell was sitting there, waiting to be interviewed by Charlie Gibson. Someone came in and handed me a dozen roses; they had a card from Joe Novella congratulating me on the swim and the interview. That piqued Colin Powell's interest, but he didn't say anything. I introduced myself and asked him if he was the president's assistant for national security affairs. He nodded, a little surprised that I knew this, and asked me why I was there. Once I explained, he said he had followed my story — all he wanted to talk about was the Bering Strait swim. He said that he thought the swim had already helped diminish tensions between the two superpowers. I didn't want to talk about me, though; I was more interested in him. It seemed more than coincidence that we were meeting like this. I sensed from our brief conversation that he hoped the relationship with the Soviets would change for the better.

Four months later, I got a call from a man

who identified himself only as Viktor from the Soviet embassy. He asked me what my time was for swimming the Bering Strait. I told him two hours, six minutes, and eleven years. He thanked me and hung up.

The next evening I received a call from my aunt Jeannine in New York City. "Are you watching television?" she asked. She sounded so excited.

I said yes, I was watching the news; President Gorbachev and President Reagan were meeting at the White House, and they were about to sign the INF Missile Treaty. Both of our countries were going to start reducing their stockpiles of nuclear arms.

For the next three hours I sat with my folks, glued to the television. President Gorbachev and President Reagan appeared with Raisa Gorbachev and Nancy Reagan. President Reagan spoke about this first history-making meeting at the White House, and then President Gorbachev made a toast. They raised their glasses and President Gorbachev said, "Last summer it took one brave American by the name of Lynne Cox just two hours to swim from one of our countries to the other. We saw on television how sincere and friendly the meeting was between our people and the Americans when she stepped onto the Soviet shore. She proved by her courage how close to each other our peoples live." Later in the toast he would add that he saw the swim as a symbol of improving relations between the United States and the Soviet Union.

Shortly after that, Italian television invited me to Rome for television interviews. A few days later, Pope John Paul asked me to meet with him at the Vatican. Meanwhile, through Claire Richardson, at a party at my home, I had met Dr. Gabriella Miotto. She was a longtime friend of Claire's, who spoke fluent Italian. Even though we had talked for only five minutes, I thought she was a fine person. So when I got the invitation to go to Rome, since I didn't have a spouse or agent, I called up Gabriella and asked if she would like to accompany me as my interpreter. Gabriella was in the middle of doing her residency in a small farming town near Bakersfield, working with people who couldn't afford medical care. She said she would talk to a friend and see if she could get her to cover her schedule for the ten days that Italian television had invited me to be in Rome.

Our trip to Rome would be unbelievable. I got to talk to the pope about swimming. A fine swimmer himself, he told me his favorite places to swim. He knew all about the

Bering Sea swim and gave me a special blessing.

Then I was asked to meet with President Reagan at the White House in the Oval Office. While I was waiting to meet with him, Ted Turner from CNN came out of the office. He was with a colleague. I had worn a Goodwill Games pin on my dress as a way to acknowledge Walsh's and Turner's support, and he saw the pin. Turner was an avid sailor, and he appreciated the significance of swimming across the Bering Strait.

22

Siberia's
Gold Medal

Swimming across the Bering Strait changed everything for me. Now my goal was not only to do something that had never been done before while providing data for cold research, but also to establish bridges between borders. My swims became more three-dimensional, more complex, and, in my mind, far more significant. It seemed to me that a relationship with a country is like a relationship with a person; it's something that one must continue working on and developing. Even before I made the Bering Strait swim I knew that if I succeeded, I had to continue to try to do another difficult and symbolic swim that would bring our countries together. And so I looked at Lake Baikal, the jewel of Siberia, the deepest lake in the world, and the source of inspiration for Russian poems, literature, and songs.

Because of the success of the swim across the Bering Strait, in spring of 1988, the Soviets invited me to Moscow to talk about future projects. They were willing to listen to any idea I had. Actually, as soon as I had completed the Bering Strait swim, Alexander Kozlovsky, of the Soviet Sports Committee, had asked me what my next goal was, so I'd told him about Lake Baikal. I'd also said that I had other projects in mind too, projects I didn't think I could discuss with him via telex or by phone. These were ideas we would have to share when we met in person.

Bob Walsh, the man who was organizing the Goodwill Games, and who had spoken to the Soviet Sports Committee and to high-ranking people at the Kremlin to secure Soviet permission, invited me to travel to Moscow with him and a couple of other people from Seattle. We stayed in the Soviet Sports Committee hotel, a dormlike building that had been built for the Moscow Olympics, the ones the United States had boycotted because of the Soviet war in Afghanistan. Staying in Moscow was like being a character in a bad spy novel. The phone in my hotel room was tapped, the room was bugged, and I was followed wherever I went. This was standard operating procedure, according to Peter Kassander, Walsh's assistant in Washington, D.C.

The night I arrived in the Soviet Union, the country was celebrating Yuri Gagarin Day. It was a very strange sensation; I felt like I was at home in the States on the Fourth of July. Yet, in reality, I was looking out across Moscow's enormous skyline, watching fireworks exploding like blazing flowers and stars, celebrating Gagarin, the first Soviet cosmonaut and person to fly into space. Gagarin's spaceflight, along with the launch of *Sputnik* — the first satellite in space — would ignite the U.S. space race and lead up to the start of the nuclear missile buildup. Gagarin's historic flight had not only changed Russia; it had changed the United States and the world. It was not by chance that I had been invited to be in the Soviet Union on this historic day. Bob Walsh told me that when the Soviets had decided to invite me to their country, they'd chosen this date to celebrate the Bering Strait crossing as well.

It was very strange to be treated like a celebrity in the Soviet Union, to have people stopping me and handing me flowers or pins or asking for autographs. It was even stranger when I was inside the Kremlin gates, viewing the historic churches, and a man from Armenia recognized me and gave me a key chain with some rubles — an Armenian custom, he said.

When I spoke with officials of the Soviet Sports Committee, I told them about my next three goals. The first was to swim across Lake Baikal. When I said that, the eyes of the members of the committee lit up. Yes, they said, that is exactly what you have to do next. And they became very enthusiastic. They told me that Lake Baikal was the most beautiful lake in all of the Soviet Union. It was the deepest lake in the world, more than a mile deep, and at twenty-five million years old, one of the oldest lakes in the world. The lake was pristine and clear; it contained one-fifth of the world's freshwater. They knew all the statistics: the lake was four hundred miles long, and averaged between eighteen and fifty miles wide. There were twelve hundred creatures unique to the lake, including freshwater seals. To Russians, Lake Baikal was the gem of Siberia, a sort of mecca that everyone in the Soviet Union dreamed of visiting one day in their lives. Once I saw their reverence for the lake, I couldn't wait to see it either, or to swim across it.

During that same meeting, I proposed

two successive swims. One would go from Hokkaido, Japan, to Kunashir, one of the Kuril Islands to the north, controlled by the Soviet Union. The other proposed swim was across the Heilong Jiang–Amur River border, from the Soviet Union to China. The reason for these swims was to promote further cooperation and understanding between these countries.

The Soviet Sports Committee immediately began working with me on all three projects and set up meetings for me with embassy representatives from Japan and China. For the next few years I worked on gaining Japanese and Chinese support, but because of political complications between the Soviet Union and Japan, and within China, I finally decided to move on to other projects.

The swim across Lake Baikal, however, was as successful as it was amazing. Thousands of Siberians came to the town of Listvyanka, a village on the edge of the lake, to celebrate the finish of the ten-mile swim. They threw long-stemmed pink roses into the water as I swam by, and they cheered, "Welcome, Lynne Cox. Welcome, USA." A few months later, to commemorate the swim, officials placed a plaque at the starting point and named the cape beside

Cape Tolstoy Cape Lynne Cox.

Buoyed with these successes, I decided to try other swims, ones that had never been attempted, that could be vehicles for opening borders and for furthering cold research. In 1990 I decided to attempt a swim across the forty-two-degree waters of the Beagle Channel. To do this, though, I had to gain support from both Argentina and Chile and cross a border that had been contested at one time or another by both countries. It took a lot of work to get both countries to agree to support the swim, and at one point while I was in Argentina with my crew, I nearly had to walk away from the swim because of the political tensions. Fortunately, the commanders of both navies were able to work out the logistics, and with their support, I became the first person to swim across the seven-mile-wide Beagle Channel from a beach in Ushuaia, Argentina, to Puerto Williams, Chile.

From there, I decided to swim across the Spree River, from East Berlin to West Berlin, at a time when the Berlin Wall was still intact. My idea was to get support from East and West Germany as well as England, France, the Soviet Union, and the United States, since they controlled various sectors of Berlin, and to promote cooperation between all of the countries.

By the time I gained permission to make the swim, the wall had been torn down, but the Spree River would prove to be one of the most dangerous waterways I'd ever swum in. The East German government had placed mines, razor wire, and large slabs of razor-sharp sheet metal in the river to prevent East Germans from swimming across it and escaping into West Berlin. Most of these devices had been cleared from the river, but the job had been done in great haste, and the East Germans weren't sure if they had removed everything. They agreed to help and had one of their police boats escort me. During the swim we made at least five rapid course changes to avoid underwater obstacles, as well as many others to avoid the dead rats, trash, and condoms floating on the water's surface. One of the most exciting parts of the swim was having people from East Germany and West Germany walking along the shore, all ten miles with us, to the finish of the swim in West Berlin.

Departing briefly from doing swims to bring countries together, I decided to instead make a swim that would highlight cooperation between countries. The Amyara people who lived on either side of Lake

Titicaca, in Bolivia and Peru, have gotten along together for centuries; many of them are related. In 1992, with help from Bob Gelbard, who was then the assistant secretary of state, I was able to quickly obtain permission to attempt a swim across Lake Titicaca from Bolivia to Peru.

No one had ever swum across the ten-mile-wide section of the lake from Copacabana, Bolivia, to Chimbo, Peru, mostly because of the extreme altitude — 12,500 feet — and the fifty-degree water temperature. But attempting this crossing really intrigued me. Training for it would be a challenge, and fortunately, I was able to work with Dr. Brownie Schoene, a pulmonary specialist who had climbed both Mount Everest and K2. Brownie helped me acclimate to the high altitude, but neither of us knew how I would react to the added stress of cold water.

It was a shock for me. When I first attempted a training swim in the lake, I suddenly couldn't breathe, which made me have big doubts about attempting the swim. In order to complete it, I would have to slow my work rate down to half speed, so I could breathe, and then hope I didn't go into hypothermia. With this strategy, and the support of my crew as well as the Bolivian navy,

I became the first person to swim across Lake Titicaca.

From there, I decided to attempt a swim that had been suggested to me years before, by two Israeli composers: a trip along the Gulf of Aqaba from Egypt to Israel, and then another from Israel to Jordan. The swims would trace the process of Middle East peace. Getting permission for this project proved to be complex and difficult, but Tom Pickering, who had been the U.S. ambassador to both Israel and Jordan, gave me guidance, and eventually I gained support from Queen Noor of Jordan, Yitzhak Rabin of Israel, and high-ranking officials in Egypt.

Working out the logistics for the swims turned out to be a challenge, but when we discovered that peace talks were under way in Eliat, Israel, between officials from Israel and Jordan, my crew and I walked into the hotel where the talks were being held, found out who was in charge of the talks, and met with them. That day we received permission, and a day later, with Egyptian navy and Israeli navy support, I made the seven-mile swim from Egypt to Israel.

The following day, the Israeli navy and the Jordanian navy, working together, supported my swim. For the first time in forty-six years, the Jordanian navy welcomed the Israeli navy, opening the border for my support crew as I swam to Aqaba. There we were welcomed and honored at a reception hosted by Queen Noor. A few days later, we were invited to witness King Hussein, President Clinton, and Prime Minister Rabin sign the peace treaty between Israel and Jordan.

In 1999 I decided to do a series of swims simply for fun. Ever since I had met the pope, and he had mentioned that his favorite place to swim was in the northern lakes of Italy, I'd wanted to swim there too. So with a group of friends, I traveled to Italy and I swam across Lake Garda, Lake Como, and Lake Maggiore. We ate Italian chocolates, listened to a friend sing opera, and immersed ourselves in reflections of Italian villas as we crossed the lakes, completely enjoying the entire journey. There was nothing challenging about these swims — no political complexities or intrigue, and no physical barriers — and while I enjoyed doing them, just for the sake of experiencing them, I felt somewhat let down. I wanted to do so much more. An idea came to mind then, one that was bigger, more complex, and more challenging than any I had ever contemplated.

23

Swimming
to Antarctica

Cody, my yellow Labrador, pulled my tennis shoe out from under my bed and followed me downstairs. He saw me set my bags down in the hallway, and he lay down in the living room with his chin resting on my shoe. He looked at me with imploring eyes.

"I'm sorry, Cody, you can't go with me. When dogs go to Antarctica they either freeze to death or get eaten by their best friends. Amundsen, Scott, Cherry-Garrard, Shackleton — all of them shot their dogs and ate them. I'm sorry, Antarctica's no place for you."

Sara, my parents' brindled whippet, raced downstairs and stretched out beside him, something she had never done before. She had come to say good-bye. I hugged my dad and he returned the hug tightly — I think he was too emotional to speak. The previous year I had planned to travel to Antarctica to attempt the swim, but my father had been very ill, and I hadn't wanted to leave him. He'd had to fight for his life. It was awful, and yet it was enlightening, being with him while he went through this siege. He always maintained a positive attitude, never wavered, and never gave up on living. Neither did my mother, who was by his side throughout the whole battle. They didn't know it, but they were my heroes. Seeing their determination to hold on to life and live it fully made me realize that I had the same drive within myself. As far as I knew, I would be here only once, and I wanted to live as much as I could.

My mother hugged me. Her voice was rich with emotion as she said, "I know you will accomplish what you want to. Good luck."

She had really come around. When I'd first told her and my dad what I was planning to do, two years before, they'd been totally against it. They said it was far too dangerous, and they were right: swimming in water temperatures in the low thirties was life threatening. But once I set a goal in my mind, I didn't want to give up without trying. I just had to figure out a way to make the swim less dangerous.

The Antarctica swim would be psychologically more difficult than any swim I had done before. There was so much emotion connected to it. Friends expressed their love and support by handing me care packages filled with hot chocolate and tea, popcorn and chocolate. Others felt concern; one of my closest friends, who had been with me on previous swims, was worried I would never return. And Laura, my younger sister, called at least a dozen times to make sure that I had a team of doctors with me and a rescue plan in place and tested in case of an emergency. David, my older brother, and Ruth, my youngest sister, were much more low-key about it, but they told me to be careful, and David told me to have fun swimming with the penguins.

For two years I had been preparing for this swim, an idea inspired by Caroline Alexander, a friend who wrote a book called *The Endurance*, about Ernest Shackleton and his attempt to reach the South Pole. I had been looking for a goal that was a really big idea, something that would intrigue me and move me far beyond what I knew. Caroline suggested I swim in the subantarctic islands — off Elephant Island or South Georgia Island — recognizable places that were associated with Shackleton. But I wasn't interested in doing a swim for the sake of it being recognized; I wanted to do something that had never been done, never been explored before in this way.

Caroline and I discussed different ideas. Ultimately, I knew, I wanted to swim somewhere on the Antarctic continent, but I thought it would be good to do a test swim ahead of time near one of the subantarctic islands. First I wanted to see what I could do, then gauge my limits and determine how much farther I could go.

For two years, I had trained very hard for this swim, and in a different manner than ever before. Instead of working on endurance, as I had in the past, my objective now was to build strength, speed, and overall cardiac conditioning. I trained by walking at sunrise with Barry Binder, my friend and the team leader for the swim, and Cody. We walked at a moderate speed from five to six miles per day. After that I went to the gym and worked out for an hour three times a week with Jonathan Moch, my personal trainer. Jonathan planned the season for me and broke it into four segments. The first quarter we worked on strength, using free weights; the second quarter on balance and stability, using a balance ball; the third quarter on a combination of balance and strength, using weights while I was balanced on the ball. During the last quarter we worked on endurance, strength, and balance to the point of complete fatigue. This last phase of my training was as much about focus as conditioning. When I got tired or overloaded with other thoughts, I lost my focus. One of my worst and best workouts was three days before I left for Argentina.

Moch was having me balance on my knees on the balance ball and toss a ten-pound ball back and forth with him. When I climbed up on the ball, I couldn't get my balance. I tried repeatedly, and I was getting frustrated.

Moch said, "Don't get frustrated; get determined."

This advice helped, but I still wasn't able to get focused and stay on the ball. Finally I said, "Why are you having me continue this? Can't we do it later, after another exercise? Right now I'm just practicing failure. When my sister coaches young kids, if they can't reach a skill after three or four times, she gives them something different to work on that will build that skill. Why can't we do that now?"

Moch smiled. "This is different. You've already done this before. You just need to slow down and focus. Stop thinking about all the people on your swim, all the problems, the logistics, the television, and everything else — it's overwhelming you. There are going to be so many variables on your swim, and you've told me you're going to have to go whenever you're given a chance. So you need to work through this now, focus here, so you can focus there."

Climbing back on the ball, I emptied my head of everything else and managed to balance for five throws. This was an invaluable lesson for me. For this swim, the mental training and the physical training were completely intermeshed.

In addition to dry-land workouts, for the past two years I had been training in the ocean all year long, and in my folks' backyard swimming pool when its water temperature got colder than the ocean. I swam one-, two-, and three-mile sprints, alternating between swimming head up and head down. Swimming with my head up would enable me to conserve body heat, since up to 80 percent is lost through the head. But this body position in the water creates drag; it was like swimming uphill, and it reduced my speed and made me tire quickly. So I decided to alternate between head up and head down.

I was to fly to Ushuaia, the southernmost city in Argentina, on the Beagle Channel, ten days ahead of my crew and train in Ushuaia Harbor. This would enable me to get over jet lag, acclimate to the cold water, and begin psyching myself up for the swim. My crew would arrive a day before the ship, the *Orlova*, sailed for Antarctica. Included in the crew would be seven friends, some of whom had been on past swims. Barry Binder would be the person I communicated with during the swim; he would help me with coordinating the logistics and navigation. Dan Cohen would be the rescue swimmer; Dan would jump into the water and help me get out in the case of an emergency. Bob Griffith and Martha Kaplan were the scouts; they would be positioned in the lead Zodiac watching the water for ice and potentially dangerous animals. Griffith, who was an expert with a lasso, would have one on hand in case I needed additional help clearing the water. He would use the lasso to pull me over to the boat. Dr. Gabriella Miotto, Dr. Susan Sklar, and Dr. Laura King would be observing me during the swim, making sure I didn't go into hypothermia. But if there was an emergency, they were trained to revive me.

CBS would be covering the swim. They

had sent their own crew, who would be traveling with us. Shawn Efran would be producing the segment with Scott Pelley for *60 Minutes II*. Casey Morgan was assistant producer, while Chris Everson and Ian Robbie would be filming the story. Adam Ravetch would film the underwater scenes, and Mark Brewer would handle the sound.

A week before leaving for Argentina, I started avoiding public places and made a point of washing my hands a lot. If someone near me sneezed, I held my breath and raced out of the area. After training so hard for this swim and working through so many details, the last thing I wanted was to jeopardize it all by getting sick. One of my greatest concerns was catching a cold or other sort of infection on the thirty-hour flight. The recirculated air in an airplane cabin dries out the nasal passages, making the area a perfect entry point to the body for rhinoviruses — which cause the common cold. I asked Laura King if there was some kind of lotion I could use to keep my nasal membranes moist. She recommended using Aquaphor, which was normally used on premature babies to keep their skin moist, and for dry, cracked lips. She also gave me a surgical mask to wear if I had the misfortune of sitting on the plane near someone with a cold.

Blood clots were also a concern. They could occur during the long flight from sitting too long in one place. My father had advised me to get up, stretch my legs, and walk around to keep the circulation going. As an added precaution, I began taking Bayer baby aspirin three days prior to departure to thin my blood. I was also concerned about health problems that could occur after my swim. If my limbs were extremely cold during the swim, my blood circulation would be greatly reduced, and there would be a chance of getting a blood clot, so I decided to continue taking the aspirin through the time of the swim and for a week afterward.

Once I was in Ushuaia, my goal was to swim for an hour a day at sprint pace. The first day I worked out in Ushuaia Harbor, the weather conditions were the worst I'd ever been in. The winds were gale force, gusting up to fifty knots, and the waves in the harbor were walls of four-feet-high rapidly breaking chop. I wasn't sure about swimming alone in the water that day. It looked dangerous, and usually when conditions are bad, they get worse before they get better. I told myself I had to get in and swim;

I needed to condition to the water temperature, and I needed to accept every challenge, because what I wanted to do would be far beyond what I did in any training swim. I decided to swim within twenty-five yards of shore so I could get out of the water quickly if I needed to. I searched for a place where I could enter the water and swim safely.

In that area, the harbor was filled with exposed rocks covered with sharp barnacles and mussels. I was afraid of swimming smack into them and slicing my hand or head open. And there was kelp, the kind that scratched like small rose thorns. I had to keep pushing myself mentally. I told myself to figure out a way to just get into the water and swim. I took off my sweats and shoes. Standing there in the wind in my bathing suit, I was freezing. *At least,* I told myself, *the water won't feel as cold now.* I found a crack between two rocks and squeezed my sweats into the crack and piled my shoes on top so they wouldn't be blown into the sea by the gale. Then I climbed down the rocky embankment, sat down on a rock, and pressed myself into the water.

It was a shock when I slipped into the forty-degree water; I turned my arms over rapidly and swam with my head up, over cresting waves, as crystal water droplets flew off my fingertips. I swam about a quarter of a mile, to an area where the Argentine navy anchored their fleet. The weather was so bad it looked as though all the ships were tied to the wharf in the harbor. Turning around to begin my second lap, I caught a faceful of water, then battled the waves the entire way back to the starting point. I did six laps, and when I turned around after the last one, an enormous and brilliant rainbow stretched from the Argentine ships. I took it as a good sign.

For the next six days, I worked out in the harbor. I had to push myself every day to get into the water, but with each day that passed, I found that I was able to stay warmer for a longer time period. After my swim, I walked back to the Albatross Hotel, where I was staying, climbed the four floors to the top of the building, where the hotel was the warmest, and walked back and forth quickly until my feet thawed, then jogged back and forth in the hallway to warm up. It felt good to work so hard, to know I had the chance to do something that had never been done before. Still it was hard being there on my own. I stayed in touch with friends and family by e-mail every day, and their words and encouragement made me realize that even though I was alone physically, they were with me in spirit.

At the end of my last solo workout, the day before my crew arrived in Ushuaia, I glanced up at the city, with its small bright red, yellow, turquoise, green, blue, and white houses built on steep hills, encircled by the end of the Andes Mountain chain, still glistening with snow. Looking up into the sky, I saw the wind tearing thin clouds apart, and encircling the sun was a huge and brilliant rainbow, formed by the sun shining through ice crystals. I thought, *This is another good sign; it's the circle of completion.*

On the Sunday morning my crew would arrive in Ushuaia, I woke up at four a.m. I tried to talk myself into going back to sleep, but I kept rolling around in bed. Finally, at five-thirty, I decided to go for an early-morning workout. It seemed like a good idea; there would be a lot of people walking around the harbor area later in the day, and I wanted to maintain a low profile, not wanting to have to explain what I was doing to anyone so I could stay focused on my training and on the swim.

As I stepped outside the Albatross Hotel, a cold, thirty-knot wind cut right through my sweat suit. This would be the last workout I did on my own, and I was happy that this part of the training was nearly over. It had taken a lot of discipline for me to swim in forty-degree water every day, and I knew having my friends there would make it easier and more fun.

When I reached the rocks where I usually began my workout, there were two men in their late twenties standing nearby, talking. I tried not to make eye contact, and I walked about a hundred yards from them and sat on some rocks. I waited, hunched over, hoping they would leave so I could maintain my low profile. But the wind was blowing harder. I had to either swim now or go back to the hotel, get warm, and return later. I wanted to get the workout over with. Unzipping my sweats, I took them off quickly and squeezed them between the rocks.

One of the men shouted at me incredulously in Spanish, "Are you going swimming?"

"*Sí,*" I told him.

"*Mucho frío?*" he said. Very cold?

I nodded, pulled off my shoes, put them on top of my sweats, and climbed quickly down the embankment. I sat down on the rock ledge and pulled my cap and goggles on, lowered myself into the water, took a deep breath, pushed off, and started swimming fast with my head up. One of the men shouted something at me a couple of times, while his friend stood beside him with his mouth wide open. I hoped they wouldn't tell anyone.

The water felt colder than it had during any other workout, probably because I was chilled by the delay. Knowing there was no one around who could help me if I got into trouble, I swam only twenty feet offshore. It was tough going. The tide was low, and the kelp beds were floating a couple of inches below the water's surface, so that I had to swim through the center of them. My arms kept getting tangled up in the kelp ropes, and I kept hitting my hands on rocks. It felt as if I were swimming through a gauntlet.

Finally I reached the Argentine ships, turned around, and swam back to the starting point. The two men had left, but another man, a tall, lean man wearing a light brown cap and uniform, was standing on the embankment. He spoke to me in Spanish, and I couldn't understand a word. So I said, "English?"

He shook his head and continued speaking Spanish, only more loudly. He said something about a marina. It was too cold to sit there and carry on a conversation, so I decided that if I just agreed with him, he would go away. I said *"Sí,"* turned around, moved farther offshore, and sprinted toward the Argentine ships.

He was startled, and he shouted at me. I again heard the word *marina,* and again shouted, *"Sí."* I laughed when I saw him jogging around the cove, trying to catch up with me. I thought the marina must have been the small beach near the pier where the Argentine navy was anchored. I wondered if he was from the harbor police or the coast guard. Maybe once he saw me swim, he would realize that I was okay, and just walk with me for the remainder of the workout. It would be nice to have company.

When we reached the Argentine fleet, the man started down an embankment toward the sandy beach. Just as he nearly reached the water's edge, I turned around and sprinted back toward the starting point. This was the most fun I'd had all week.

All of a sudden I heard him blowing a whistle. I put my head down into the water, pretended I hadn't heard, and continued swimming. He was scrambling up the rocks, blowing his whistle louder now, and jogging back along the sidewalk. People were beginning to congregate on the sidewalk above the embankment, staring and pointing at me with astonishment. A blue police car with sirens blaring and lights flashing stopped near the crowd. Two officers jumped out, a man and a woman, and they climbed down the embankment.

Another truck arrived, also with its siren blaring; two more men in brown uniforms leaped out of it and scrambled down the rocks toward the water. The first man in uniform blew his whistle in shrill bursts and waved furiously at me. I angled back toward shore, thinking, *How am I going to talk my way out of this when I can't speak the language? Swim closer to the shore,* I told myself. The man finally stopped blowing his whistle. He thought I was going to climb out of the water, but I didn't want to. There were so many rocks covered with barnacles, and there was a lot of broken glass. I was afraid of getting cut. I pointed to the opposite shore, where I knew I could climb out safely and get my sweats and shoes, but the man shook his head. I took a few more strokes toward him and pointed at the starting point again. He adamantly shook his head, then balanced on a rock five feet from me, squatted down, and extended his hand. I lifted my goggles and smiled. *"Gracias,"* I said, wondering how much trouble I was in. He continued to extend his hand, but I didn't take it; there were too many sharp rocks. *"Gracias,"* I repeated, pointing to some smoother rocks to the right. He leaped in that direction, and I climbed out on all fours.

My feet were stiff, and they hurt. The man's uniform had the word *Prefectura* written on the shoulder. He pointed near my feet, warning me where there were shards of glass. A small policewoman reached down to take my hand. I was afraid that I would slip and pull her in, so I said, *"Gracias"* again and stayed down on all fours, grabbing a rock to pull myself forward. When I reached the top, the policewoman motioned for me to get into the police car. I pointed to my swimsuit; I was dripping wet. They didn't want to get the back seat of the car wet, did they? The policewoman spoke with the man from the *prefectura,* and I think she told him that I was his responsibility. He seemed to accept that. He asked me something in Spanish, but the only word I caught was *ropa*.

Sounds like robe, I thought; *he must mean clothes.* I gestured to the place where I had started the swim. He escorted me along the street, where a crowd was watching and shouting questions. Traffic had stopped so that people could see what was going on. My feet were killing me, and I was cold, wet, and shivering.

He signaled for me to wait while he climbed down the embankment and searched for my sweat suit. He found something and held it up to show it to me. It was the key from the Albatross Hotel.

"Ropa?" he asked completely confused.

How do you say "Someone stole my clothes" in Spanish? I wondered. "No *ropa*," I said.

He didn't understand.

"No sweat suit. No shoes," I explained. I'd never had my clothes stolen before, and I'd never been arrested either.

He gestured for me to follow him back along the road to the coast guard headquarters. The wind was howling, and more people were stopping their cars to see what was happening. I was so embarrassed to be walking down what was their main street in a swimsuit. I stepped on some broken glass, grabbed my foot, and winced. It wasn't bleeding. I just wanted to get back to the hotel and get warm. But I kept trying to talk with the man from the coast guard, hoping to gain his sympathy so he wouldn't put me in jail.

"California. *Nadadora* — swimmer? You?" I asked, wishing I had studied Spanish.

"Buenos Aires. Prefectura," he said,

pointing to the word written on his shoulder. He was trying, and that made me feel a little better.

We crossed the street, climbed a hill, and entered the coast guard headquarters. It was attached to the Argentine navy base. Eleven years before, with the support of the Argentine and Chilean navies, I had swum across the Beagle Channel. No one had made that swim before, because of the cold and the strong currents, but my underlying reason for the swim was to gain cooperation from both navies and bridge the political distance between Argentina and Chile. The tall man in uniform guided me into the coast guard headquarters. There were four more men in uniform standing behind a counter. They were staring at me as if I'd just flown in from Venus. One man smirked and made a comment in Spanish. The man in charge agreed and moved over to the counter and tried to question me. When he realized I had no idea what he was saying, the tall man volunteered what he had learned from me during our walk to headquarters. The man in charge tried again, but all I could do was stand there and shiver.

A man in civilian clothes entered the headquarters. He explained in fluent English that he was a shipping agent and was there to translate. He asked me what I was doing. I explained that I was just swimming in the harbor. I had been there twelve years before to swim across the Beagle Channel and had done it with the support of the Argentine navy. Admiral López and Captain Alvarez had been in charge of the swim.

The shipping agent interpreted. The men from the coast guard shook their heads with disbelief. One of them said something. "No one could have swum across the Beagle Channel," the man in civilian clothes translated.

"In 1992 I became the first person to swim it. I swam from Ushuaia to Puerto Williams. Admiral López was in command, and Captain Alvarez was in charge of the swim," I repeated.

They still didn't believe me, so I dropped it, realizing that arguing with them wasn't going to help.

The man in charge said something to the shipping agent and he interpreted for me: "You are not allowed to swim in the harbor without a permit."

"Who do I need to talk with to get a permit?" I asked.

The shipping agent mentioned a name. It was the name of an officer from the coast guard I had met twelve years ago when I was going to swim the Beagle. How wonderful it would be to see him again.

The shipping agent told me to come back on Sunday, the following day, or during the week; I could get a permit at that time. The tall man and the shipping agent offered to drive me back to the Albatross Hotel.

People turned and stared when they saw me jogging through the lobby of the hotel and racing upstairs. I think I stood under the hot shower for forty-five minutes; I was cold to the core. I packed my bags and moved to the Los Niros Hotel, where I would be staying with the crew that evening. All day long, I hiked around the city, burning off energy, anticipating their arrival.

When I saw my crew entering the baggage-claim area at Ushuaia Airport, I was so excited. The baggage claim was on the other side of a floor-to-ceiling glass wall. There was a sign that said NO ENTRY, but there wasn't any security. Susan Sklar kept waving at me. Finally, she came over to the sliding doors and I explained that I didn't want to get arrested twice in one day. My excitement grew each time I saw one of my friends. Everyone was there. As they came through the glass doors we hugged. Yes, it was really happening. We were finally together and almost on our way.

The next morning, with the help of an Argentine woman named Gabriella who worked for the Bureau of Tourism, my crew and the CBS crew met with the coast guard officials. Gabriella acted as our translator. Because I was writing a story about the swim for *The New Yorker*, and because CBS's *60 Minutes II* was doing a segment on it, we could not tell the coast guard about my plan to swim in Antarctica. We were concerned that other members of the media would pick up on the story. Through Gabriella, we told one of the coast guard officials that CBS was doing a documentary on me. They wanted to film me swimming in Ushuaia Harbor. The coast guard official said they would like to help. They said their only concern was for my safety, and they offered to provide us with a Zodiac escort boat, a driver, and a rescue swimmer. They wanted to know if I had a doctor who could accompany me. Gabriella Miotto, one of the team physicians, immediately offered to sign a release form stating I was in good health. As we walked to the harbor, they drove the boat over, and I slid into the water and began my training swim. The two men from the coast guard in the Zodiac couldn't believe I could swim in forty-degree water.

For the first time I could swim a quarter of a mile offshore, through the harbor, in clear, clean water. I could explore the city and mountains from the water. I felt great after that workout, and the following day, in addition to the support from the coast guard, we had the Argentine navy offering to provide backup boat support, as well as allowing the CBS crew to film from one of their ships. After that workout, one of the rescue swimmers from the Argentine navy came over to congratulate me, to tell me how impressed he was with my swimming in the harbor. At the same time, José, a local man who had climbed Mount Everest the year before, came over to tell me that he was amazed by my swim in the harbor. He told me that many people had climbed Mount Everest, but no one else could do what I had done. I thanked him and smiled, thinking, *If he only knew what I was really training for.* Their comments gave me a real boost, and I could feel a momentum was building; we were on track, and we were ready. I was so excited.

That night, we boarded the *Orlova*, a three-hundred-foot-long icebreaker leased by Quark Expeditions, which was partially sponsoring the swim, and set sail for

Antarctica. We traveled through the Beagle Channel and into the Drake Passage, where the waves were as high as twenty-five feet — as tall as a two-story house. They pounded, tossed, turned, and rolled the ship. Sleeping that night was impossible for me; I was in the upper bunk, and I was afraid that I would fly out of bed and land on top of Martha Kaplan across the room. My fears weren't unwarranted: at two a.m. a large wave hit the ship with so much force that the dresser drawers between the beds flew open and everything on top of the desk was tossed across the room, while two chairs crashed onto the floor.

In the morning, we were still in the center of a storm. Waves were hitting the porthole and spinning so quickly that it looked like we were riding in a washing machine set on the spin cycle. Many of my crew were using medicated patches to prevent seasickness, but I couldn't. I was afraid the drug would linger in my system and somehow affect me negatively during the swim. Still, I was also concerned about getting seasick. If that happened, I would deplete electrolytes from my system and stress it out. I couldn't afford to get sick, so I stayed in bed, telling myself to relax, and imagined I was being rocked in a giant cradle.

Finally, by noon, the storm subsided, but the majority of my crew remained down in their cabins. I met with Susan Adie, the expedition leader for Quark. She was the person who would work the logistics out with me and determine when conditions were safe enough for a swim. Susan told me she had some concerns; her biggest was ice. She explained that we had to stay away from glaciers. "There could be a catastrophic calving," she said. "That's when an iceberg breaks off a glacier and hits the water — you get a mini tsunami. That wave can swamp a boat, and if you're in the water with brash ice — ice as small as a fist or as big as a VW — it will kill you."

She continued: "You and your crew will have to wait until the other passengers are ashore before you make your swim, and if the weather changes during that time, you won't be able to go."

"What about tides? Is there any way we can look at tidal charts and figure out the best time to swim?" I asked.

"You're fortunate because you're here on a neap tide, so there's less water movement. But tidal charts won't help. We don't have any for this area. Even though scientists have been studying tides at Palmer Station, the American research base, for twenty-seven years, no one knows what the tides here are doing. Some days we get two tides; other days we get only one. Sometimes there's a strong tidal current, and sometimes you don't have much current at all. You just have to go when the weather looks good," she said.

This was something I had never done before. Usually the tides were a large factor in planning a swim. I guessed I would just have to go with whatever I was given and make the most of it. I understood that this swim would draw on everything I knew and many things I didn't know. That's what made it exciting to me, exploring and extending beyond myself; but I did have some concerns. "What about wildlife? Will leopard seals or orcas be a problem?" I asked. I didn't mention that Jack Baldelli, a friend of mine who had dived for nine seasons in Antarctica for the National Science Foundation, had told me that he had watched leopard seals rip penguins out of their skins. Once, a leopard seal had pinned him to the bottom of the ocean; he waited until the thousand-pound animal swam away before he surfaced. He also said there was only one incident of an orca killing a person. Experts thought it was a case of mistaken identity, but if he saw orcas in the area, he got out of the water and recommended I do the same. I wasn't sure if I could get out of the water quickly enough in an emergency, or if I would be able to get out at all.

The doctors — Gabriella Miotto, Laura King, and Susan Sklar — were to be positioned in two Zodiacs so they could monitor me during the swim. If one Zodiac broke down, the other could pull alongside me so I could continue. If a life-threatening situation developed during the swim, Anthony Block, the ship's physician, would be in charge on board the ship.

We figured out where to position each of my crew members, as well as the CBS crew. Then Dr. Block had a request: he wanted to go through a drill with the doctors on the ship so they would know where everything was (medications, IV fluids, defibrillator, and so on) in case they needed to work with him on me. He asked me if I went into cardiac arrest during the swim and they brought me back aboard the ship did I want CBS to film it? I tried to think of how it could be useful, and the producer for CBS tried to convince us it was the right thing to do. Fortunately, Dan Cohen was sitting beside me. He could see that I was very uncomfortable with this, and he whispered, "Is this what you want?"

I shook my head.

"Then tell them," Dan encouraged me.

My voice went kind of weirdly deep from the stress. "I don't want anyone filming me if I'm like that," I said.

The producer nodded. He said they would be able to document my being pulled out of the water, and that would be enough to show what happened.

This was tough stuff for me. I understood we had to be prepared, to have an emergency plan, but all this focus on death was pushing my mind to a place it didn't want to go.

Dr. Block's run-through drill with my three doctors — Laura, Gabriella, and Susan — made sense to me, but then he asked me to participate in a stretcher drill. I would lie on a stretcher while Barry Binder and Scott Pelley carried me up the gangway to the ship.

I couldn't practice my own death, especially if I was going to do a test swim immediately afterward. All of my thoughts about the swim had been focused on success. I had looked at George Butler's films on Shackleton and used them as scouting reports. I had imagined myself swimming in Antarctic waters, past icebergs, and onto the shore. I had imagined success, not death.

This talk about death was something I balked against. I felt I would be okay if I paid attention the whole time, listened to my body, and had the courage to stop swimming if necessary, even if it meant I'd only be in the water a short amount of time. That would be the difficult part, but I knew I'd have to do it; otherwise I couldn't make the attempt.

The day after my crew's logistics meeting, we planned to do a test swim if the weather cooperated. I was eager to find out how far I could swim in the cold. More than that, I just wondered what it would be like to swim Antarctic waters.

During this test swim, we would rehearse what we would do on the actual swim. The doctors would get water temperatures and stroke rate, Bob Griffith would get air temperature, and Martha would have the clothes and blankets on hand and would be watching for wildlife. Barry would be giving me directions, Gabriella would be watching my responses to the cold, and Dan, sitting on the pontoon in a dry suit, would be prepared to jump in and drag me toward the boat if need be. At the end of this test swim, while I was strong and doing okay, Barry and Scott Pelley would pull me out of the water to simulate a mock rescue in case they needed to do it during the official swim.

Half an hour before the test swim, Dr. Block asked me to come with him so we could go through the stretcher drill. I told him I was sorry, but I just couldn't do it. He thought about it for a moment, then apologized. He said he was just trying to go through a drill and make sure the crew knew what they were doing. He hadn't considered how it would affect me. It disturbed me so much that I didn't want to see the stretcher drill. I didn't want to have that image in my mind. Martha Kaplan volunteered to be my body double. I retreated to the ship's lounge — as far as I could get from the drill — and started drinking four eight-ounce mugs of hot water, to warm my body from the inside out. That way I could make myself into a human thermos. It would also counteract the possible dehydration caused by exposure to extreme cold.

We had anchored off Admiralty Harbor, near the Polish research station called Arctowski Base. The base was made up of seven small, bright yellow buildings, set on a rocky beach encircled by steep, curvaceous mountains covered with ice and snow. There were thick glaciers along the mountains' peaks and deep within their recesses, set against a light blue sky filtered by moving clouds. The roof of one building had blown off in the same storm we'd experienced going through the Drake Passage. Studying the geography, I picked out places on land, ones I could use as reference points. I replayed the voices of friends and their encouraging words in my head. I had prepared as well as I could for this swim, down to the last details. I had grown my hair long to insulate my head; I had let the hair grow on my legs, which would make me less sensitive to the cold; I had even let my toenails grow to the edge of my toes to protect them from rocks at the end of the swim.

My friend Arthur Sulzberger, who has read more about Antarctic exploration than anyone I know, had suggested that I pay attention to my teeth. He pointed to the story of Apsley Cherry-Garrard, one of the early explorers of Antarctica in the Scott expedition, whose teeth had shattered in weather sixty-six degrees below zero. While I knew I wouldn't be in air that cold, I wondered if my teeth would conduct the cold through my body, since I knew it could be conducted through the mouths of mammals. Studies done by Dr. John Heyning at the Natural History Museum of Los Angeles County had shown that humpback whales divert blood flow away from their tongues when they are feeding so that their core temperatures are not cooled down. I went to my dentist, Dr. William Poe, and asked him about my teeth. He explained that teeth are porous, and the more porous they are, the more likely they are to be sensitive to the cold. He said that Cherry-Garrard's teeth might have been filled with tiny droplets of water; when he opened his mouth in the subzero weather, the water instantly froze, and the quick expansion of water into ice shattered his teeth. Dr. Poe gave me three fluoride treatments to fill in the pores in my teeth. He also removed three old silver fillings and replaced them with enamel crowns.

One other concern was protecting my eardrums. I was worried that intensely cold water would damage them and possibly cool down my brain temperature. Dr. Poe came up with a solution; he made formfitting earplugs out of dental-impression material to protect my eardrums.

While I sat in my cabin trying to stay calm and mentally preparing myself, Barry and Scott had been trying to lift Martha Kaplan on a stretcher up the gangway. She'd bravely lain there on the stretcher with her eyes closed while they'd tried numerous times to bring the stretcher up the gangway, once nearly dropping her overboard. They finally realized that the gangway was too steep to get her up that way. Barry and Dan then suggested that if necessary they put me in the Zodiac, get back to the ship, and use the ship's crane to lift the Zodiac onto the deck. This was the way Zodiacs were put into and taken out of the water every day. They felt certain they could get me out of the water in this fashion. I had been waiting for nearly two hours to start the test swim, and they decided it would be better to get me now rather than delay any longer.

I had been sitting still in the cabin, focusing on my breathing, working on staying calm and relaxed. Barry came down to my room and threaded a short rope through the top of my swimsuit and tied it in a double knot. It would serve as a handhold in case he needed to pull me into the boat. As backup, Bob had made a lasso, which he gave to Dan, because he would be closer to me in his Zodiac. If Dan couldn't grab the loop on my suit, he could leap into the water himself, slip the lasso over my head and shoulders, tighten it under my arms, drag me back to the boat, and inflate his dry suit to bring me to the surface, after which the crew would pull me into the boat.

At the ship's door, I pulled off my shoes, then took off my sweat suit and folded it. I held on to the railing and walked slowly down the ramp, so I wouldn't slip and fall. I stepped outside the icebreaker. Glacial winds hit my body at thirty knots. The hairs on my arms and neck stood up as goose bumps raced up my legs and back and out along my arms. My skin turned red. The Zodiacs were moving into position, one on either side of a platform at the base of the long ramp, and one out in front. In their three layers of heavy clothes and water-proof outer gear, I could not distinguish one crew member from another, but I knew they would be where they were supposed to be. Martha Kaplan and Bob Griffith were in the lead Zodiac. They would be watching for killer whales, leopard seals, icebergs, and brash ice. Adam Ravetch, who was shooting the underwater footage for the story for CBS's *60 Minutes II*, would also be watching the water and let us know if he saw anything.

If Martha or Bob spotted a killer whale while I was swimming, the crew member from Quark Expeditions who was operating the Zodiac would radio the other two Zo-diac drivers in the boats that would be on ei-ther side of me. If the orca or leopard seal was moving in close and looked threatening, the crew would immediately pull me out of the water.

None of us knew how long I could swim. None of us knew how I would react to water temperatures ranging from thirty-three to thirty-five degrees. None of us knew if I would push too far without realizing it. Dr. Gabriella Miotto was in the Zodiac to my left, and she would be watching me to make sure I wasn't becoming disoriented or losing fine motor control, letting my fingers splay. Dr. Laura King and Dr. Susan Sklar, in the Zodiac to my right, would observe me during the swim, taking water temperatures and measuring my stroke rate — counting the number of strokes I was taking each minute to see if I was on or off pace. If my stroke rate fell off rapidly, it could indicate that I was going into hypothermia. Laura and Susan would also serve as backups for Gabriella in case her boat broke down. That way they could take over as the main observers, enabling me to continue swimming.

Knowing that we had a rescue plan in place and a team of experienced, fast-thinking, and quick-reacting friends who were there, gave me the confidence that I could push as far as I could go. Without them, I wouldn't have attempted an Antarctic swim.

Quickly I retreated inside, divided my long hair in half, wound one half around my left hand, and pushed it into the right side of my swimming cap, then did the opposite with the other half. *Your long hair will help keep your head warm; it will be like penguin feathers,* I told myself. *Leave a little space on top so you can trap some air; it will give you more insulation. Remember to keep your head up as long as you can; that will give you more time in the water.*

I stuck my head outside again, determined to maintain my calm. It was so cold. They still weren't ready. The waiting was nearly the hardest part — the hardest part would be jumping into the frigid water and making the swim. I smiled. I thought back to what a friend had told me: "You're so ready for this. Have no doubts." He was right. I was ready. I didn't doubt. Taking another deep breath, I looked out again. Everything was set. I started down the gangway, holding tight to the ice-cold railing with my right hand, hanging on to my goggles with my left hand, and watching my feet, making sure I placed each solidly on each step. When I reached the bottom of the stairs, I sat down on a platform and looked at the crew. They were smiling reassuringly. They were as ready and as apprehensive and excited as I was. I smiled at them, and then I retreated deep into my mind and took one last moment to focus within myself. I didn't want to remain there long; the platform was so cold I felt like I was sitting on a giant ice-cube tray. My feet dangled inches above the water.

The waves looked molten. They rose to two to three feet, coming from my left side, then flowed slowly forward as if they were melted glass. They were Payne's gray, the same color as the blue-gray highlights on emperor penguin feathers. I was afraid looking at the water for too long would psych me out. I placed my hands on either side of my body and reminded myself not to press the air out of my swim cap, the way I normally did. I wondered if I should lick my goggles so they wouldn't fog up. I had thought this through before, but I still wasn't sure what to do. If I licked them, would that help keep them clear, or would that moisture turn to ice? If they iced up, I'd have to take them off to see, and how would the frigid water affect my eyes? It would be painful, and I'd lose the heat more quickly through my unprotected eyes. But the most troubling question was, Would the extreme cold permanently damage my eyes? I decided to do what I normally did and licked the goggles, then pulled them over my head. If I couldn't see through them, I'd just have to swim the whole way with my head up.

This was the hardest part, the first step. I was afraid, but I wanted to be there; I wanted to see what I could do. A wave rose to within an inch of my feet and instinctively I lifted them up. I didn't want to touch the water before I slid in, afraid it would psych me out. The wind was blowing at around thirty knots right off the glaciers, right into me. I was already losing body heat.

I took a deep breath, leaned back, and threw my torso forward, keeping my feet under me. In flight, my body braced itself. My feet hit first, then my knees, thighs, chest, and face. I didn't want my head to go under, but I couldn't help it. I rapidly dog-paddled myself to the surface, got my head above the water, and gasped for air as the molten ice water shattered around me. All I could feel was cold. All I could do was turn over my arms as fast as they would go and breathe. All I could think about was moving forward. There were so many alarming sensations that my mind could not distinguish what was happening to my body. I just kept swimming.

The water was searingly cold, pervasive, and it stung. It was so cold I had to constantly tell myself to keep going, that I could do this. Gradually, I lowered my face into the water, and my body shuddered and stiffened like a block of ice. I turned my head, drew in a deep breath, put my face back into the water, and for the first time, I looked at my watch on my left arm to check my time. I thought I had been swimming for at least ten minutes. I looked again. I had been swimming for only one minute. I thought, *Oh my God! How am I ever going to keep going at this rate?* I told myself, *You've got to. You can't bring these people with you all the way to Antarctica and swim for only a minute. You've got to keep going.* A wave hit me in the face and I experimented; I let the water fill my mouth. It didn't hurt my teeth, and it tasted surprisingly more sweet than salty. It must have been because the sun was shining and the glaciers were melting.

I was swimming at eighty strokes per minute, working harder than I had ever worked before, fighting the cold, going as fast as I could. This was taking everything I had. The crew watched me closely. Their expressions were tense and worried. I continued sprinting. When I reached the ten-minute mark, I thought, *Okay, I can stop now.* But it occurred to me that if I was going to swim a full mile in another day or two, I needed to swim at least five more minutes, at least half a mile, today. *Come on, you can do it, you're ready for this,* I coached myself, and I pulled more forcefully with each stroke.

A few minutes later, I lifted my right foot and waved to Laura and Susan in one Zodiac. They smiled, and I heard Shawn laugh. Shawn waved back with his hand. I took a big breath and shouted to the crew in the other Zodiac: "Are you doing okay?"

Chris, the cameraman, said, "Did she just say what I thought she said?"

I extended my reach into the water. The crew couldn't believe I was still swimming. And I was surprising myself. Lifting my right foot, I waved again. The crew waved back. I checked my watch. I had completed fifteen minutes. My skin was freezing cold and I was tired, but I thought, *This was supposed to be a test swim, and the crew was supposed to practice pulling me out, but I don't want to practice being pulled out. I'm very cold on the outside, but on the inside, I feel warm. I want to push farther. Besides, this may be the only swim I get to do. The weather could turn bad in the next day or so. I think I can keep going.*

I stretched out my pull and looked down into the water. Seventeen minutes, nineteen minutes. We were paralleling large icebergs, some as big as houses; others were the size of hockey pucks. Some were box-shaped, as if they had snapped off the glaciers; others were exquisitely carved and curved by the wind and smoothed by the sea. They were dancing ice sculptures, gliding and spinning on the current.

As we neared shore we turned to the right. The crew began pointing and yelling.

I heard Dan shout, "Lynne, ice!"

I just missed a block the size of a refrigerator. It was hard to judge the speed of the icebergs. They moved at different rates, like meteors, and I was trying to cut across their path.

The crew shouted again, pointing at small pieces of brash ice. This ice was transparent and hard to spot. I spun to my left.

"Watch out!" Barry pointed to my right.

I didn't react quickly enough; I swam headfirst into a piece the size of a big dog, and hit it hard. The impact brought hot tears to my eyes. I wondered if I would have a bump. We were moving into a field mined with ice. From the boat on my right, I heard Susan yelling, "Lynne, watch out!" as Laura pointed to my right. I swerved to the left.

Shawn was shouting, repeating, "Ice, ice!" to make sure I heard him, and Casey was directing me around a large chunk. I was breathing only on my right side now, focused on that side because the ice chunks and bergs seemed to be flowing in from that direction. I didn't realize the ice was all around us until I heard Barry on my left side. He was leaning way over the side of the Zodiac, waving me away from the boat. I was swimming within inches of a large piece, and its edges were as sharp as broken glass. I could tell that if I got any closer to it, Dan was prepared to jump in and push it away. Clear ice the size of a hall mirror was barely visible on the surface, but it expanded below the surface, like an eight-foot-wide upside-down snow cone. I looked at the base of the iceberg, then saw the shore. I couldn't help myself; I started sprinting faster. I should have been more careful, but I just wanted to get clear of the ice field and finish. I wasn't paying attention to the crew, and I slammed headfirst into a round chunk of ice the size of a soccer ball. My forehead registered a sort of blinding pain. I wanted to stop and rub it, but I decided instead to swim the last few yards with my head up; that way I would take the hits to my chest instead of my head.

When the passengers from the *Orlova*, who had no idea what we were doing and had been exploring King George Island, saw the Zodiacs landing, they ran down to the water's edge to greet us. Our youngest crew members were standing onshore, cheering and clapping. I saw their smiling faces beneath their hoods, and I smiled too. I tried to stand up gradually. It was difficult moving from a horizontal position to a vertical one; it put a lot of stress on my heart, and I felt unsteady. The rocks, small as pancakes, flat, and blunt-edged like shale, were shades of terra-cotta, gold, white, and brown. As I hobbled forward, the rocks stuck into my feet. My feet were numb and stiff, but walking on those rocks hurt a lot, and I wondered if my body was magnifying the pain. I saw Susan Adie, the expedition leader, who had helped us plan out the swim. She was cheering and offering me her hand. I waved her off, wanting to completely clear the water first on my own, then reached for her hand. Someone else grabbed me under my left arm, supporting me. All I could see of his face beneath a furry hat were two very bright blue eyes. I leaned heavily on him, taking the pressure off my feet, so the rocks wouldn't hurt so much.

"Who are you?" I asked.

He laughed and said something, and I recognized him as Bob Griffith. He had thought I was joking, but I really hadn't recognized him; my brain was not working normally. It was operating at a mechanical level again. My brain was trying to filter out the multitude of sensations my body was experiencing; my brain was focusing on survival. I was colder now than I had been during the swim, and all I could think about was getting warm.

The three doctors surrounded me. Susan Sklar hugged me, helping me stand up. Laura King wrapped a blanket over my shoulders, and Gabriella Miotto supported me on the right side. I hunched over and closed my eyes, as if that would help shut out the cold. The wind was gusting through the glacier peaks at perhaps thirty knots. There were hands on my body, drying me off, and I smiled. I felt so pampered, so happy, so tired.

"Do you want me to take your swimming cap off?" someone asked.

I shook my head. "I want to keep it on to keep my head warm," I said, not wanting to lose any more heat. Someone else was helping me pull on some boots. Yet another person was holding me under the arm and asking if we could start walking again. I looked at my legs. They didn't seem to be part of my body. They were stiff, red, and wobbly. There were three bleeding scratches on my left thigh; I must have gotten them from the ice crystals in the water column when I'd jumped in. I was glad I hadn't dived in headfirst.

The doctors and crew and I staggered across a one-hundred-yard-wide beach and forded a fast-moving stream to one of the huts of the Polish research base, where we climbed three stairs and walked inside. Three tall Polish men, who were working in the lab, examining plankton, were astonished to see me. They immediately offered me a place on the floor to lie down as well as a cup of hot tea. I was shaking too hard to drink or hold on to anything. Anthony Block, the ship's doctor, appeared and checked to see if I was okay.

I lay down on a wool blanket on the floor while Dr. King covered me with another blanket. My whole body was shaking. It was working as hard as it had worked during the swim. I was breathing very shallowly and rapidly. And as the circulation opened to my skin and extremities, I could feel waves of cold pouring into my core. My body was shaking so hard, my head was bouncing up and down. Before I'd started the swim, my temperature was 99.5 degrees; immediately after I'd finished, it was 97.7 degrees.

For the next twenty minutes I curled into a ball on my side on a blanket on the floor and shivered. When Gabriella and Laura offered to lie down on either side of me, sandwiching me between them and giving me their body heat and comfort, I gladly accepted, but when Laura offered to come underneath the blanket, I declined. Both Laura and Gabriella were thin, and I was concerned that my cold skin and wet swimsuit would give them a chill. I was too cold to take my suit off. My fingers weren't functioning properly and I was shaking too hard.

It was exhausting and yet amazing to feel what was happening. Dr. Laura took my core temperature every twenty minutes and recorded it. My body was systematically regulating its circulation, opening up blood flow from one area, shivering to create heat to compensate for the cold blood that rushed in from there, allowing for a few minutes of rest, and then beginning the sequence again with a new area. This was something I'd never experienced before, but I'd never been this cold. Still, in only forty-five minutes my temperature was back to normal.

Once I stopped shivering and was able to hold a mug, the three doctors and I drank a toast of tea to our new Polish friends. We took some photos together, got a quick tour of their lab, and said good-bye. The wind outside the hut had increased to forty knots. A storm was moving in rapidly from the south, and we needed to get out to the ship before it broke or we would have to spend the night in the hut and delay the ship's sailing.

Barry was waiting outside the hut for us. He gave me a huge hug. He was as thrilled as I was. He and Susan held me under each arm and helped me walk across the beach. I was deeply fatigued. My legs kept slipping out from underneath me, and if Barry and Susan hadn't been holding on to me, I would have taken two or three nosedives.

The Zodiac operator who had been driving the Zodiac on my left side during the swim was waiting for us. Amazed, he said to me, "If I hadn't seen it with my own eyes, I wouldn't have believed it." He shook my hand and directed me to sit on a pontoon beside him. On the ride back to the *Orlova*, the waves were steep, three to four feet, and it felt as if we were flying down a roller coaster. Each time a wave slammed into the bow, icy water flew into the boat.

Brad Stahl, the Zodiac driver, had positioned me behind Barry so I could duck behind him and stay dry; that way I wouldn't get chilled or experience an afterdrop.

When we reached the ship, the passengers on the *Orlova* cheered as we climbed back up the ramp. I had swum for twenty-two minutes and fourteen seconds, covering .92 mile in thirty-three-degree water. No one had known that I would be able to swim that far on my first attempt, not even I, and I felt like we had achieved a lot. Now I believed that we could move forward with the larger goal, the one I had been contemplating for the past two years. I believed I was ready to attempt the first Antarctic mile, the first swim to the continent of Antarctica. And I believed the crew now had the confidence in me to help me achieve it. In spite of my fatigue, I felt a surge of energy.

As I walked back to my cabin, passengers and crew members hugged and congratulated me. I took a very long, hot shower and rested on my bunk. I needed to recover as quickly as I could from the swim, replenish my fluids, and flush out the lactic acid. I drank two twelve-ounce servings of a solution of maple syrup and water. My thinking was that when a maple tree goes from dormancy to budding, it uses sap as energy, so why shouldn't I use it for rewarming and for energy?

That night when I ate dinner with my crew, everyone's spirits were high. I had swum for twenty-two minutes and I had surprised them as well as myself. It was a much longer test swim than any of us had expected. We celebrated with toasts and tales and a lot of laughter. This gave me time to pause and relax. But that night, as I lay in bed, in anticipation of the big swim, I reflected on the day and the things I wanted to do better. I had never shivered so hard in my life, and it had been extremely uncomfortable. I wasn't looking forward to doing that again. And since the water closer to the mainland would be colder, I suspected the shivering would be more violent or more prolonged or both. I decided that if I got the chance to swim a mile, I would need to crank my arm speed up and move faster to generate more heat; that way I wouldn't be as cold at the end of the swim and wouldn't have to shiver so hard. The bottoms of my feet were black and blue and tender from being bruised on the rocks. It still hurt to walk. I would ask Dan to jump into the water with me in his dry suit when I was making the transition from swimming to standing and have him help me climb out of the water. And I'd ask him to let me lean heavily on his shoulder to take the weight off my feet. Before the test swim, I had thought of doing a second training swim the following day at Deception Island, but now I decided against it. My main goal was to swim to Antarctica, and I was beat. I needed more time to recover.

The following day the weather conditions were rough. Sixty-knot winds churned the sea into white waves and flying spray, and when we reached Deception Island waterspouts whirled around the ship like small watery tornadoes, rising up to twenty feet above the water's surface. All day long we traveled south, toward the Antarctic Peninsula, and I wondered if I would get another chance to swim. I felt a tension growing within me. I had to keep talking to myself, reminding myself that the weather changed rapidly here and the situation could be better in the morning.

That evening on the bridge I met with Susan Adie and the Russian ice master, Valery Eremin, who monitored ice movement and weather conditions. We looked at charts and studied satellite information on the weather. Susan pointed out three possible sites on the continent of Antarctica where we could land. The northernmost one was called Water Boat Harbor, the middle site Neko Harbor, and the third choice Paradise Harbor. We wouldn't know until we got there which of these sites would be possible.

When I returned to my cabin, I thought for a long time about what I was about to attempt.

I had mixed feelings about the test swim. In some ways, it had given me confidence; I now knew that I could swim for twenty-two minutes in thirty-three-degree water. But it had also made me feel uncertain. It had been the most difficult and probably the most dangerous swim I had ever done. Part of me wanted to be satisfied with it. Part of me didn't want to attempt the mile. I was afraid. The water temperature on the big swim would be a degree colder. Thirty-two degrees. That was a magic number, the temperature at which freshwater froze. I wondered if in thirty-two-degree water the water in my cells would freeze, if my body's tissues would become permanently damaged. I wondered if my mind would function better this time, if I would be able to be more aware of what was happening, or if it would be further dulled by the cold. Would my core temperature drop faster, more quickly than I could recognize? Would I be able to tell if I needed to get out? Did I really want to risk my life for this? Or did I want to risk failure?

The other part of me wanted to try, wanted to do what I had trained for, wanted to explore and reach beyond what I had done. That part of me was excited about venturing into the unknown. That part of me knew I would have felt a tremendous letdown if I didn't get a chance to try. I wanted to do it now.

The next morning, on December 15, 2002, Susan called me up to the bridge. She pointed out Water Boat Point. The tiny gray beach between steep glaciers was completely blocked by icebergs and brash ice. There was no place to land.

We continued sailing south through the Gerlache Strait, past mountain-high glaciers and by ship-sized icebergs ranging in shades of blue from juniper berry to robin's-egg to light powder blue. In the protection of the Antarctic Peninsula, the wind dropped off and the sea grew calmer. When we reached Neko Harbor, about an hour later, Susan called me up to the bridge. She was excited. The beach was free of icebergs and brash ice. A landing was possible.

Now I would have a chance to swim the

first Antarctic mile. I was thrilled and scared, but I tried to remain calm; I knew that the weather could suddenly change and the swim would be off. I met with Barry Binder, who said, "I'll get the crew into the Zodiacs and come and get you when everything's set."

I walked to the ship's library, drank four eight-ounce cups of hot water, and ate two small croissants for breakfast — they were high in fat and carbohydrates, two sources of energy I would need for the swim. Then I started through the hallway to my cabin, where many of the *Orlova*'s passengers were waiting, eager to find out if I was going to swim. They wished me luck and said they would wait for me at the finish. I stopped by Dan's cabin to ask him if he would jump into the water with me at the end of the swim. He was already in his dry suit, prepared to go. Everyone was doing what we had practiced. All I could do was to go back to my room and wait. Gabriella came in to take a core temperature; it was up to 100.4 degrees. Knowing I was venturing into unknown waters, I must have psyched myself up so much that I increased my body temperature. Gabriella left me alone while I put on my swimsuit and sweats. I rubbed sunscreen on my face, but not on my arms or legs; it could make my skin slippery, and if my crew needed me to get out of the water quickly, that would create a problem. The night before, three of the crew had spotted a pod of eight killer whales swimming into the Gerlache Strait. They hadn't been moving fast. I hoped they were still north of us.

I stared out the window at the brown crescent-shaped beach. There were snow-covered hills directly above the beach, and massive glaciers on either side. I picked out landmarks, places I could aim for, so I'd know if I was on or off course.

Dr. Block caught me at the top of the stairs, just before we stepped out the door and onto the ramp, and asked if I would sit down on a step so he could trace two veins on my hands with a blue Magic Marker. It was just a precaution, he said, in case I needed emergency assistance; this way he would easily be able to find a vein to start an IV. I gave him my right hand and watched him draw the blue lines for the television camera. It gave me the creeps. Why did he have to do this now, right before I swam? Didn't he realize this kind of stuff psychs people out? *I know the swim is dangerous, but he could have done this hours ago, not just before I swam. Get over it,* I told myself. *Shake it off. Take a deep breath. Refocus. Take another breath. Good. Now think about the swim.* I smiled. *I'm so ready for this.*

Walking to the door, I peeked out and felt a blast of icy wind hit my face from the northwest. It was blowing in off the glaciers in gusts to twenty-five knots, and the air temperature was thirty-two degrees. I felt the hair rising on my arms and my jaw tighten to suppress a shiver. I was much more nervous than I had been during my first swim. I had greater expectations of myself now. I wanted to swim the first Antarctic mile, and I knew I would be very disappointed if I didn't succeed.

I stared across the icy water at Neko Harbor's beach and felt excitement building within me. Quickly, before I could lose my chance, I pulled off my sweat suit and shoes and stuck them in a corner of the ship, climbed down the gangway, sat on the platform, and dangled my feet in the water. Surprisingly, it didn't feel any colder than it had two days before. I didn't realize then that the nerves on my skin's surface had been damaged from the first swim. I didn't know that the nerves that signaled danger weren't firing. I wasn't aware that my first line of defense was gone. I had no idea that prolonged exposure in thirty-two-degree water could cause permanent nerve and muscle damage.

And I didn't know then that when an untrained person is immersed in water colder than forty degrees, their nerves are cooled down so they can't fire at the neuromuscular level. After only seven or eight minutes the person's body seizes up and they can't move. It was a good thing I didn't know any of this. All I knew was that I was ready. I took a deep breath, leaned back, and threw myself forward into the thirty-two-degree water.

When I hit the water, I went all the way under. I hadn't intended to do that; I hadn't wanted to immerse my head, which could overstimulate my vagus nerve and cause my heart to stop beating. Dog-paddling as quickly as I could, I popped up in the water, gasping for air. I couldn't catch my breath. I was swimming with my head up, hyperventilating. I kept spinning my arms, trying to get warm, but I couldn't get enough air. I felt like I had a corset tightening around my chest. I told myself to relax, take a deep breath, but I couldn't slow my breath. And I couldn't get enough air in. I tried again. My body wanted air, and it wanted it now. I had to override that reaction of hyperventilating. I had to concentrate on my breath, to press my chest out against the cold water and draw the icy air into my lungs.

My body resisted it. The air was too cold. My body didn't want to draw the cold air deep into my lungs and cool myself from the inside. It wanted to take short breaths so the cold air would be warmed in my mouth before it reached my lungs. I was fighting against myself.

I noticed my arms. They were bright red, and I felt like I was swimming through slush. My arms were thirty-two degrees, as cold as the sea. They were going numb, and so were my legs. I pulled my hands right under my chest so that I was swimming on the upper inches of the sea, trying to minimize my contact with the water. I was swimming fast and it was hard to get enough air. I began to notice that the cold was pressurizing my body like a giant tourniquet. It was squeezing the blood from the exterior part of my body and pushing it into the core. Everything felt tight. *Focus on your breath,* I told myself. *Slow it down. Let it fill your lungs. You're not going to be able to make it if you keep going at this rate.*

It wasn't working. I was laboring for breath harder than on the test swim. I was in oxygen debt, panting, gasping. My breath was inefficient, and the oxygen debt was compounding. In an attempt to create heat, I was spinning my arms wildly, faster than

I'd ever turned them over before. Laura later told me that I was swimming at a rate of ninety strokes per minute, thirty strokes per minute quicker than my normal rate. My body was demanding more oxygen, but I couldn't slow down. Not for a nano-second. Or I would freeze up and the swim would be over.

An icy wave slapped my face: I choked and felt a wave of panic rise within me. My throat tightened. I tried to clear my throat and breathe. My breath didn't come out. I couldn't get enough air in to clear my throat. I glanced at the crew. They couldn't tell I was in trouble. If I stopped, Dan would jump in and pull me out. I still couldn't get a good breath. I thought of rolling on my back to give myself time to breathe, but I couldn't. It was too cold. I closed my mouth, overrode everything my body was telling me to do, held my breath, and gasped, coughed, cleared my windpipe, and relaxed just a little, just enough to let my guard down and catch another wave in the face. I choked again. I put my face down into the water, hoping this time I could slow my heart rate down. I held my face in the water for two strokes and told myself, *Relax, just turn your head and breathe.*

It was easier to breathe in a more horizontal position. I thought it might be helping. I drew in a deep breath and put my face down again. I knew I couldn't do this for long. I was losing too much heat through my face. The intensity of the cold was as sharp as broken glass. I'd thought that swimming across the Bering Strait in thirty-eight-degree water had been tough, but there was a world of difference between thirty-eight degrees and thirty-two. In a few seconds, the cold pierced my skin and penetrated into my muscles. It felt like freezer burn, like touching wet fingers to frozen metal.

Finally I was able to gain control of my breath. I was inhaling and exhaling so deeply I could hear the breath moving in and out of my mouth even though I was wearing earplugs. I kept thinking about breathing, working on keeping it deep and even; that way I didn't have time to think about the cold.

My brain wasn't working as it normally did. It wasn't flowing freely from one idea to another — it was moving mechanically, as if my awareness came from somewhere deep inside my brain. Maybe it was because my body was being assaulted with so many sensations, too different and too complex to recognize. Or maybe it was because my blood and oxygen were going out to the working muscles. I didn't know.

For the next five or six minutes, I continued swimming, telling myself that I was doing well, telling myself that this was what I had trained for. Then something clicked, as if my body had gained equilibrium. It had fully closed down the blood flow in my skin and fingers and toes. My arms and legs were as cold as the water, but I could feel the heat radiating deep within my torso and head, and this gave me confidence. I knew that my body was protecting my brain and vital organs. Staring through the clear, silver-blue water, I examined my fingers; they were red and swollen. They were different than when I'd been swimming in the Bering Strait, when they'd looked like the fingers of a dead person. They looked healthy, and I thought their swollenness would give me more surface area, more to pull with.

I smiled and looked up at the crew, who were in the Zodiacs on either side of me. Each of them was leaning forward, willing me ahead. Their faces were filled with tension. Gabriella, Barry, Dan, and Scott were leaning so far over the Zodiac's pontoon I felt as if they were swimming right beside me. I was sprinting faster than I ever had before, moving faster than the Zodiac, and I was getting fatigued quickly. The water was thicker than on the test swim, and it took more force to pull through on each stroke. My arms ached. I didn't feel right; I couldn't seem to get into any kind of a rhythm. Then I sensed that something was wrong.

We were heading to the left, toward some glaciers. This didn't make sense; we couldn't land there. It was too dangerous. The glaciers could calve and kill us.

"Barry, where are we going?" I shouted, using air I needed for breathing.

He pointed out our direction — right toward the glaciers. I didn't understand. I didn't want to go that way. I wanted to aim for the beach. I was confused. I was moving my arms as fast as they would go, and it was taking all I had. From each moment to the next, I had to tell myself to keep going. The water felt so much colder than on the test swim. It had already worked its way deep into my muscles. My arms and legs were stiff. My strokes were short and choppy. But I kept going, telling myself to trust the crew and focus on the glaciers to watch the outcropping of rocks that was growing larger. I couldn't get into any kind of pace.

Abruptly the Zodiacs zagged to the right.

I looked up and thought, *Wow, okay; we're heading for the beach now.* For a moment, I started to feel better. I was able to extend my reach farther, and I could see passengers from the *Orlova* walking along the snowbanks. In the distance, their clothes lost their color and they looked black, like giant penguins. I saw smaller black figures, too — real penguins nesting near the edge of the shore. For a few moments, I felt like I was going to be okay, like I was going to make it in to shore, but then the Zodiacs abruptly turned farther to the right, and we were headed past the beach for another range of glaciers.

Finally, it occurred to me that the *Orlova* had anchored too close to shore for me to swim a mile, so Barry was adding distance by altering the course. And the ship's captain was on the bridge monitoring our course on his GPS and radioing our Zodiacs, updating them on the distance we had traveled. One of the passengers, Mrs. Stokie, who was on the bridge with him, told me later, "The captain was watching you and he was shaking his head. He was an older man, and he had experienced everything. And now he was seeing something new. It was good for him. Still, I think he couldn't believe it."

We continued on right past the beach, toward more glaciers.

"How long have I been swimming?" I asked.

"Fifteen minutes," Barry said.

I had swum a little more than half a mile. I looked up at the shore. If I turned left, I could make it in. I could reach the shore. This struggle could be over. But I wouldn't complete the mile. I had swum farther two days before. But I was tired now, and this was so much harder. I just didn't feel right. I couldn't figure out what the problem was. I kept talking to myself, coaching myself to keep going. Then I felt it; it was the water pressure, and it was increasing on my back. It meant there was a strong current behind me. I looked at the glaciers onshore, using the fixed points to gauge how fast the current was flowing. It was flowing at over a knot. I wondered if I would have enough strength to fight it when we turned around and headed back for the beach. It would cut my speed by half and could cause me to lose heat more rapidly.

Barry and the crew in the Zodiacs couldn't feel what was happening. They had no idea we were moving into a risky area. If the current grew any stronger, it could cost us the swim. Barry motioned for me to swim past a peninsula and across a narrow channel. I lifted my head and pulled my hands directly under my chest, to gain more lift, so I could look across the bay and see if we had any other options for landing. There were no alternatives. This made me very uncomfortable. Chances were good that there would be a strong current flowing into or out of the narrow bay. And if we got caught in that current, all would be lost.

We started across the inlet, and within a moment I could feel that second current, slamming into our right side at two knots, pushing us into the inlet. Without any explanation, I spun around, put my head down, dug my arms into the water, and crabbed into the current. I focused on repositioning myself so I could parallel shore again and head toward Neko Harbor. Barry knew I knew what I was doing. But the abrupt course change caught the Zodiac drivers by surprise. They scattered in different directions, trying to avoid ramming into each other and trying to catch up with me. The motor on the lead Zodiac on my left sputtered and stopped. The second Zodiac immediately pulled up beside me. I sprinted against the current.

"How long have I been swimming?"

"Twenty-one minutes," Barry said. He

and all the crew were watching me intently, their faces filled with tension and concern.

I put my head down, and something suddenly clicked. Maybe it was because I knew shore was within reach, or maybe because I got a second wind; I don't know. But I was finally swimming strongly, stretching out and moving fluidly. My arms and legs were as cold as the sea, but I felt the heat within my head and contained in my torso and I thrilled to it, knowing my body had carried me to places no one else had been in only a bathing suit. I looked down into the water; it was a bright blue-gray and so clear that it appeared as if I were swimming through air. The viscosity of the water was different, too; it was thicker than any I had ever swum in. It felt like I was swimming through gelato. And I got more push out of each arm stroke than I ever had before. I looked at the crew. They were leaning so far over the pontoons, as if they were right there with me. I needed to let them know I was okay.

I lifted my head, took a big breath, and shouted, "Barry, I'm swimming to Antarctica!"

I saw the smiles, heard the cheers and laughs, and I felt their energy lift me. They were as thrilled as I was. I swam faster, extending my arms, pulling more strongly, reaching for the shores of Antarctica. Now I knew we were almost there.

The crew was shouting warnings about ice. I swerved around two icebergs. Some chunks looked sharp, but I was too tired to care. I swam into whatever was in my path. It hurt, but all I wanted now was to finish.

As we neared shore, I lifted my head and saw the other passengers from the *Orlova*, in their bright red and yellow hats and parkas, tromping down the snowbanks, spreading their feet and arms wide for balance, racing to the water's edge to meet us. I lifted my foot and waved and saw my crew break into bigger smiles.

I'm almost done, I thought. *I feel okay. I feel strong. I feel warm inside. My arms and legs are thirty-two degrees. But I feel good. I can stretch out my strokes and put my face in the water. Maybe I can go a little farther. Maybe I can see what more I can do. Maybe I can swim five or ten more minutes. Or maybe I should be happy with what I've done. My skin is so cold I can't feel it, and when I stop swimming, I don't know how far my temperature's going to drop.* I looked at my watch. Twenty-three minutes. I'd been in a minute longer than two days before. *How much difference would a minute make?* I asked myself. *How much difference is there between thirty-two-degree and thirty-*

three-degree water? Remember what Dr. Keatinge said: once your temperature starts to drop, it will drop very fast. If you continue swimming, you're going to cool down even more. Remember how hard you shivered last time? Remember how much work it was? Remember how uncomfortable you were? This is the place where people make mistakes, when they're tired and cold and they push too far into the unknown. You could really hurt yourself. Finish now. You've done a good job. Be satisfied with what you've done. Go celebrate with your friends.

Turning in toward shore, I again lifted my foot and waved it, and my friends waved back and cheered. One hundred yards from shore, I saw chinstrap penguins sliding headfirst, like tiny black toboggans, down a steep snowbank. When they reached the base of the hill, they used their bristly tails like brakes, sticking them into the snow to stop their momentum. They waddled across the beach at full tilt, holding their wings out at their sides for balance. Reaching the water, they dove in headfirst, then porpoised across it, clearing it by one or two feet with each surface dive. They tucked their wings back by their sides so they would be more aerodynamic. When they neared the Zodiacs, they dove and flapped their wings under the water as if they were flying through air. It was amazing to think this was the only place they would fly. They zoomed under me in bursts of speed, and their bubbles exploded like white fireworks. More penguins joined in. One cannonballed off a ledge, another slipped on some ice and belly flopped, and three penguins swam within inches of my hands. I reached out to touch one, but he swerved and flapped his wings, so he moved just beyond my fingertips. I had no idea why they were swimming with me, but I knew it was a good sign; it meant there were no killer whales or leopard seals in the area.

When I reached knee-deep water, Dan jumped in, ran through the water, looped his arm through mine, and helped me stand. "Are you okay?" he asked.

"Yes. We made it!" I said.

Everyone around me was crying. Susan Adie helped Dan pull me up the incline. Martha wrapped a towel around my shoulders. Barry hugged me tightly. Laura and Susan began drying me off. I was so cold I was already starting to shiver hard. My legs were stiffer than after the other swim. The crew helped me into the Zodiac and I flopped onto the floor. Laura and Susan piled on top of me to protect me from the wind, and we pounded across the water, my head slamming into the Zodiac's floor. I managed to lift my head so that someone could place a hand under it to buffer the impact. I was so cold and stiff and shaking harder than before.

When we reached the *Orlova*, it took me a minute to stand, to gain my balance, and as I climbed the ramp's steps I clung to the railing and pulled myself up, shaking hard. By the time I reached the top of the ramp, my teeth were chattering and I was breathing harder and faster than when I had been swimming. I didn't like being so cold. I didn't like my body having to work so hard. My temperature had dropped to 95.5 degrees, and I couldn't control my shaking. I just let go, and my body bounced up and down with shakes and shivers.

Quickly Martha and Dan and the three doctors huddled around me like emperor penguins, and their combined comfort and body heat began to warm me. It seemed as if I would never stop shaking, and I was completely exhausted. Within half an hour my shivering had subsided to small body shudders. Once I was able to stand and maintain my balance, the doctors helped me pull on a special top and pants that had been designed by a friend. She had sewn pockets under the arms, in the groin area, and into a scarf and had placed chemical packs that emitted heat inside the pockets. Their placement in the clothing warmed the major blood-flow areas of my body so that I was heated from the inside out. It was effective, and within an hour my temperature was back to normal.

That night we celebrated with everyone aboard the *Orlova*. I had swum the first Antarctic mile — a distance of 1.06 miles, in fact — in thirty-two-degree water in twenty-five minutes. I had been able to do what had seemed impossible because I'd had a crew who believed in me and in what we as human beings were capable of. It was a great dream, swimming to Antarctica.

AFTERWORD

When we sailed into Ushuaia harbor, Dan Cohen and I were standing on the bow of the *Orlova*, watching the Andes Mountains that embraced the city become steeper as the city grew larger and the gap between the sea and land diminished. Off to the right of the *Orlova*, we saw an Argentine coast guard cutter racing toward us, and it pulled up alongside us. Eight or nine men in uniform moved to the ship's stern. The men onboard jumped up and down, waved, and cheered. It took me a few minutes to realize what they were doing. Someone blew the cutter's horn three times. Dan and I waved and applauded them. I wondered how they had known about the swim, and then I remembered that I had seen the bright red Argentine navy ship, the *Antarctica*, in the Gerlache Strait. When I completed the swim in Neko Harbor, Susan Adie had radioed the other ships in the area, including the *Antarctica*, to let them know about our success. The navy must have called the coast guard, who in turn escorted us all the way to the docks, giving us a hero's welcome.

For the next month few people knew about the swim, but when the story came out in *The New Yorker* and on *60 Minutes II* and I was invited on the *David Letterman* show, I heard from friends and family I hadn't heard from in years.

I gave a lecture to a group of elementary and high school teenagers in Callaway, Nebraska, and was asked countless questions about the Antarctica swim and my other swims before it. One of the questions that made me pause was from a seven-year-old boy. He asked, "If you had a goal and worked very, very hard toward it, but you didn't accomplish it, would you still be happy?" I wondered what kind of goal a seven-year-old could have worked so hard toward and not achieved, and how such a young boy could have such a profound question.

I answered him as best I could: "I would have been happy that I tried to reach my goal, but if I didn't succeed, I would want to go back and figure out what I thought I needed to do to accomplish it, and then try again."

He smiled and nodded; he appeared to understand so much beyond his years. I still wonder about him and if what I told him was helpful. One friend said I should have told him to reevaluate his goals and to lower the bar if the goal was too high. I asked myself if I would follow that advice, and I decided that's not the way I do things. I don't lower the bar. Maybe it's because the bar's not high enough or maybe it's because I work toward goals in reachable steps. The swim to Antarctica was the culmination of thirty years of swimming and two years of complete focus on one big goal. Achieving it was satisfying, and I know that that success will now allow me to do something more. It may be in swimming or another adventure — I don't know yet. I do know that the nerves in my fingers, toes, and skin are regrowing, and I'm gradually getting the sensation back; it will just take time for my body to fully recover. Until then I'll be thinking about what's next, and beginning to work toward it.

VW'14